Second edition

OCR
RECOGNISING ACHIEVEMENT
HODDER EDUCATION
Official Publisher Partnership

OCR ICT for AS

Glen Millbery and Sonia Stuart

DYNAMIC LEARNING

HODDER EDUCATION

The Publishers would like to thank the following for permission to reproduce copyright material:

Photo credits
p.iv © Image Source/Getty Images; **p.6** Jalite Plc; **p.7** © vario images GmbH & Co.KG/Alamy; **p.11** MGM/ The Kobal Collection; **p.30** © Art Directors & TRIP/Alamy; **p.31** © Anne Wanjie **p.32**/© Marianna Day Massey/ ZUMA/Corbis, r © AGphotographer-Fotolia.com; **p.34** © Steven May/Alamy; **p.40** © Glen Millbery; **p.42** /© Pieter Goossens/iStockphoto.com, r www.PurestockX.com; **p.43** Jerry Bergman/Rex Features **p.44** /© Steve Connolly, c © Beaconstox/Alamy, r © David R. Frazier Photolibrary, Inc./Alamy; **p.47** r © Art Directors & TRIP/Alamy /© iStockphoto.co/Mike McCune; **p.51** r © Picture Contact/Alamy,/Realistic Reflections/Getty Images; **p.82** /© Electronistock/Alamy, c © geogphotos/Alamy, b Hodder Education; **p.90** Rex Features

t = top, b = bottom, l = left, r = right, c = centre

Acknowledgements
p.13 BBC.co.uk; **p.26** Young Person's Railcard; **p.67** Croner; **p.69** NCH Software; **p.70** Ticketmaster; **p.72** Automobile Association

Every effort has been made to trace all copyright holders, but if any have been inadvertently overlooked the Publishers will be pleased to make the necessary arrangements at the first opportunity.

Although every effort has been made to ensure that website addresses are correct at time of going to press, Hodder Education cannot be held responsible for the content of any website mentioned in this book. It is sometimes possible to find a relocated web page by typing the address of the home page for a website in the URL window of your browser.

Hachette UK's policy is to use papers that are natural, renewable and recyclable products and made from wood grown in sustainable forests. The logging and manufacturing processes are expected to conform to the environmental regulations of the country of origin.

Orders: please contact Bookpoint Ltd, 130 Milton Park, Abingdon, Oxon OX14 4SB.
Telephone: (44) 01235 827720. Fax: (44) 01235 400454. Lines are open 9.00 – 5.00, Monday to Saturday, with a 24-hour message answering service. Visit our website at www.hoddereducation.co.uk

© Glen Millbery, Sonia Stuart 2012
First published in 2012 by
Hodder Education,
An Hachette UK company
Carmelite House,
50 Victoria Embankment,
London EC4Y 0DZ

Impression number   5 4 3
Year   2016 2015

Cover photo Victoria-Fotolia
Illustrations by DC Graphic Design Limited
Typeset in ITC Usherwood 11pt by DC Graphic Design Limited, Swanley Village, Kent

Printed in Slovenia

A catalogue record for this title is available from the British Library.

ISBN: 978 1444 168600

Contents

Contents

Introduction

This book has three sections – G061 – the exam, G062 – the structured tasks and exam technique. G061 is worth 60%, G062 is worth 40%.

The theory chapters follow the specification, going through it bullet by bullet. The coursework chapters look at tools, tips and techniques. It does not look at skills, these come from your teacher, instead it focuses on how to interpret the tasks and present the evidence required to gain the marks.

There are three main aspects to a good examination, knowledge, application and exam technique. Unless all three are present you will not gain high marks. The aim of this text book is to assist you in getting the grade that you deserve.

The knowledge is a basic understanding of the facts and the specification, it is rote learning and regurgitation. This will assist you in gaining marks in the identify and describe questions.

The application is how the knowledge that you have is applied to the context. It is taking the rote learning and tailoring it to fit the specific context of the question.

The exam technique is how the keyword in the question tells you what the examiner is looking for in the response and how it will be marked.

When all three elements come together you will achieve a good mark, if one of them is missing then the marks will fall dramatically.

This book does not give you all the answers. It gives you the knowledge and allows you to practice that knowledge in a given context. It helps you along the road but it does not replace your own learning. The exam will be in a context, you need to make sure you understand the theory so you can apply it.

In G062 the paper changes every year but there is always a core set of skills you need.

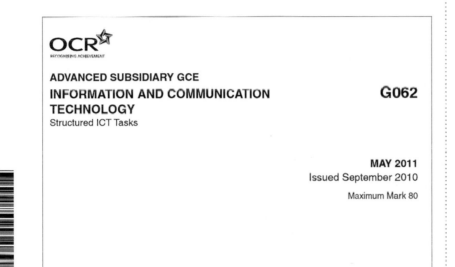

Make sure you understand the context and the skills being asked. There is a difference between having the skill, applying the skill explaining the skill. Just because you have high level skills, unless you provide the evidence required you will not score highly. Make sure you look through the examples in the book and are absolutely sure what evidence is required before you start the task.

Presentation counts – this is ICT AS Level, you should be able to use the computer to produce work that looks good. Is it fit for purpose? Could it be used in the target environment? Would you be proud to stand in front of a manager and hand them the work?

Lastly, good luck and enjoy the course.

1 Data, information, knowledge and processing

Introduction

This chapter covers the fundamental knowledge required to support all the other chapters in this book. You will need to make sure you know the concepts and definitions covered here so that you can understand future chapters.

This chapter covers:
- Data, information and knowledge
- Representation methods
- Data types
- Sources of data
- Static and dynamic data
- Quality of information
- Encoding data
- Validation and verification
- Backup and archive
- Cost of information
- Input–Process Output feedback loop

Describe the term data, using an example, clearly identifying the fact that the term has no meaning

Data is a big part of our lives – anything that is written or spoken is made up of data. If you break any words down you eventually, at the bottom of the pile, find data.

The official definition is.

Data is the raw facts and figures before they have been processed.

"Raw facts and figures" means without meaning. It should not be possible to understand what the letters and figures stand for. For example:

BAT45&&7

478GH89"

These are examples of data. There is no way to tell what they mean – at this time they are just a random series of numbers and letters.

The key facts you need to know are that:
- data can be alphanumeric characters (letters and numbers), sound or graphics
- data is raw facts before it has been processed
- data has no meaning.

If you have to give an example of data, make sure that it is just a set of random numbers and letters and there is no meaning to it.

Questions

1 Using an example, describe the term data.

2 Identify **two** characteristics of data.

3 What is meant by alphanumeric character?

Describe what is meant by the term information

Information is made by taking data and processing it.

Processing is performing some action on the data. This might be sorting, searching or editing. The act of processing gives the data meaning. It is not possible to search the data unless you have some idea of what you are looking for.

There is a formula that you need to know that shows how data can become information:

Information = Data + [Structure] + [Context] + Meaning

In some cases, the data (raw facts and figures) does not need to have a structure and a context in order to become information. However, it is always better to know the complete formula.

Key words

Data – the raw facts and figures

Structure – how the data is presented. Are the numbers actually numbers or should they be read as text? Should the data be organised in any way (e.g. grouped by numbers of characters)? What, if any, encoding system has been used?

Context – an environment where our prior knowledge and understanding can make sense of the data.

Meaning – data in the correct structure and placed within the context.

Knowledge – the application of information to a situation.

Examples of converting data into information

Data	Structure	Context	Meaning
12102005	12/10/2005 NN/NN/NNNN	UK date	Date of hotel room booking
31 32 34 32 31	Numbers	Celsius	Temperature over 5 days in Venice
SKBL10	First 2 letters – type of garment Second 2 letters – colour Last 2 numbers – size LLLLNN	A shop stock code	A black skirt, size 10
1	Selected from a scale of 1–4 N	How enjoyable was the film? 1 being good, 4 being bad	The film was good

Activities

Copy and fill in the following table, showing how data can be turned into information. Use the context given at the top of the table.

	Context		
	Fish shop	**Holiday website**	**TV programme listings magazine**
Data			
Structure			
Context			
Meaning			

Questions

1 Give a definition of information.

2 Within the definition of information, what is meant by structure?

3 Within the definition of information, what is meant by context?

4 Within the definition of information, what is meant by meaning?

5 Within the context of a car sales garage, show how data can become information.

Tip

You will need to be able to give an example of information. The example you give must be relevant to the context of the question being asked in the examination. If the question is about hotels, give an example to do with hotels.

Representation methods to convey meaning

For people to be able to use information they must be able to recognise, extract and pass it on. If information is only known by one person and is not passed on to anyone else then its value is limited.

Ideally, information should be available in many different formats. However, there are restrictions. Some information needs to be kept secure and if it became known then it could cause problems, for example:

- secret service intelligence
- business information.

Another restriction is the language barrier. If information is presented in one particular language then someone who does not understand that language might have difficulty acquiring the information.

People who are disabled are likely to be restricted in acquiring information. This will depend on their disability, for example people who have visual (seeing) or aural (hearing) problems may have problems acquiring information if it is in the wrong format.

It is not possible to give all information in all formats. Some decision has to be made about which format to use within each situation.

It can be difficult to select and justify different methods (known as representation methods) of conveying information for different situations. The main representation methods are:

- text (including writing)
- graphics (including pictures)
- sound (including voice)
- moving pictures (animation or video)
- light-emitting diode (LED).

Each method has its advantages and disadvantages. However, the user (i.e. the individual who needs to acquire the information) and the location where the information is being given must be considered when selecting a representation method.

General examples of the advantages and disadvantages of each of the representation methods are given in the next table.

Activities

Give examples of information that should be kept secure. Explain who should have access to this information and the implications of other people finding it out.

Representation	Advantages	Disadvantages
Text	• Clear to understand • Lots of detail	• Need to be able to read • Need to understand the language • Can be confusing – level of language • Lots of text cannot be read quickly – road signs

Representation	Advantages	Disadvantages
Graphics	• Multilingual – do not need language to understand an image – e.g. male and female	• Can be confusing if you do not know the symbols – does everyone know the road signs?
	• Can match what you see – physical shapes	• Some symbols do not mean the same thing in different countries
Sound	• No fixed position • No line of sight required • Good for visually impaired people	• No good in large areas – distortion of sound • Usually language based • May not know the sound – e.g. different alarms have different sounds • Need to be able to hear
Moving pictures	• Lots of information conveyed • Not language dependent • Can exemplify text	• Linear – if you do not see the beginning you may not understand • Problems if sound attached
LED	• Can allow data to be kept secure • Can be used in noisy places • Similar to graphics	• Need to be able to see the lights • Combinations of lights may need to be known to be understood

Activities

Make a copy of the table below. Look around the room that you are in and fill in your table. Add as many rows as required. Identify the type of representation (text, sound, pictures, moving pictures, LED); a description of the representation; how it is used; and the intended audience. The first one has been done for you.

Type of representation	Description	Use	Audience
Light	LED on the keyboard	To show when the Caps Lock key has been pressed	All users of the keyboard who can see

The context in which the information is being acquired needs to be considered:

• User manuals are often provided as text and graphics, not sound.
• Fire alarms are sound rather than text based.
• Electronic tills are text and sound based.
• Early-learning toys are sound, picture and text based.

These are only examples. User manuals might be computerised and include sound. Fire alarm systems can include LED arrows pointing to an exit.

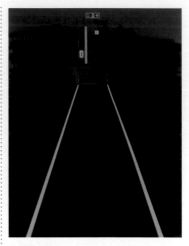

Figure 1.1 Light is a method of representation directing people to the exit

Questions

1 Identify **three** different representation methods.

2 What are the advantages of using graphics instead of sound in a software user manual?

3 Give **three** situations where the use of sound to convey information would be appropriate.

4 Give **three** situations where the use of text to convey information would be appropriate.

5 Explain, using examples, why it might be advantageous for an electronic till to use graphics as well as sound and text.

6 Why are road signs symbols and not text?

Describe what is meant by the term knowledge and distinguish between information and knowledge

Data on its own is meaningless. When we add context, structure and meaning to data we get information. Knowledge is the application of that information to a situation – in other words, putting the information to use.

For example:

Data:	46, 54
Information:	Scores for team 1 and team 2, respectively, in a pub quiz.
Knowledge:	Team 2 won.

It is easiest to think of knowledge as being the action that you need to take or a general rule you can determine from the information.

For example:

"I know what I need to get to win the quiz."

"How do you know?"

"Because the quiz master just told me that team 1 got 46."

This is taking information and applying it to acquire knowledge.

Data	Information	Knowledge
2 and 4	Ice cream shop in Lynton, Devon. 2 kg of ice cream sold in January, 4 kg of ice cream sold in July.	More ice cream is sold in July – the hotter the temperature the more ice cream is sold. More ice cream is sold in July because there are more tourists around.
101	BBC1 channel number	Sky number to input to get BBC1.

Information is based on certainties. There is a formula that allows us to determine where the information has come from and how it is derived. It has a context, a structure and raw data. If we take all of these we can associate a meaning with the data, then it becomes information.

Certainties are things that will occur the same way every single time, or mean the same thing every single time. They do not change or alter for that event.

Knowledge can change. It does not mean that every time it will or does, but it can change. More information can be added to our knowledge and as we add more information we revise our knowledge.

When distinguishing the difference between information and knowledge, the following comparisons are useful:

- Information is based on facts. Knowledge is opinion.
- Information can be quantified and judged against. Knowledge can be quantified with success criteria.
- Information is independent of a person's viewpoint – it is factual. Knowledge depends on the perspective and belief of the individual.

Figure 1.2 Using information

Imagine you are driving towards a junction for the first time and you see some traffic lights turn from green to amber.

Data	Information	Knowledge
The amber light is the data	The information is that you will need to stop.	The knowledge is how to stop the vehicle you are driving and when you need to start braking to stop the vehicle where you need it to.

As you approach the traffic lights you will need to be aware of conditions that determine your knowledge of the situation. For example:

- the proximity of traffic behind you
- the road conditions
- tyre grip
- the weather.

All these will affect your knowledge of the situation. Individual pieces of information will affect the knowledge that we have of the current situation and affect the action that we take (in this example, when to brake and with how much force, whether to be aware of possible aquaplaning or skidding etc.).

Questions

1 What is the difference between information and knowledge?

2 Using an example, show how data can be turned into knowledge.

3 What is meant by the term knowledge?

4 Within the context of using mobile phone call charges, show how knowledge can be adapted by the user being given additional information.

Describe different data types (Boolean, real, integer, string, date/time), selecting an appropriate data type for a given situation

The fundamental building blocks, the facts and figures, are made up of alphanumeric characters. An alphanumeric character is any character that can be displayed on a computer screen. It could be a letter, number or symbol.

Alphanumeric characters can be grouped into different data types.

A data type is the sort of alphanumeric character that can be allocated. There are five data types that you need to be aware of:

- Boolean
- Real
- Integer
- Text/String
- Date/Time.

Boolean

The Boolean data type is one which can contain one of only two values – true and false. These two values can be used to represent anything containing two states, for example:

- Male/Female
- Yes/No
- L6th/U6th.

It is used to hold data where the response can only be one of two values. It is often phrased as a question, for example:

- Is the motorway open yet?
- Does the property have a garden?
- Are you male?

Real

This data type contains numbers that will have decimal places, for example:

- 45.78
- 123.0323
- 12.00.

It is used to hold numbers where precision is important, for example:

- measurements in a house/building (2.7 m wide)
- prices of goods (£1.75)
- height of people (1.82 m).

Integer

The integer data type contains whole numbers with NO decimal places, for example:

- 45
- 125
- 1250.

It is used where the accuracy may not be of vital importance or the value allocated is specifically a whole number, for example:

- TV channels
- Large amounts of money – house prices
- Coding responses – 1–4.

Currency may be real or an integer. If it is a small amount of currency then it will be real (£16.99), however if the amount is large, then it is an integer (house prices: £175 000). In general the units used may influence whether a number is represented as a real or an integer – a price in pence may be an integer (75p), but the same price in pounds is real (£0.75).

Text/String

This is any alphanumeric character. This includes numbers, text and symbols, for example:

- 12345
- Examination
- 123GD56
- 10 Downing Street
- ⌂☺✈✄

Text is used to convey basic information, for example on labels:

- forename of a person (Eleanor)
- postcode (B17 4BH)
- telephone number (01234 567890).

As the examples show, text/string is used to hold telephone numbers. In a computer, telephone numbers are stored as text. This is because the telephone number contains a leading 0, spaces and, most importantly, no mathematical calculations are performed on telephone numbers, so there is no need to store it as a number.

Date/Time

This contains numbers and letters, which, depending on the format used, displays the date or the time to different degrees of accuracy, for example:

- 12:45:45
- 1995
- 7th September 2007.

Tip

When storing numbers and prices, if there is a leading or trailing identifier (a currency symbol (e.g. £) or a measurement (e.g. cm)), the data type does not change. The identifier is not included as part of the data type. Do NOT then think that £2.99 or 32 cm should be stored as text because of the pound sign or unit – they are not. They would still be stored as real or integer as appropriate.

In reality, the computer works out a date from a number.

A predetermined date, 1st January 1900, is given a value −1. Every date is then calculated numerically, so 1st January 2000 is stored as 36526 – the number of days that has passed since day 1.

	Boolean	Real	Integer	String	Date/Time
Definition	One of only two values	Numbers with decimals	Whole numbers	Alphanumeric characters	Numbers and letters
Example	True	123.32	87	Hello	03/05/1988

Activities

Within the context, give an example of how each of the data types could be used.

	Context		
	Estate agency	Removal company	School
Boolean			
Real			
Integer			
String			
Date/Time			

Why is it important to allocate the correct data type to the data?

Various processes are carried out on data, including sorting, searching and mathematical processes (addition, subtraction etc.).

Some of these processes can only be carried out on some data types. For example:

- Text can only be added together to form a longer string such as "hello" + "there" = "hellothere". This is called concatenation.
- Boolean could not store the results of a survey with many choices.
- Multiplication cannot be carried out on text.

Questions

1 Using an example, describe the Boolean data type.

2 Give **three** examples where the use of an integer data type would be more appropriate than a real data type.

3 Give **two** reasons why a telephone number is stored as text.

Give examples of different sources from which data can be derived and explain the advantages and disadvantages of using each source

Data has to come from somewhere – it does not just appear. If you need some data, you must consider where to get it from.

If you have been given the task of creating a leaflet for a local cinema, you will need to find some data to go into the leaflet.

Where this data comes from is known as the source.

Figure 1.3 Source of data

Direct and indirect data

Direct (primary) data is data collected from an original source. It is often easiest to think of direct data as data that has been physically collected by you.

Indirect (secondary) data has two interpretations:

- Data that has been used for a purpose different to that for which it was originally collected. For example, collecting data on how many tickets have been sold for a film to make sure it is not oversold, and then using the data to find the most popular film.
- The people/companies involved in collecting the data are different to those using the data. Typically this might be organisations that conduct market surveys and then sell the results to other companies who use it in advertising.

Activities

Using the context given, identify four direct sources of information and four indirect sources of information for producing leaflets.

	Context	
	Estate agency	Removal company
Direct		
Indirect		

Questions

1 What is the difference between direct and indirect sources of data?

2 Give **two** examples of archives that would need to be accessed to find data.

3 Information on the number of girls who play football in a town is required. Describe **one** direct and **one** indirect method of collecting data that will provide this information.

Advantages and disadvantages of collecting data from different sources

The choice of the data collection method is often taken out of the hands of the individual, for example it is not possible to collect historical data from an original source. The advantages and disadvantages will depend on the situation.

	Advantages	Disadvantages
Direct	• The source and collection method is known and verified. • The exact data required can be collected. • The data being collected can change in response to answers.	• May not get a large range of data. • Data may not be available – location/time.
Indirect	• Large range of data is available that could not have been collected directly. • Data can be available from different locations and time periods. • Analysis might already have been completed on some of the data.	• Do not know if any bias was placed on the collection. • Cannot be certain of accuracy of the recording of data. • May not have all the information about how, when and where it was collected to make a valued opinion on its usefulness. • If the information was not originally collected, may not be able to get hold of it.

Questions

1 Describe **two** advantages of using an original source to collect information on how good different MP3 players are.

2 Give **two** situations where using indirect data is a better option than direct. For each situation, give a different reason why.

3 Describe **one** situation where there is an advantage to using both direct and indirect methods of collecting data.

Compare the use of static information sources with dynamic sources

An information source is a repository of data that can be accessed when required. There are two main types of information source: static and dynamic.

A static information source is one where the data, once created, does not change. A dynamic information source is one where the data can change and be updated.

Static information sources include books and CDs. Dynamic sources include pages on the World Wide Web and CD-RW.

With static information sources, the data contained within it does not change. This means that it can be found when it is needed. For example, if a teacher had created a worksheet based on the source they would know that the student could find the information.

If the teacher used a book as the source they can be confident that the content has not changed since they last looked. If they used a web page as the source, there is no guarantee that it will be the same – in fact it could even change halfway through the lesson.

Figure 1.4 Changing content

The data stored on a CD-ROM is static. Once the data is burned on to the CD-ROM it cannot be changed. A common use of a CD-ROM for storing static data is an encyclopedia. Companies may also promote their products by producing a catalogue or brochure on a CD-ROM and sending it to all their customers or clients.

It is likely that static information sources have gone through some editing process. If it is a book or a CD there is a rigorous system for checking the data. The end result is content that can be relied on to be accurate.

Dynamic information is information that changes or can be changed. A dynamic web page contains content that a user can interact with, such as information that is tied to a database. The user can request information, such as ticket availability or product information, for retrieval from a database. The information retrieved will be up to date but not necessarily accurate.

There will be static and dynamic elements to a website. Take the BBC website for example, the structure is static (it may undergo refreshing and changing periodically, but between those times it remains the same); it is the content within the structure that is dynamic – the news is different each day.

Anyone with a computer and a telephone line can create a website. They can put whatever they want on the website and it can be viewed worldwide. Just because something is on the Web does not make it correct. Any information found on the Web needs to be treated with caution until it is verified by a separate source.

Activities

Some CD-ROMs, especially those for encyclopedias, can appear to update their content. Investigate how this is possible. Is this really dynamic content?

A book or a CD (static) has limited accessibility. Only one person can see a single copy of a book and possession of a CD requires a CD drive to view its contents. Information on the web is accessible by thousands of people simultaneously.

Questions

1 What is the difference between static and dynamic data?

2 Describe, with examples, **two** reasons why websites are classified as dynamic sources of data.

3 Describe **two** situations where the use of static data is preferable. Give reasons for your choices.

4 Describe **two** problems of using dynamic data.

Comparison of CD-ROMs and websites

There are advantages and disadvantages to data being held in a static form, on a CD-ROM, and in a dynamic form on websites.

CD-ROM	Websites
There is a limited amount of information available.	The web provides a large volume of information.
Does not require internet access.	Only people with internet access can access the information.
More reliable source of information.	The information is not always reliable.
Does require a suitable computer with CD-ROM drive.	You do not need a CD-ROM drive or a computer – can access using a mobile phone.
Data cannot be updated very quickly.	Data can be updated very quickly.
The CD can be scratched/broken or lost/stolen.	Internet access might not be working. Difficulty accessing the pages.
Software to search the data on the CD can be included with the CD along with any additional necessary software.	The user may not have the correct browser software.
If there are errors, correction notices would have to be sent out to people.	The web provides many different opinions.
There is a cost involved in making and sending the CD-ROMs.	Can potentially reach everybody.
A required CD-ROM can take time to arrive.	People come to a website rather than the CD-ROM being sent to a person.
Several CD-ROMs may need to be looked at to find the required information.	Hyperlinks can lead the individual to related sites.
The CD-ROM is in a single location – have to possess it to look at it.	The same web resource can be accessed from anywhere as long as the address is known.

Describe how the following can affect the quality of the information produced: accuracy, relevance, age, completeness, presentation, level of detail

Garbage In Garbage Out (GIGO) is a well known concept in ICT. It means that if the data that is input into the system is not very good, then you will not be able to translate it into information that is useful.

Or, put another way, if you put incorrect data into a system you will get incorrect information out of it.

There are six factors that determine how good the data is. Different factors are applicable to different scenarios.

- Accuracy
- Relevance
- Age
- Completeness
- Presentation
- Level of detail

These six factors are explained below and an estate agency is used as an example.

Accuracy

The data needs to be accurate. If it is not accurate you cannot rely on the information it provides.

If you ask for the price of a house and you are given an incorrect figure, the information is worthless.

Relevance

The information must be relevant. If you have some information but it does not relate to the topic it is worthless.

Having information that is not relevant can be a disadvantage. It increases the volume of data and this could mean a longer time is required to look at it.

If you ask for the distance of a property from different places within town, to be told how far it is from a bus stop on the other side of town or how far it is to the mayor's house is irrelevant.

Age

The information might be too old. Information can change over time. If you know the information is from the past it may not be relevant now.

If you ask for the price of a house, to be given a figure that is five years old is of no value to you.

Completeness

If you only have part of the information then it is worthless. Think back to the formula for information – data requires a context, structure, and meaning for it to have value and be useful.

If you want to view a house and you are only given the house number but no road name, or the date of the viewing but not the time, then the information is not worth anything.

Presentation

If the information is not presented in such a way that you can understand or find what you want it loses value. The presentation might be improved by sorting or using a different method of representation, for example a picture or graph instead of text.

Pictures of a property make house brochures easier to digest. Also, house brochures are presented in an organised way (as if you were walking through the house). This consistent presentation makes it easier to compare properties.

Level of detail

You can be given too much or too little information. The volume of data determines whether you have enough to make a decision or too much. If you have too much it can be difficult to find what you require.

If you are buying a house, having every minor alteration and samples of different colour schemes used in the house is too much information.

On the other hand, being told how many bedrooms there are but no details, for example the length and width, is too little.

There is a balance between too much and too little and it can be difficult to get it correct.

Activities

HOUSE FOR SALE

Price: between £200,000 and £290,000

In Grove Street

The garden is 102.12 m long. It is a delightful area with a post-modern design. The grass used has been imported from China from a small grass grower who supplies the grass seeds to many different countries, including Hawaii.

The house has 4 bedrooms, a few reception rooms and some toilets. When the house was built in the 1800s the walls were a lovely crimson colour.

If you are interested in viewing this house, give us a ring.

Figure 1.5 Quality of information

Using the above leaflet, go through each of the six factors affecting the quality of information and analyse how well the leaflet addresess them.
Redesign the leaflet to take into account the factors.

The six factors are not usually present just on their own. For example, level of detail is linked to completeness, presentation can be linked to age.

Activities

Within the contexts given, give examples of how the six factors can affect the quality of information produced.

	Context	
	Removal company	Exam results
Accuracy		
Relevance		
Age		
Completeness		
Presentation		
Level of detail		

Questions

1 Describe each of the six factors affecting the quality of information.

2 For each factor, give an example of how it affects the quality of information produced.

3 Demonstrate, using examples, how one factor can have a knock-on effect and influence other factors.

There is a link between the factors affecting the quality of information and direct and indirect sources.

	Direct source	Indirect source
Accuracy	● Confidence in the accuracy because you have collected it yourself.	● Do not know if it is accurate. ● Need to cross reference.
Relevance	● Can collect only the information that you need.	● Information collected may have additional material that is not relevant and that will need sorting through.
Age	● You know the exact age of the information because you collected it.	● Reliant on what could be found – could be old.
Completeness	● You collect all the information that you need.	● Restricted to what has been collected by others. ● It may not be complete for your purposes.
Presentation	● Can collect it in whatever format you require – text, table, graph, pictures, photograph.	● Can change the format from what has been collected occasionally – numbers to graph, for example – but not always.
Level of detail	● Will cover everything you require in the appropriate depth.	● May be too much information and so requires editing or too little information, which leaves a gap.

Explain the advantages and disadvantages of encoding data

We collect data for a purpose. If the data that has been collected cannot be organised in such a way that it can be used for the original purpose then it is worthless.

There needs to be some method of standardising the information so that it fulfils its purpose and is organised. One method is known as encoding data (putting data into code or shorthand data). This is nothing to do with secret messages (ciphers, which are often called codes).

Encoding data is taking the original data and storing it in a different representation. What is stored is not the actual data but a representation of it. An everyday example is using a postcode to represent an address or part of an address.

The following are examples of representations of data. It is easy to work out what the codes stand for.

Mon	Tue	Wed	Thu
Jan	Feb	Mar	Apr

Tip

Try and describe the terms without using them. For example describe completeness without using the word 'complete'.

Other codes are not as easy to understand.

BLTR36

RDSK16

It is not possible to interpret the data unless you have the key:

BL = Blue, RD = Red

TR = Trouser, SK = Skirt

Last two digits = size

Disadvantages and problems of encoding data

The precision of the data entered is coarsened. This means that the data entered into the computer is not as accurate as the data originally given.

Imagine you are doing a survey of hair colour and the options that you give people are:

- black
- red
- blonde
- grey
- brown.

This may cover most of the major colours, but most people do not categorise their hair in these precise terms. They may think of themselves as chestnut or strawberry blonde.

This will mean that the actual data entered into the computer is inaccurate. If the data is seen to be inaccurate then the integrity of the system will be questioned – how can the results be believed if the data is not correct?

If you were to ask a question, the response that you are given is unlikely to fit exactly into any encoding system you try to come up with. This is why many surveys ask you to give marks on a scale instead of allowing you to comment freely.

However, if you are trying to encode free comments you will need to make some value judgements. Value judgements are where an absolute value is placed on some vague text. Different people will apply different value judgements to the same text.

You are doing a survey outside a cinema about the film that has just finished. You ask the people coming out of the cinema: 'Did you enjoy the film?'

The responses might include:

'Yes, it was great.'

'It was OK.'

'Most of it was excellent, but some bits were rubbish.'

'Complete rubbish, except for the end.'

Activities

Create **three** different sets of codes. Hand them to another student and get them to try to understand what the codes represent and how they work.

If you have a scale of 1–4 (1 being excellent, 4 being rubbish) how do you code these statements? Different people will give the same statement a different mark on the scale.

It would be difficult to set up and analyse a database where all possible values were allowed, therefore we need to try and organise the data. However a balance needs to be achieved between having enough categories to get most of the responses, thereby making the data usable, and not having enough and so having to coarsen the data or make too much of a value judgement.

There are some other disadvantages to encoding data. If the user does not know how the codes are being used, they will not be able to encode any new data or be able to interpret the data that is currently held on computer.

It is possible that if some encoding system was devised that uses a system of numbers and letters to identify objects, for example:

BL36TR   **meaning Black Trousers 36" waist**

then eventually the number of codes will be used up and a new encoding system will need to be developed. This will of course mean re-encoding all of the existing data.

Once a survey has been done and all the information encoded and entered into the computer, it is unlikely that the computer operator will have access to the original survey forms. This means that they have to accept what is on the computer. If there are any errors, value judgements that are incorrect or codes that have been input incorrectly they would not know. This means that any information that is extracted will be taken as being correct.

Advantages of encoding

Encoding data is not all doom and gloom. There are some advantages as well.

The computer memory requirements are a lot less when information is encoded. Instead of storing **Black Trousers 36" waist**, you would only need to store **BL36TR**. This may not seem a lot, but when you are storing thousands of records, the space saving is considerable. This means you do not need as large a hard drive and back-up capability and this in turn costs less money.

It can be quicker to enter a code into the computer than to type in all the details. Of course, with new users, there is a delay as they work out the codes. The code is also more suitable to bar code tagging that allows the code to be scanned (probably automatically) into the database.

Activities

Create an encoding system to encode people's facial features: hair colour, eye colour, skin tone etc.

Try out the encoding system. What are the advantages and disadvantages of the system you have created? Is it easy to understand and use?

Investigate the Dewey Decimal system of encoding for libraries. Is it easy to follow? Could it be improved?

Hopefully, there will be fewer errors. As the codes follow a set pattern, it is possible to apply validation to the different parts of the code. In the example:

BL36TR

- the first two letters must match a colour code in the database;
- the second two numbers must be between two values;
- the final two letters must match an item code in the database.

This cannot ensure that the data is correct, but it does ensure that it matches the codes. Fewer errors will occur than with free text data entry.

The data takes on a very precise structure when encoded. It is easier to sort and search the data because it is organised. It is also possible to analyse and graph data if it is tightly structured.

Summary of encoding

Advantages	Disadvantages
Less memory requirement Storing less information therefore less memory is required.	**Precision of data coarsened** For example, Light Blue encoded as Blue.
Security If the codes are not apparent then it is difficult to know and understand the meaning of the codes (not encryption).	**Encoding of value judgements** For example, 'Was the film good?' to be encoded as a judgement of 1–4. This will be encoded differently by different people and makes comparisons difficult.
Speed of input The codes take less time to enter therefore it is quicker to input large amount of data.	**The user needs to know the codes used** If the user does not know the codes they cannot use them.
Data validation Since the codes follow a strict set of numbers and letters they are easy to validate.	**Limited number of codes** If codes are made up of a range of letters and numbers the options will be limited.
Organisation of data If the data is in a standardised format then it can be compared and organised.	**Difficult to track errors** Validation will ensure the code is entered correctly but the nature of the code will make it difficult to see if the code is actually correct.

Questions

1 What is meant by encoding data?

2 Describe **three** advantages of encoding data.

3 Describe **three** disadvantages of encoding data.

4 Explain, using an example, how data can be encoded.

5 Give **two** situations where the encoding of data is appropriate. For each situation, explain why data needs to be encoded.

Describe and give examples of a range of validation methods and their purpose

In order for it to be useful within a computer system, the data first has to be entered into the system. Errors can occur at the point of entry of data into the system.

Validation is a check that is performed by the computer as the data is being entered. It tries to prevent entry of any data that does not conform to pre-set rules.

There are many different rules that can be created, however they will not stop incorrect data being entered, they will just ensure that the data that is entered is:

- sensible
- reasonable
- within acceptable boundaries
- complete.

The checks that can be applied fall into several categories:

- Range
- Type
- Presence
- Length
- Lookup
- Picture
- Check digit

Range checks

A range check sets an upper and a lower boundary for the data. The data entered must lie between these two values.

For example, in a secondary school a student can be in Years 7–13. A lower boundary of 7 and an upper boundary of 13 can be set.

Type checks

This makes sure that the data entered is of the correct type. Types of data include: Numeric, String, Boolean and Date/Time.

Type checks will not allow you to enter the wrong data type. For example if you try to enter text into a numeric field it will be rejected.

Presence checks

These are also called existence checks. Not every field or question will need to be answered. However there will be some that must have an answer and be filled in.

By applying a presence check, the computer will insist that a value is entered for that field.

For example, if you are storing details about a student, you need to know their name, address and phone number. These are vital pieces of information. You may not need to store an email address as not every student has one.

Length checks

When any data is entered into a computer it has a length. A single character has a length of 1, 'Hello' has a length of 5.

A length check ensures that the data cannot be more than a set number of characters.

Lookup checks

This is where the data is cross referenced against a list to make sure that it is valid and acceptable. In some cases, the cross referencing may give additional information. For example, a postcode can be checked against a list and if there is more than one property then a choice is given. It is a confirmation of correct entry.

Lookup validation is not a search, it is a comparison against known data.

Picture checks

This is also known as a format check. Some data entries might be a combination of numbers and letters, therefore you cannot apply a type check. However the location of the numbers and letters within the data might be in the same place every time.

For example, some item codes might look like:

RT678H

FD634K

FG789E

- The first two entries are letters.
- The next three entries are numbers.
- The last entry is a letter.

This would allow a format check to be applied to the field, for example:

LLNNNL

where L is letter and N is number.

This makes sure that only letters can be entered for the first two characters and the last character and numbers for the middle three.

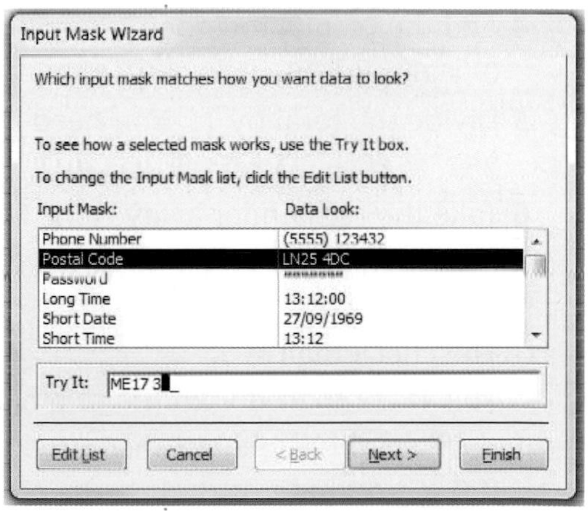

Figure 1.6

Check digit

A check digit is calculated using a set of numbers and then added to the end of them.

When the code is created, the check digit is created and added to the code. Before the code is then processed, the check digit is recalculated and compared with the one in the code. If they are the same processing continues. If they are not an error has occurred and the code value needs to be re-entered.

Check digits are commonly used when data is transmitted. Corruption can occur during transmission of data and the check digit is used to ensure that the data received is the same as that sent.

The International Standard Book Number (ISBN), the number that uniquely identifies a book, has a check digit. A 10-digit ISBN is calculated using Modulus 11.

The following example shows how to use Modulus 11 to calculate a check digit. An ISBN is 0-7487-9116-7

1 Remove the last digit from the ISBN: 0-7487-9116

2 Write out the remaining numbers. Starting from the right-hand number, put a 2 under it. Put a 3 under the next one and so on.

Number	0	7	4	8	7	9	1	1	6
Code	10	9	8	7	6	5	4	3	2

3 Multiply the number by the code.

Number	0	7	4	8	7	9	1	1	6
Code	10	9	8	7	6	5	4	3	2
Result	0	63	32	56	42	45	4	3	12

4 Add the results together.

$0 + 63 + 32 + 56 + 42 + 45 + 4 + 3 + 12 = 257$

5 Divide the total by 11. You need to write down the remainder.

$257 \div 11 = 23$ remainder 4

6 Take the remainder away from 11. The value that is left is the check digit.

$11 - 4 = 7$

The check digit is 7.

This is compared with the original check digit. If they are the same then the data has been transmitted correctly.

If the remainder is 0, then the check digit is 0.

If the remainder is 1, then the check digit is X.

A check digit calculation is very good for finding transposition errors. If two numbers were swapped around then they would have different weightings and the check digit would be different.

Activities

1 Configure a spreadsheet for a user to confirm whether or not an ISBN check digit is correct.

2 Use the Modulus 11 calculation to confirm the check digit of the following ISBNs. For any that are incorrect, give the correct check digit.

   a) 1-854-87918-9

   b) 0-552-77109-X

   c) 0-330-28414-3

   d) 0-330-34742-X

   e) 0-330-35183-3

3 Examine the form below and identify all the different validation methods that could be applied to it. Give a reason for each method of validation used.

```
Application for Climbing Course

Surname _____   Forename(s) _____

Address _____

       _____

Postcode _____   Tel No. _____

Date of birth ___/___/___   Age _____   Male ☐   Female ☐

Previous experience:   Experienced ☐   Moderate ☐   Beginner ☐

Signature of applicant _____   date ___/___/___

_____

Consent of parent or guardian (for young people under 18 years of age)

I agree to my son/daughter/ward participating in the Climbing Course

Signature of Parent/Guardian _____

Name _____

_____

For office use only:

Applicant accepted: Yes/No          Date of course: ___/___/___
```

Figure 1.7 Example of a form

Describe and give examples of a range of verification methods and their purpose

If you have collected some information on paper, at some point it will need to be entered into the computer.

Once you have entered it into the computer you will have two copies: the paper-based original and that stored in the computer.

The paper-based copy is known as the source document.

The copy on the computer is known as the object document.

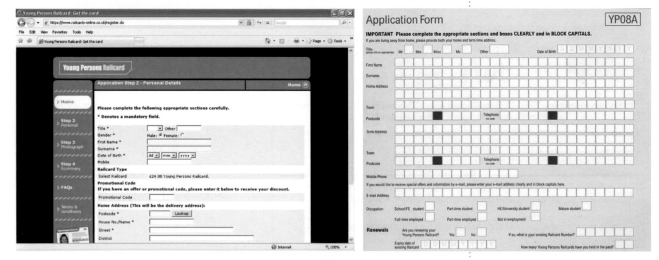

Figure 1.8 Electronic and paper documents

Verification is making sure that the information on the source document is the same as the information on the object document.

Put simply, it is making sure that the same information that is on the paper has been entered and not changed in any way. It does not ensure that the information is correct.

There are two main methods of verification:
- double entry
- manual verification.

Double entry

This is essentially entering the data twice. The computer then compares the two sets of data and if it finds any differences it informs the user who can then make appropriate changes.

Passwords are one method of double entry that you will have come across. Often you are asked to enter a password twice so correct entry can be verified.

Figure 1.9 Confirming a password

Double entry could be by the same person or different people.

The main problem with double entry is that if the same error is made both times then the computer will not find a difference.

Manual verification

Manual verification is essentially proofreading the data.

This involves visually comparing the source data with the entry typed into the computer. It relies on a person being able to follow two sets of data and find any differences.

Unfortunately, this is not a very reliable method. It is very difficult to transfer attention between paper and screen. It is also difficult to keep track of where you are on the paper and where you are looking on the screen.

Questions

1 Describe **two** methods of verification.

2 Give **two** disadvantages of double entry verification.

3 Give **one** advantage of manual verification.

4 Explain why verification cannot ensure that the data is accurate.

Common errors

The two most common errors caused when entering data into a computer are transcription errors and transposition errors.

Transcription errors are where you have made a mistake copying the data. For example, it may be by striking the wrong key on the keyboard or hitting two keys at once.

Examples of transcription errors include:

	Wrong	Correct
Postcode	TN**18** 7TH	TN**28** 7TH
Surname	Stua**e**t	Stuart
Date	2**5**th March 2004	26th March 2004

Transposition errors are where you have reversed two numbers or letters.

	Wrong	Correct
Postcode	TN**82** 7TH	TN28 7TH
Surname	St**au**rt	Stuart
Date	26th March 20**40**	26th March 2004

No degree of accuracy

Neither validation nor verification can ensure that the data that has been entered is accurate.

Validation, as stated earlier, can make sure the data is:

- sensible
- reasonable
- within acceptable boundaries
- complete.

However, it is still possible to enter data that meets the validation rules but is wrong. In the table, all the data examples entered would pass the validation rule but in every case it is incorrect.

Rule	Data entered	Data intended to be entered
Presence	24 Apple Court	23 Apple Court
Range: between 0 and 5	4	2
Type: Numeric	244	245
Length: 4 characters	Help	Held

Similarly, verification methods also cannot make sure that the data entered is correct. They can make sure that it is the same as what was written down but can give no certainty of accuracy.

For example, imagine that on a data capture form the individual has written down that their birthday was 26th February 1965. If their birthday was actually 16th February 1965, then verification methods would not pick up the error.

Describe the difference between backing up and archiving of data and give reasons why they are necessary

Backing up is keeping a copy of the current data. If there is a failure of the computer system (e.g. a power failure leading to corruption, a virus, files accidentally deleted etc.), then the backup can be used to restore the data.

A backup is important so that data is not lost. Data is valuable and needs to be protected. It is suggested that the data held on the computer system is one of the most important assets of a business. There are many different back-up devices and strategies, such as:

- external memory: floppy disk, memory card etc.
- external hard drive
- tape
- making a second copy on a different disk, possibly storing it off site.

The backup needs to be organised and it must be possible to locate the files that you need. If you have several copies of the file, it is important to know which one is the latest backup. There are many different programs that will automate backups and restore data for you.

Archiving is for long-term storage of data that is not required immediately. In fact, archived data is often not required at all. It is taken off the system and stored in case it is required for an investigation in the future. When archiving, data is written to a large capacity storage device at long intervals, unlike backups, which should be written at short intervals.

Files should be archived when they are no longer needed immediately, but should be readily available if needed so they cannot be permanently deleted. Examples of these types of files are:

- last year's financial or sales records
- completed projects
- other materials not required on a day-to-day basis.

In a school, leavers' records are not required on a day-to-day basis but might be required in the future (for up to seven years after leaving) to write a reference for a student. The leavers' data would be archived.

The general procedure that should be used for archiving files is:

1 Copy the file onto the archival media (disk or tape).

2 Verify the copied files (make sure that the two copies are exactly the same and the copy has worked).

3 Delete the original files.

When you archive old files, you eliminate the waste of time and media that results from backing up unused files, free up hard drive space, and improve the performance of the system.

Activities

Investigate two different back-up programs. What facilities are available on them and why are they required?

Tip

Archiving data does not make a copy of the data. It is removing the data from the current system.

Backing up is making a copy of the data.

Questions

1 Using an example, define what is meant by the term backup.

2 Using an example, define what is meant by the term archive.

3 Why is it important to back up data?

4 What is the difference between archiving and backing up of data?

5 What storage medium should be used for archiving?

Describe the costs of producing information

Information needs to be produced. It does not just appear.
Information is not free – it costs money to produce it. It takes time to
collect the data, input it, process it and produce an output that meets
the required purpose.

There are four main areas where costs are incurred in the
production of information:

- Hardware
- Software
- Consumables
- Personnel

Hardware

Figure 1.10 Hardware

Hardware can be used to collect information, process it and output
it. It can also be used to store data for use at a later date. It may be
necessary for the organisation to purchase items of hardware.

The initial costs of the hardware are expensive but these can be
offset by the length of time the hardware is kept. Also, once it has
been acquired, it can be used for other tasks, again spreading the
costs.

Ongoing hardware costs include repair and maintenance costs
as well as upgrade costs. It is necessary to keep the hardware in
good working order and the organisation could have a maintenance
contract or have the equipment repaired when required.

As time progresses, the storage requirements of the organisation
will increase. If, for example, they are producing a newsletter, they
will want to keep all back issues on the computer. This will have an
implication on disk space and they may need to increase the capacity
of the hard drive. This has a knock-on effect on backups, which will
therefore also require greater capacity.

Activities

Copy and fill in the following table giving examples of what the hardware could be used for, the cost of the hardware and its estimated life.

Device	Use	Cost	Life
Scanner			
Printer			
2 GB memory key			
Digital camera			
Digital tablet			
LCD monitor			

Software

Figure 1.11
Software

Software licences need to be purchased. This will include the operating system and utilities, as well as that used to produce the information. The licences can be purchased as a one-off cost or re-licensed year to year.

The software might also require a technical support agreement so if there are difficulties, support is available to solve the problems. Support might be bought from the software manufacturer or from a third-party: both are likely to cost money.

There may be training costs associated with the software, such as courses that the users will need to go on. They may also require reference manuals.

Over time the software may need to be upgraded. If the software is upgraded, there are more puchasing costs, though it may be possible to acquire the new version licence at a lower cost. There are also potential costs associated with upgrading software, not only for installation time, but possibly to purchase new hardware to make the system work efficiently.

Activities

Investigate the cost of training courses for a piece of software such as InDesign or Adobe Photoshop.

Consumables

Figure 1.12 Paper and ink cartridges

Consumables are items that get used. Paper and printer ink/toner are the two main consumables.

Personnel

Personel costs are the costs related to people working in the organisation. Employees' salaries need to be paid or people may need to be hired to produce the information. This is a long-term cost. They may be required to collect, collate, enter, process and output the information.

When staff first begin to work on a project, it is likely that they will take longer than staff who have been doing the work for some time. They will need some time to get used to the system and software. Over a few months, as they get used to procedures and software, the time will reduce until they eventually meet the deadlines. This 'bedding in' time needs to be built into the costs.

When the people using the software go on training courses there may be costs associated with covering their job whilst they are away, as well as the training costs.

Depending on the information that is being produced, there may be additional costs that involve checking the accuracy of the data.

Personnel costs are likely to be the most expensive costs incurred in producing information.

Activities

Imagine that you are producing a leaflet for a new vegetable delivery service.

Using the four costs discussed, list all the expenditure associated with producing a leaflet and give a cost to each item.

Questions

1 Describe the hardware items required to collect and input data for a fashion magazine.

2 Explain why an organisation might need to upgrade the software it uses to produce information.

3 Explain the personnel costs incurred by an organisation that produces a leaflet completely from scratch.

Describe clearly the terms input, processing, output, storage and feedback, drawing a diagram to illustrate how they are related

Any ICT system can be broken down into:

- input
- processing
- storage
- output
- feedback.

This can be represented as a diagram. Some of the elements may be manual.

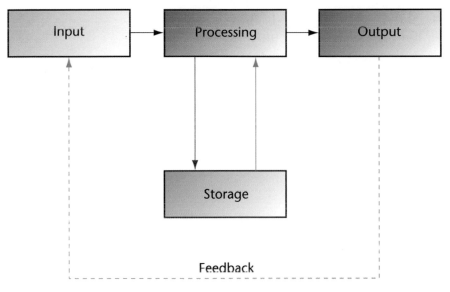

Figure 1.13 ICT system block diagram

Input

This is taking information that is external to the system and entering it into the system. This may be manual input (e.g. keyboard) or automated input (e.g. OMR). It may also be input by electronic means (e.g. via a network or CD/disk).

Processing

This is an action performed on the data. Processing can include sorting, searching or performing calculations on the data.

Storage

This is where data is held. It may be the data that has been input, data required during processing or the results of processing. This is data that is still within the system.

Output

This is taking information that was in the system and outputting it. The method used may result in printed output, output on screen or electronic output (e.g. disk/CD).

There is always a problem when looking at input, storage and output. Where do CDs and disks fit in? In themselves, they are storage devices. However, if the data stored on them is being entered into the system via the storage device then they are input media and if the data on them is being taken outside of the system they are output media. If they are storing data within the system then they are storage devices as well!

Feedback

This is where the output from the system forms part of the input to the system. Feedback is usually applied to real-time situations. If the response to the feedback is automatic then the process is a closed loop. If there is an operator involved then the process is an open loop.

A feedback example is taking the register at school using a computer.

1 The teacher takes the register for their class. This is input into the computer.
2 The data is processed. The student is found on the system and the correct response marked by their name: present, absent etc. This data is stored in the system.
3 The system can then generate an absence list for the session. This is the output.
4 The teacher can look at the absence list at a later time, question the offending student and find out why they were absent. The teacher then updates the list with the reason. This is feedback.

Turnaround documents

In some systems a turnaround document is used. This is a document that has gone through the system and is output. It is printed by the computer. Additional data is recorded on the document and this is then input into the system at a later date.

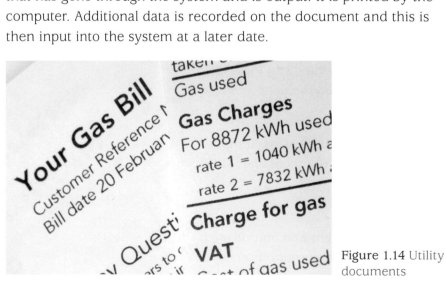

Activities

Using the following scenario, describe the terms input, processing, storage, output and feedback.

A school trip to The Lake District is being organised. Letters are sent each week to all parents whose children are going, with how much they need to pay. If they send money in during the week, the records are altered. Once they have paid the full amount no more letters are sent to the parents.

Figure 1.14 Utility documents

Turnaround documents are used by utility companies to allow the home owner to record meter readings. The document has the name, address and account number of the home owner already on it. The home owner adds the meter reading and sends it back.

Figure 1.14 shows an example of feedback. The document is output from the system and forms part of the input at a later date.

Questions

1 Describe these terms: input, storage, processing, output and feedback.

2 Draw a diagram to show the input, storage, processing, output and feedback for a vehicle cruise control system.

3 What is the difference between closed-loop and open-loop feedback?

4 What are the advantages of using a turnaround document?

Chapter summary

Data, information and knowledge
Data is made up of alphanumeric characters.
information = data + structure + context + meaning
Knowledge is the application and use of the information.

Representation methods
Text (including writing)
Graphics (including pictures)
Sound (including voice)
Moving pictures (animation or video)
LED (sequence of lights)

Data types
Boolean: true or false
Real: numbers with decimals
Integer: whole numbers
Text/String: alphanumeric characters
Date/Time

Sources of data
Direct and indirect
A direct source is where you have collected the data.
An indirect source is where someone else has collected it, either for the same or for a different purpose.

Static and dynamic data
Static data cannot be changed (e.g. CD-ROM).
Dynamic data can be updated (e.g. web pages).

Quality of information
Accuracy
Relevance
Age
Completeness
Presentation
Level of detail

Encoding data
Validation and verification
> Neither can ensure the accuracy of the entered data.

Validation
> Ensures that entered data is reasonable, complete, sensible and within acceptable boundaries. This is achieved by:
>> Range check
>> Type check
>> Presence check
>> Lookup check
>> Check digit
>> Length check
>> Picture check

Verification
> Ensures the source and object data are the same. This is achieved by:
>> Proofreading
>> Computer verification

Backup and archive
Backing up is making a copy of the data.
Archiving is removing the data from direct access.

Cost of information
Hardware: specialist equipment such as scanner, camera, graphics tablet etc.
Software: desktop publishing or graphics software etc.
Personnel: new employees and the training of individuals
Consumables: electricity, ink and paper

Generic ICT system
Input: external data placed into the system
Process: manipulating the data
Storage: holding the data for later use
Output: data being passed outside the system
Feedback: output influencing the input

Chapter tests

Test 1

Answer the following questions in the context of a rugby supporters' club that needs to keep data on its members.

1 Describe the term 'data' and give an example of data. [2]

2 Show how data can become information. [3]

3 The club is producing a leaflet for its members. Identify **two** different methods of representing information they could use and give an advantage of each method. [4]

4 Describe **three** different costs the club would incur if they decided to produce the leaflet in house. [6]

5 The club is setting up a database to hold details of its members. The data needs to be encoded before it is entered into the database. Describe **three** advantages of encoding data. [6]

6 Describe and give examples of **three** different methods of validation the database could use. Identify an appropriate field for each type of validation. [9]

7 Data is input into the system, processed, stored and output from the system. Draw a diagram to show how the terms: input, process, storage and output are related. [4]

Test 2

Answer the following questions in the context of a small company that writes online user manuals for different application software.

1 The manuals contain text, graphics and sound. Describe the advantages of each type of representation method and give an example of its use in the manual. [9]

2 The manuals are designed to give the reader information that they can turn into knowledge. Describe the difference between information and knowledge. [4]

3 The content of the manual could come from a direct or an indirect source. Describe what is meant by a direct and an indirect source of data. Give an example of each that could be used to get information for the manual. [6]

4 The manuals will only sell if the quality of the information contained within them is high. Identify **three** factors that affect the quality of information and, for each, use an example to describe how it could affect the information in the manual. [6]

5 The information in the manual has value. Explain under what circumstances the manual may lose its value. [2]

6 The manual can contain static and dynamic data. Describe the difference between static and dynamic data and give an example of each that could be used in the manual. [4]

7 Describe what feedback the company could receive on its manuals and how it could use the feedback to improve future manuals. [4]

Software and hardware components of an information system

2

Introduction

This chapter covers the hardware and software that make up a computer system. You will need to make sure that you understand the type of question and the answers required as the hardware devices will change and improve.

This chapter covers:

- The difference between hardware and software
- Standardisation and its impact
- Input, output and storage devices
- Specialist hardware devices
- Specialist software
- Different types of software
- Characteristics of different user interfaces

Describe the difference between hardware and software, giving examples of each to illustrate the description

Hardware is things you can touch. It is the physical components that make up the computer. Examples include the mouse, keyboard, processor, monitor, printer etc.

Software is the programming code that makes the computer work. There are two main types of software: system software (operating systems), which control the workings of the computer; and applications, such as word-processing programs, spreadsheets and databases.

Any examples you give must be in general terms. You must not give proprietary (makers') names. For example, 'Word' is not acceptable, but 'word processor' is.

The following table gives the correct terms.

Allowed	NOT allowed (examples of)
Word processor	Word WordPerfect
Spreadsheet	Excel Quattro Pro

Allowed	NOT allowed (examples of)
Database	Access Paradox FileMaker
Presentation	PowerPoint
Email / PIM	Outlook Lotus Notes
Operating system	Windows Linux Mac OS

Questions

1 Using an example, define what is meant by the term hardware.

2 Using an example, define what is meant by the term software.

3 What is the difference between software and hardware?

Explain the lack of standardisation affecting both hardware and software

Standardisation is the imposition, by a third party, or with agreement, of a set of standards on manufacturers.

There is a set of standards (rules and benchmarks) that both software and hardware must adhere to if it is to be recognised by certain bodies.

There are different standards in other parts of business, such as standards for food preparation, voltage and measurements etc. In ICT there are several organisations that monitor and develop standards:

● W3C: the World Wide Web Consortium develops standards for the Internet.
● ISO: the International Organization for Standardization currently has over 14 000 standards.

In a perfect world, everything would meet the same standard. This means that everything is built and works to the same level of quality. A standard will ensure that items of a similar type, but from completely different manufacturers, perhaps on different sides of the world, will work together using the same protocols.

Unfortunately there is a lack of standardisation in ICT. This is not to say that it is missing altogether. There are standards for hardware and software, but there are many different standards and they are not always compatible with each other.

A lack of standardisation amongst hardware has the following disadvantages.

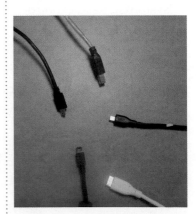

Figure 2.1 Different USB connectors

Cost	If you purchase a computer that is not part of a global standard then all the subsequent upgrades and parts you buy will have to come from specific sources and are likely to be very expensive. If you do not buy items that are compatible with your computer, then they might not work correctly, or at all.
Availability	If there is limited availability of a piece of hardware then the supply itself may be limited. Limited supply has a knock-on adverse effect on cost.
Technical support	If availability is limited, then the support for it is also likely to be limited and expensive.

The standardisation of hardware is not just about different types of computers. It may be about computers of the same type but of different ages. Computers purchased three or four years ago will probably not be able to use new processors, RAM or graphics cards because the standard itself has moved on. This is seen in the rapid development in wireless network devices.

Software standards are a little different. Although there is a set of standards released by the operating system manufacturers (so that application programs can be written to work with the operating system and be accredited) there is limited compatibility between the standards.

Think about word processors. In an ideal world, every document written in any word processor would be able to be viewed in any other word processor.

Software standards are not just linked to operating systems. Web pages are written for different computers, running different operating systems and different browsers, and standards mean that the pages can be viewed on many different platforms. However, there are elements of web pages that cannot be viewed correctly in different browsers (e.g. colours and alignment).

A lack of standardisation amongst web browsers means that you might not see the page exactly as the designer intended it. In many cases this might not matter, but it could mean that the corporate colours of a company are displayed slightly differently, that some text does not appear where it should, or that some code may not work properly thereby limiting the functionality of the website.

From a manufacturer's point of view, lack of standardisation is not necessarily a bad thing. It means they can continually release new hardware, resulting in built-in obsolescence in the devices and they can make more money because of it.

Takeovers

When one company takes over another there are likely to be incompatibilities with the computer systems used. The two companies might have standardised within themselves, but a lack of

Activities

1 Launch your word processor and look at the different files that can be imported.

2 Do some research to see if there are any word-processor types missing.

global standards might mean that systems do not function with one another. This can have the following negative impacts:

- no communication between systems
- miscommunication between systems leading to incorrect data being shared
- new equipment having to be purchased
- staff needing to be trained to use the new systems
- lack of technical support on the new system.

Questions

1 What are standards?

2 Describe **two** effects on a user of having different hardware standards.

3 What are the problems of having different standards?

4 How does standardisation affect how web pages are displayed?

5 What are the advantages of a lack of standardisation to a company?

Identify an appropriate input device for a given situation and justify the choice made

An input device is a piece of hardware that gets data from outside the computer system into the computer system.

Any manual input device increases the risk of inaccurate data being entered.

There are many different input devices and it is not possible to list them all. Different input devices are suitable for different uses, so it is important to choose the most appropriate. This can be determined by the cost, the volume of data to be input and the number of mistakes you can allow to be made.

Keyboard

A keyboard is a typewriter-like set of keys that are used to input data and control commands to the computer. A keyboard has a set of letter and number keys, and may also have a calculator-like numerical keypad, as well as a set of cursor-movement keys.

Keyboards are good for inputting small quantities of data.

There are three main keyboard layouts: QWERTY, alphabetical and Dvorak. Most keyboards use the QWERTY layout.

Activities

Make a template (or download one) of a Dvorak keyboard and an alphabetical keyboard. What are the advantages and disadvantages of using the Dvorak layout and the alphabetical layout?

Figure 2.2 Types of keyboard

Keyboards do not always have to have capital letters on them. Primary school keyboards are available with lowercase letters and concept keyboards are programmable.

A concept keyboard/overlay is a sheet that goes over a flat pad and you can create your own individual keys. These are used in bars and restaurants where the keys represent items for sale, such as drinks and meals.

Concept keyboards are good in situations where language is a problem (pre-school, physically impaired) or there is a set number of options (on tills).

Figure 2.3 Using a concept keyboard

Keyboard design has evolved over the last few years and now there are several different ergonomic varieties. These include curved keyboards, split keyboards and complete keyboard desks to ensure good posture.

Mouse

A mouse is a pointing device that can be used to select items on a screen. It has buttons on top to make the selection and a sensor underneath that allows the pointer (cursor) to move on the screen following the physical movement of the mouse.

Mouse shapes have evolved over the last few years and it is now possible to get ergonomically shaped mice that fit into the palm of the hand. The movement is sensed by a ball and rollers (on a cabled mouse) or by using an optical sensor (on a cable-less mouse).

A mouse needs some surface area to operate on. This is not always convenient with laptops, so these are fitted with touch pads that sense the movement of the user's finger.

Alternative pointing devices are the trackerball and the joystick. Both of these devices remain stationary on the desk surface.

The trackerball is effectively an upside-down mouse, so the ball is moved directly by the user instead of moving it along a surface.

Activities

Create a concept keyboard that could be used in your school canteen by the till operator.

The joystick directly controls the cursor on the screen. Ergonomic joysticks are moulded to fit the hand. They are commonly used for games software and flight simulators.

Scanner

A scanner translates information into a form the computer can use. There are many different types of scanner, for example:

- Bar code. This reads the bar codes and translates the bars into numbers. Bar codes are used to identify an item, for example products in supermarkets, so stock and price can be analysed, or parcels by couriers, so that the location of a delivery can be tracked.
- Optical Mark Reader (OMR). This detects the presence or absence of a mark in a predefined area on a page and translates it into a value, for example on Lotto number selection forms, school registers and multiple choice questions.
- Magnetic card reader. This can take the information on a magnetic stripe and convert it into usable data, for example on credit cards and secure access cards.
- Flatbed scanner. This digitises an image so that it can be processed later as a picture or, by using optical character recognition (OCR), as editable text.
- Magnetic Ink Character Recognition (MICR). This detects magnetic ink marks and turns them into numbers. They are used to read bank details on cheques.

Figure 2.4 OMR, MICR and bar code

Graphics tablet

A graphics tablet is a flat working area like a sheet of paper with a stylus that resembles a pen. Both have evolved ergonomically in recent years. The movement of the stylus is detected by the tablet so the user can manipulate images on a screen and create free-hand drawings. Classroom interactive whiteboards can be thought of as very large graphics tablets.

Graphics tablets are used by designers and anyone involved in drawing directly on a computer.

Digitiser

Any device that converts analogue data to digital data is a digitiser. It is a generic description of many devices. A scanner, digital camera and graphics tablet are all types of digitiser.

Activities

1 There are many other data input devices that have not been covered above. Research the following devices, focusing on their purpose and ergonomic features.
   - Digital camera
   - Microphone
   - Sensor
   - Touch screen
   - Switch
2 Investigate the use of biometric devices as input devices. Describe the devices and list their advantages and disadvantages.

Questions

1 Why are keyboards not suitable for inputting large amounts of data?

2 What are the advantages of concept keyboards?

3 Describe a digitiser.

4 Describe **two** different types of scanner and give examples where they should be used.

5 What is the most efficient input device for a newspaper reporter and why?

Identify an appropriate output device for a given situation and justify the choice made

Output devices are used to display the result of processing to the user. They are designed to get data from within the computer to outside of the computer system. As we move towards the paperless society there is less reliance on hard copy and a lot of output is now being produced electronically (emails, transferred to CD etc.).

There are many different output devices and it is not possible to list them all. Different output devices are suitable for different uses, so it is important to choose the most appropriate.

Monitor

A monitor is a device that takes signals from a computer and displays them on a screen. Monitors come in a variety of sizes and resolutions. The resolution is the maximum number of dots (pixels) that can be displayed on the screen at any one time. A screen resolution is given as the number of horizontal dots and then the number of vertical dots, for example 800 × 600 or 1024 × 768.

Printer

Printers produce hard copy output (most often on paper). There are several different types of printer.

Dot matrix

These are impact printers. This means there is physical contact between the print head and the paper through an inked ribbon. Dot-matrix printers can print in colour as well as black and white and their main advantage is that they will print on multi-part stationery (carbon forms).

Inkjet

These spray ink onto the paper and are relatively quiet. They are available in black and white or colour. They are relatively cheap to run as the only replaceable component is the cartridge. They are used in homes and offices where the cost of a colour laser printer can be prohibitive.

Laser

These are high-resolution non-impact printers that use a similar process to photocopiers. A laser printer uses a rotating mirror to reflect laser beams onto a photosensitive drum, where the image of the page is converted into an electrostatic charge that attracts and holds the toner (ink). A piece of charged paper is then rolled against the drum to transfer the image, and heat is applied to fuse the toner and paper together to create the final image.

They are reliable and produce excellent quality in both colour and black and white. Toner will frequently need replacing so running costs are high. Drum and fuser unit replacements are also expensive.

Laser printers are used where high-quality fast output is required. Once mainly found in businesses, they are becoming cheaper to buy and are now often used in homes. Colour laser printers are often now found in schools.

Activities

1 Copy and complete the following table.

Printer	Description	Advantages	Disadvantages
Dot matrix			
Inkjet			
Laser			

2 There are other types of printer. Research the following types of printer:
   ● Daisy wheel
   ● Line
   ● Thermal

There are several factors that need to be taken into account when choosing a printer.

1 How much output?

2 What speed is needed?

3 Is heavy-duty equipment necessary?

4 Quality of output needed?

5 Letter quality?

6 Near letter quality?

7 Draft?

8 Location of printer?

9 How big a footprint can be handled (i.e. what surface area does the printer cover)?

10 Is noise level important?

11 Multiple copies needed?

12 Colour print needed?

Plotter

A plotter is a mechanical device which produces printout using vector or coordinate graphics. They are used to draw accurate lines diagrams, such as maps and building plans.

There are two types of plotter: the flat-bed plotter where the paper stays still and the pens move, and the drum plotter where the paper is on a drum which moves in one direction whilst the pens move across it at right angles.

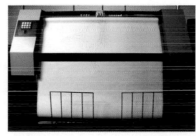

Figure 2.5 Flat-bed and drum plotters

Identify an appropriate storage device for a given situation and justify the choice made

Storage devices are used to hold data and programs. They are non-volatile (they keep the stored data after the computer has been switched off). Storage capacity is measured in bytes.

kilobyte (kB)	1024 bytes
megabyte (MB)	1024 kB
gigabyte (GB)	1024 MB
terabyte (TB)	1024 GB
petabyte (PB)	1024 TB
exabyte (EB)	1024 PB
zettabyte (ZB)	1024 EB
yottabyte (YB)	1024 ZB

There are many different types of storage device on the market. The main ones are discussed here.

Hard disks

Hard disks are the main storage devices for a computer and hold the data and programs.

A hard disk comprises a flat, circular, rigid plate with a surface that can be magnetised on one or both sides and on which data can be stored. The disk is sealed in a case to prevent dirt entering and potentially crashing the drive read/write heads. Hard disk drives can be internal (fixed in the computer) or removable. Portable hard disks allow large amounts of data to be transferred easily between machines (which perhaps are located far apart), and they are often used as external back-up units.

Optical discs

CD-ROM

The CD-ROM (compact disc read-only memory) is similar to a music CD. They have a storage capacity of about 700 MB and come in two varieties: a CD-R (recordable) and CD-RW (rewritable). CD-Rs are WORM (Write-Once, Read-Many) storage devices, and once the data has been written to them it is fixed and cannot be removed. CDs that you buy in shops (music, games and program CDs) have already been written. You can buy blank CD-Rs and copy (write) data to your own CDs. CD-RWs can be written to, erased and rewritten to many times.

DVD

The DVD (digital versatile disc) again looks similar to the CD. It has a storage capacity of 4.7 GB (or more) and, like CDs, comes in recordable (DVD-R) and rewritable (DVD-RW) forms.

Tape drive

Tape drives use tape cassettes to store data and have very high storage capacity. They are used for backing up large amounts of data.

Memory sticks

These are a series of solid state devices. They were originally developed for digital cameras but have found a market replacing the floppy disk. They have a large storage capacity and come in a variety of formats

Activities

1 Copy and fill in the following table.

Media	Description	Use	Capacity	Transfer speed	Cost per megabyte
Hard disk					
CD					
DVD					
Tape					
Memory stick					

2 Describe **five** characteristics that you should be looking for in order to make a comparison between devices when choosing a storage device.

Describe specialist hardware devices for physically disabled users: puff-suck switch, foot mouse, eye-typer, Braille printers and keyboards, speakers and microphones

There are a number of input and output devices for physically disabled people. There are two main groups of physically disabled people who require special devices to use a computer: the visually impaired and the motor impaired.

Devices to help the visually impaired

A person might have a total loss of vision in one or both eyes (blindness) or a partial loss. Hardware devices that can assist include:

- a Braille keyboard (a keyboard with Braille dots on the keys)
- a microphone (an input device used with voice recognition software)
- a loudspeaker (an output device for hearing signals and text read out for someone who cannot see it)
- a Braille printer (an impact printer that can create Braille on a page).

Activities

Investigate other hardware devices that have been created for visually impaired people and draw up a table like this:

Device	Use

Devices to help the motor impaired

Motor impairment is a loss or limitation of function in muscle control or movement, or a limitation in mobility. This can include hands that are too large or small for a keyboard, shakiness, arthritis, paralysis and loss of a limb.

Hardware devices that can assist include:

- a mouth-stick (a stick to control input with the mouth)
- a puff–suck switch (or blow–suck tube – a tube placed in the mouth and blown/sucked through)
- a tongue-activated joystick (placed in the mouth and manipulated with the tongue)

- an eye-typer (a device that fits onto the muscles around the eye and when the eye is moved a pointer on the screen moves)
- a foot mouse (a mouse that is controlled by the foot).

Figure 2.6 Helping the impaired

Questions

1 Describe **two** input devices that can be used by a visually impaired person.

2 Describe **two** input devices that can be used by a motor-impaired person.

3 Describe how a foot mouse works.

4 Describe how an eye-typer works.

Describe specialist software for physically disabled users: predictive text, sticky keys, zoom, voice recognition

One way of making the computer more usable for physically disabled individuals is to install specialist software. Some software comes pre-installed with computers.

The most common aid for the visually impaired is a screen reader: a program that reads out a computer display. The screen reader can read text that appears in dialogue boxes, menus, icons and text-editing windows. The screen reader may output information in Braille, use voice output or use other audio signals to indicate graphics on the screen.

Other tools that can be useful in place of or in addition to a screen reader include:

- Text-to-speech system. This takes written text and outputs it using a speech synthesiser. A text-to-speech system is useful for the visually impaired and in situations where users are not able to view the computer screen at all times, for example when driving.

- Speech-to-text system. This takes spoken words and inputs them into the computer, where they can be used to run commands or they can be converted to text in a word processor.
- Auditory feedback system. This plays sounds in response to user activity, for example noises for key presses, opening windows and menus, deleting files etc. This is useful as it confirms an action.
- Screen magnifier. This is a utility that can zoom in on portions of the screen to make it easier for the visually impaired to view information on computer monitors.
- Predictive text. This suggests the required word as the letters are typed so the user does not have to type the whole word.
- Sticky keys. These are useful for people who find it difficult to hold down more than one key at a time. Sticky keys allow keys to be pressed once and the system to act as if it was being held down.

Questions

1 Explain how software could be used by a visually impaired person to improve their computer use.

2 Describe **two** items of software that could be useful to a motor-impaired person.

3 Describe how a voice recognition system works.

4 Explain how the use of specialist software for disabled users could be used to improve computer use for the elderly.

Activities

Investigate the software that is pre-installed on a standard computer. Experiment with the software and consider whether it is useful only to physically disabled users or if other people could also benefit.

Describe different types of software (operating systems, user interfaces, utilities, applications software) and give examples of how and where each type of software would be used

Software is a computer program that provides the instructions enabling the computer hardware to work.

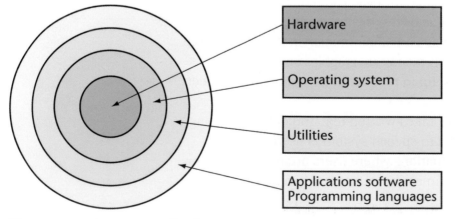

Hardware

Operating system

Utilities

Applications software
Programming languages

Figure 2.7

There are various types of software.

Operating system

The operating system is software that controls the allocation and use of hardware resources, such as memory, central processing unit (CPU) time, hard disk space and peripheral devices (like speakers or a mouse). It performs basic data management tasks such as recognising input from the keyboard, sending output to the display screen, and keeping track of files and directories on the hard disk.

The operating system is the core software on which programs depend. There are many different operating systems available, for example Microsoft Windows, BEOS, Linux and Unix.

User interface

The user interface is the means by which the user can interact with an application or operating system.

There are different types of user interface:

- Menu: an on-screen list of options
- Form: an on-screen form in which to type data
- Command line: a space to type instructions
- Natural language: a voice-based interface

A user interface is often termed as being a GUI and a WIMP interface.

A GUI (graphical user interface) is the term for an interface that is based on graphics and pictures rather than text.

A WIMP (Windows Icons Mouse Pointer) interface is a particular type of GUI. Not all GUIs use windows, icons, menus and pointers, but might use one or two of them.

All WIMPs are also GUIs, but not all GUIs are WIMPs.

Utility

A utility program is a small program that assists in the monitoring and maintaining of the computer system. Many utilities are now included with operating systems.

Examples of utility programs include:

- printer monitoring software
- virus checkers
- file compression software.

Application software

These are programs that allow the computer to be used to solve particular problems or perform particular tasks for the end user.
Application software includes programs such as:

- word processors
- spreadsheets
- databases
- communications (email)
- graphics packages.

Activities

1 List as many pieces of software that you can.

2 Using an athletics club as the scenario, copy and fill in the following table (an example has already been done). You can use the same type of software more than once.

Name of software	Type	Use
Word processor	Application	Writing letters to members letting them know when the next meeting is to be held.

Questions

1 What is the role of the operating system?

2 Identify **two** different types of application software.

3 Describe **two** different user interfaces.

4 What does WIMP stand for?

5 What is a GUI?

6 Describe **two** different utility programs.

7 How could a library make use of a spreadsheet, database and word processor?

Describe the characteristics of different styles of user interface (command-based, forms, dialogue, natural language, WIMP) and their appropriate uses

The user interface is the method by which the user communicates with the computer. When deciding which user interface to implement, the situation where it is going to be used and who is going to be using it must be considered.

Command-based

The user types instructions at a command prompt to control what the computer does. This means that you need to have a good knowledge of the commands and the effect of those commands. It is possible to do a lot of damage to the computer because the operating system can often be controlled directly unlike through a GUI. The screenshot example in Figure 2.7 shows the MS-DOS command `dir/p` typed at the command prompt `C:\>dir` to output a directory listing of a computer's C: drive, pausing after each page length is displayed.

Figure 2.8 A command-based instruction

The commands available will depend on the operating system, but often allow instructions to:

- output a directory listing
- show the difference between two files
- display environment variable.

If the interface is command-based only, then it takes up less memory than a GUI and so has the effect of running the commands faster.

A large number of commands have switches. These are parameters (additional commands) that can be added to the end of the main command to slightly change how it operates. In the screenshot example **/p** is a switch to output the directory one page at a time.

Command-based systems are used by expert users with a good understanding of the operating system. They are useful for running commands that cannot be accessed from a menu or form.

Activities

Investigate **five** different commands from two different operating systems. Describe what the command does and its syntax, including the switches.

Forms

A form is a limited area on screen with boxes to fill in.

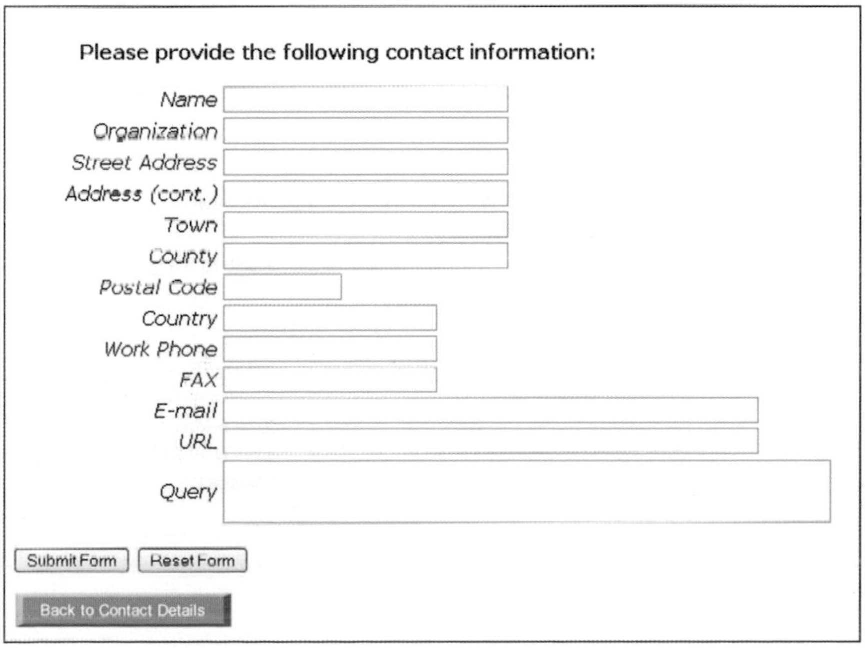

Figure 2.9 An on-screen form

A form has labels to give help to the user (for example stating what data to type in the box) and spaces to enter data. The latter might be drop-down boxes giving choices or open text boxes for free-form type. The form might also include option buttons to give further choices.

Forms can guide the user through typing relevant information in a structured manner. They can include default options for the user and give context-based assistance. The data entry boxes can also be validated.

Sometimes an on-screen form is designed to look like a paper-based form. This can make entering data easier.

Another type of interface that makes use of forms is a dialogue interface. This is one which asks questions and requires a response before continuing. Error messages that appear and must be dealt with are part of a dialogue interface.

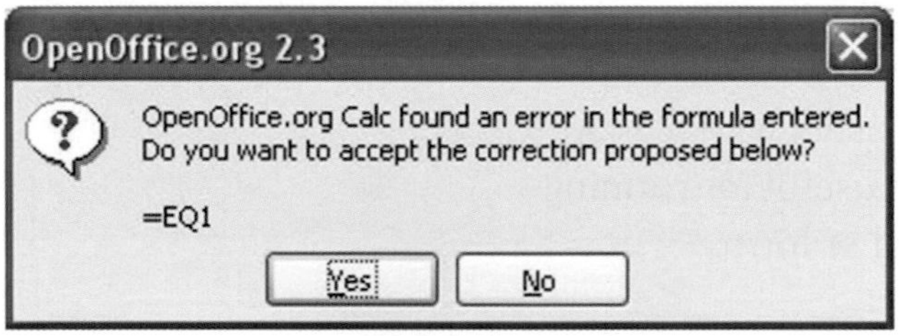

Activities

Design a form to be used for entering a customer order when purchasing a car.

Figure 2.10 An on-screen error message

Menus

- Menus are a series of related items that can be selected. Menus are either pop up (when you press a button or key a menu appears next to the cursor) or pull down (when you click a heading the rest of the menu appears below the heading).
- Menus are usually structured. This means that the menu items are categorised by the top word in a pull-down menu which gives an indication of what the menu is about. For example, 'File' contains all aspects to do with the file itself, 'Format' is about changing the appearance.
- Menus can be cascaded, that is one menu leads to another menu. Items on menus can appear faded to show they cannot be used in a particular context.
- Menus can also be context sensitive. Depending on what you are doing within the application, a different set of menus might appear. If you are working with tables you will get a menu for tables and if you are working with pictures you get a picture menu.
- Menus can use a GUI or be text-based.
- Menus are part of a WIMP interface.

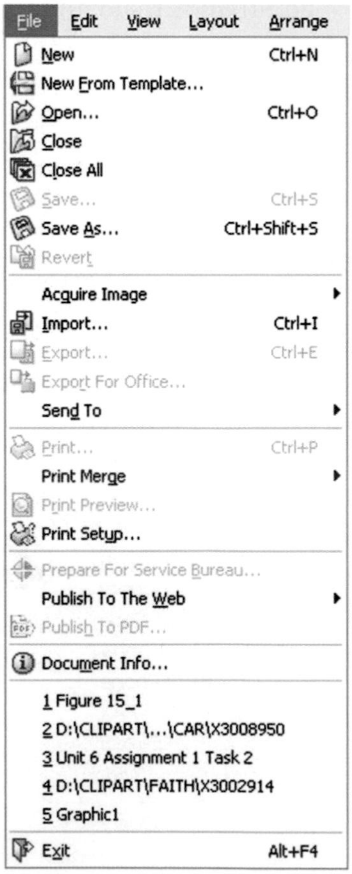

Figure 2.11 A file menu

Natural language

Natural language interfaces allow the users to use their own language to communicate with the computer. To some extent, this type of interface is still being researched and current offerings are still in their infancy.

There are two main types of natural language interface: spoken and written. Spoken interfaces are typified by voice recognition software that allows you to speak words into a word processor. Typed natural language interfaces include Microsoft Help and Ask.com. Software that recognises handwriting is also available for tablet PCs and Portable Digital Assistants (PDAs).

When natural language interfaces eventually become common place they will allow users of all abilities to access computers and this will revolutionise ICT.

Activities

1 Investigate the history of the WIMP interface.

2 The Apple Mac and Microsoft Windows computers use a WIMP interface. Compare and contrast the interfaces on both types of computer.

3 Investigate and write a report on the problems of voice recognition and using voice activated software.

Questions

1 Describe **three** advantages of using a command-based interface.

2 Where would the use of a forms interface be appropriate?

3 What are the disadvantages of a natural language voice interface?

4 Describe **three** characteristics of a menu interface.

Chapter summary

The difference between hardware and software
Hardware: something you can touch
Software: the programs used on the computer
Examples: NOT proprietary

Standardisation and its impact
Incompatibilities and cost implications

Input, output and storage devices
Input: getting data external to the system into the system
    Keyboard
    Mouse
    Graphics tablet
    Scanner
    Digitiser
    Microphone
Output: getting data within the system out of the system
    Printer
    Plotter
    Monitor
    Speakers
Storage: holding data
    Internal and external hard disk drives
    CD / CD-R / CD-RW / DVD / DVD-R / DVD-RW
    Memory stick
    Tape

Specialist hardware devices
Puff-suck switch
Mouth stick
Foot mouse
Eye-typer
Braille printer
Braille keyboard

Specialist software
Text-to-speech
Speech-to-text
Magnifier
Predictive text
Sticky keys

Different types of software

Operating system: core software

Utilities: additional programs to make the use of the computer easier

User interface: method by which the user communicates with the computer

Applications software: programs that solve particular problems and replace manual methods

Characteristics of different user interfaces

Command line: types commands at a prompt, can use switches, low memory overheads but specialist knowledge required

Forms: structured areas for responses, validated and logical

Menus: drop-down, pop-up and context sensitive, can be part of WIMP

Natural language: written or spoken everyday language, computer translates into commands needed to operate

Chapter tests

Test 1

1 A local newspaper has many computers advertised for sale within it. The computers have hardware and software. Describe, with examples, the difference between hardware and software. [4]

2 One of the adverts claims that an advantage of buying a PC from them is that they conform to industry standards. Explain the problems that would be brought about by a lack of standardisation in hardware. [4]

3 Justify the use of a plotter when producing orienteering maps. [6]

4 Describe how a home user would make use of **three** different output devices. [6]

5 Identify **two** different utilities that could be found on a PC. For each utility state how it would be used. [4]

6 Describe **two** characteristics of a command line interface. [4]

Test 2

An employee of an insurance company has recently been given the opportunity to work from home.

1 The software used at home is often different to the software used at work. Describe **two** problems that might arise as a result of this lack of standardisation. [4]

2 The employee has been given a QWERTY keyboard. Give **two** reasons why this is a more appropriate keyboard layout than DVORAK or alphabetical. [4]

3 Identify **three** different input devices that could be used by the employee, and for each **one** give an example of its use. [6]

4 Describe **two** items of software appropriate for a physically disabled user. [4]

5 How would the employee make use of:

a) a rewritable DVD [2]

b) a memory stick. [2]

6 Identify **three** different types of software found on a computer. [3]

7 Describe **three** different types of interface found on a computer and, for each, give an appropriate use. [9]

Characteristics of standard applications software and
3 application areas

Introduction

This chapter covers the characteristics, purpose and uses of the commonly used standard application software. You will need to make sure that you understand the specific purposes, characteristics and uses of each type. You should also be able to apply your knowledge to a specified scenario.

This chapter covers:

- Types of applications software used for basic tasks
- Characteristics of systems
- Wizards, style sheets, templates and macros
- Design considerations and tailoring of data-entry screens
- House style
- Master documents and slides
- File types

Describe different types of application software and justify their use for given tasks

Word processor

A word processor is a generic applications package that allows the entry, editing and formatting of text to create a range of documents. Word-processing packages are amongst the most commonly used computer software. We use the term 'word processing' to mean the activity of writing with the aid of a computer. Writing, when used in association with word processing, is generally used to mean the production of business or personal documents. These documents may include:

- letters
- memos
- reports.

The use of word-processing packages has replaced the use of pen and paper and typewriters in many businesses. These packages enable the user to enter data using a keyboard so that the data appears on the monitor as though on a piece of paper. The data may also be input by speaking into a microphone. The text on the screen can then be formatted to meet the needs of the user, edited, saved and printed.

Most word-processing packages have WYSIWYG (pronounced 'wizzy-wig') features. This means:

What You See Is What You Get

WYSIWYG means that the user can be sure that the screen layout will match the printed layout.

Desktop publishing

Desktop publishing (DTP) packages allow users to combine images and text to create publications.

The main difference between a word-processing package and a DTP package is that of emphasis. A word-processing package focuses on the creation of text-based documents whilst a DTP package focuses on the manipulation and accurate positioning of graphical objects on the page, including text, to create a composite publication.

A DTP package incorporates specific features to enable the end user to design, create and produce professional looking publications.

Amongst the publications that can be produced using a DTP package are:

- flyers
- brochures
- posters
- business cards.

There are many similarities between word processing and DTP packages. Many of the features, such as style sheets, wizards, templates and macros, found in a word-processing package are also found in DTP packages, and other packages such as spreadsheets, databases and presentations. However, the options presented to the user are likely to be different and will depend on the package being used.

Spreadsheet

Spreadsheet packages enable the user to produce both mathematical and financial models, and to produce graphs to diagrammatically represent the data. They display and process data and are capable of performing a wide range of calculations and so are generally used to process numerical data. However, a spreadsheet package can also handle text. They are used to create graphs, to make 'What if…?' calculations and for goal seeking, forecasting (including trend lines) and data pattern analysis. Any task that involves the manipulation of numbers is suitable for a spreadsheet. (Chapter 4 gives more detailed explanations on the use and purpose of spreadsheets.)

Database

Database packages enable the user to handle data, such as sorting and searching. The data can be split into tables and relationships created between the tables to allow the data to be joined together. The data can be sorted by different methods and different fields – one field, or more than one, as required. (Chapter 5 gives more detailed explanations on the use and purpose of databases.)

Spreadsheet and database packages can be linked with a word-processing package to complete the process of mail merge. (The process of mail merge is discussed in Chapter 6.)

Web authoring

Web authoring, the creation of web pages, can be achieved through the use of a web-authoring package or by using a word-processing package and converting the document produced to a web page. Web-authoring software has built-in functions to enable well-designed web pages to be created with a variety of features to meet the needs of the users.

The user interface of web-authoring software is similar to that of a standard applications package but there are some functions that are different, for example changing the font style. Some technical ability is, therefore, needed and training may be required to use the software.

Web pages are visual representations of code, generally HTML (Hypertext Mark-up Language). Most web-authoring software packages do not require the user to write any code as pages are created using a graphical interface where objects are dragged and dropped on to a page template. It is then possible to access and amend the code, to tidy it up and make it more efficient, if the user has sufficient knowledge.

The majority of web-authoring software packages are aimed at the general user. Templates are available in the packages (usually an outline website structure that just requires details to be added) and wizards (a series of questions/dialogue boxes that take the user through a procedure one step at a time).

The user can determine the final look and structure of a web page by formatting. Most web-authoring software packages offer formatting facilities such as:

- colour options for background, text, lines and boxes
- font and point size options for text
- the positioning of objects on the web page and layout items such as columns, tables and forms.

As well as text and layout items web pages contain graphical objects. A web-authoring software package will allow the user to access these objects, for example by providing a clipart library. The user can then import these graphics into a web page and manipulate them, so they meet the needs of the web page and its users. Other objects, such as animation, video and sound clips, can also be used in the creation of web pages.

Web pages normally contain links to other pages within the site or to other related and linked sites. These are hyperlinks. When the user activates these hyperlinks, a request is sent for the page to be downloaded. The web-authoring software package will allow the user to create and add new links to their page(s). The hyperlinks may show the URL (Uniform Resource Locator) that is being activated or may be activated by clicking a graphic.

Many web pages allow user interaction. The web page may contain an interactive form. This form may allow the user of the web page to, for example, register their details or place an order. This facility requires the use of CGI (Common Gateway Interface) script. Most web-authoring software packages will enable the creator of the web page to produce forms without having to write any code.

Another approach to creating web pages is to use a standard application package and use the built-in facility to convert the document to a web page. This is a quick and simple method of distributing a document on a website, and it requires very little knowledge of web authoring and HTML. Also, as very little technical ability is needed and it is likely that a standard applications package will be used, no training will be involved.

The pages are created in the standard applications package, saved using the web page option and then viewed using a browser. Figure 3.1 shows the option of saving a document as a web page.

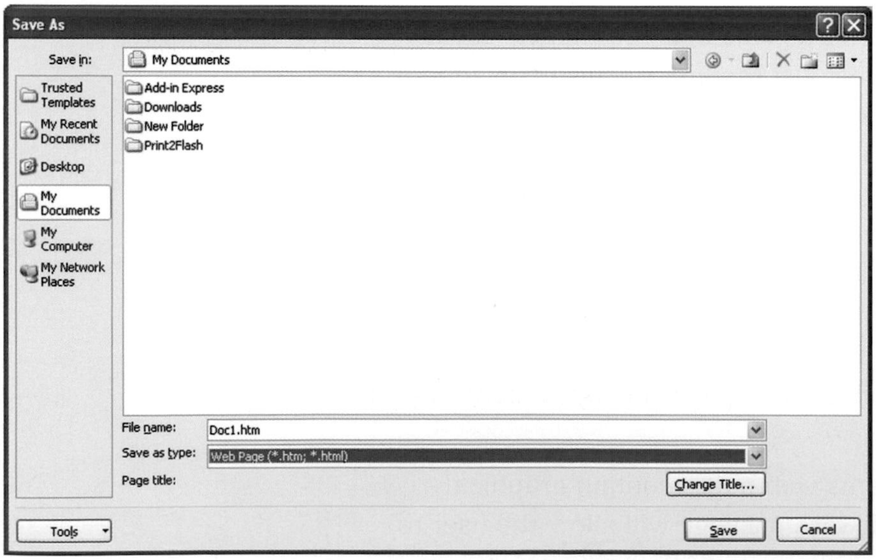

Figure 3.1 Saving a document as a web page

Some of the benefits and limitations of using web-authoring software rather than other applications are given in the table below.

Advantages	Disadvantages
• The exact effects required can be developed. • Wizards for specific tasks are built in, for example creating HTML tables. • WYSIWYG. Some web-authoring software also allow the representation of different screen sizes and different browsers. • Some packages include website management tools, for example to assist the user to check versions of pages. • A site manager can be used – if the name of a page is changed then all links to that page within the site are automatically updated. • Specialist software, code samples/scripting language, can be integrated and tested. These can then be integrated into other packages within the authoring software, for example you can integrate Adobe Flash and Fireworks into Adobe Dreamweaver. • Editing of the code can be done by either using the WYSIWYG feature or editing the HTML directly.	• Some degree of knowledge and technical ability are required as not all concepts from word processing will apply (e.g. changing the size of the font). • Often more expensive to purchase than a standard applications packages.

Some of the benefits and limitations of using standard application software rather than web-authoring software are given in the next table.

Advantages	Disadvantages
• Very little technical knowledge is required. If a standard word processor can be used then a web page can be easily created and saved using the automatic conversion facility. • It is likely that a standard applications package is already installed, so there will not be an additional cost.	• It is very difficult to get the page to look exactly how it is wanted, as this method of creating web pages is not true WYSIWYG. • The code that is created is 'messy'. It is bloated and often not very good or compatible with all browsers. • Available tool sets are limited – there is likely to be no site management or uploading tool, very few wizards and no tools to assist in script generation.

Questions

1 What are the advantages of using a word processor to create web pages?

2 What are the advantages of using web-authoring software to create web pages?

Presentation

Presentation software can be used to produce presentations to be shown, on printed acetate or by using a computer and projector, to a target audience. They can be for kiosk applications or presentations for speeches. They can run without intervention on a timer or with user intervention. Presentation software, its use and purpose is discussed later in this chapter.

and other events that may increase sales. Manufacturing stock control systems need to know all the components that are required to create a product. They need to be linked into the ordering system so that they can see how much stock they require to meet demand. They also, as with the shops, need to be linked to the sales so that they can identify trends and prepare for surges in sales, for example Christmas and forthcoming promotions. The system must:

- have a list of all stock items and the suppliers
- have a list of all components for the item if the stock is manufactured
- know the minimum and maximum stock levels
- work out how much to order
- know the delivery times for stock items that have been ordered
- have links to the orders database
- update the stock records when deliveries are received
- link with the budgeting system
- store previous sales figures
- predict stock requirements based on previous sales
- have manual override on items being ordered.

Invoicing

An invoice is a document issued by an organisation to a customer. The invoice usually shows the products, quantities, and agreed prices for products or services which have been provided. An invoice also shows how much is owed to the organisation by the customer. The invoice may also show the date the payment is due and whether any discounts are available if the payment is made before the due date. The invoicing system will create and produce the invoices to be sent to customers.

The invoicing system should link to other systems within the organisation such as ordering and delivery.

An invoicing system must:

- generate invoices/credit notes for orders
- calculate VAT/delivery costs
- calculate any discounts which may be available
- record and store payments against the invoice number
- produce customer statements showing details of paid and outstanding invoices
- flag any outstanding payments to the finance department/staff of the organisation.

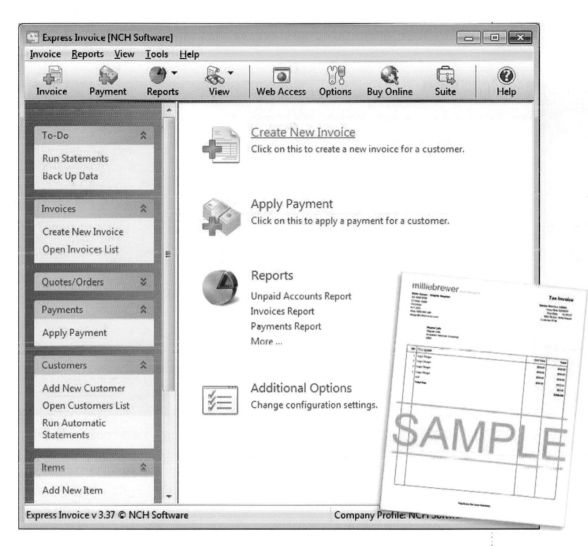

Figure 3.3 An invoicing system

Booking

There are many different things that can be booked, for example, theatre tickets, cinema tickets, doctor's appointments etc. There are three main ways of booking: the telephone, the internet and by person/post/fax. Booking systems require an event, a person and a date and time. Booking via the internet is becoming more popular. The combination of emails to notify individuals of events, with direct links to booking systems and the ability of the online systems to retain settings, means that mail shots can be tailored to individual choice.
A booking system must allow the user to:

- select a time and date
- select an event
- specify a number (adults, children)
- check availability of event for time, date and number
- check price of selected booking
- change options
- confirm and pay (via email or booking number).

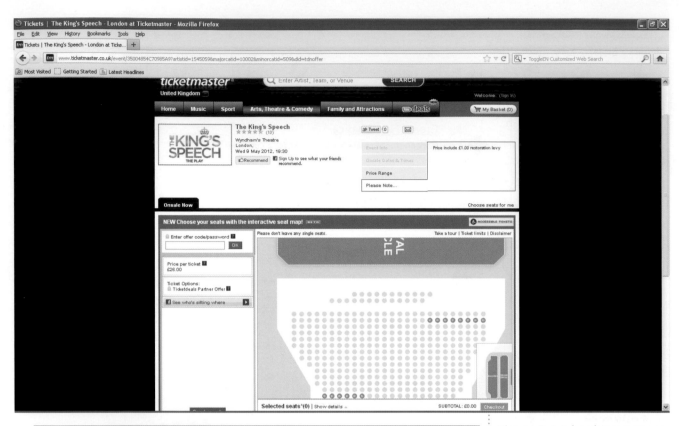

Figure 3.4 A booking system

Question

What are the advantages and disadvantages of booking via the internet as opposed to in person/by post?

Timetabling

Timetabling systems enable an end user to enter data to find, for example, train or plane times which meet specified criteria. For example, an end user may need to find the times of planes from Glasgow to London, Heathrow.

To be able to provide the end user with the correct feedback the timetabling system will require inputs from the user. These inputs may include:

- start and destination (end) points
- day of travel
- time of departure/arrival including depart after/arrive before times
- single (one way) or return journey

Other criteria which may be specified could include a via point to either avoid or go through, any connections which need to be considered, the class of travel (e.g first or standard class on a train), how many tickets are required and a maximum price for the tickets.

Following the input of these by the end user the timetabling system will then search for the most appropriate results. If the journey is possible the timetabling system will provide an output in the form of the most appropriate journeys for the specified inputs. Most timetabling systems will provide a range of different journeys, all based on the input from the end user, to allow the user to select the journey they require, this can include a range of options for the one-way (single) and return journey. The user will then be able to book the journey(s) they need, get a booking reference number and a copy of the details for their journey. Most timetabling systems will also provide, following successful completion of the booking process, an email confirmation providing all the details.

Route-finding

These are systems which allow the user to enter a variety of information about the starting and destination places and plot a route between the two as shown in Figure 3.5. This can be done prior to the journey and printed out, requested and printed from an organisation's website or through the use of in-car navigation systems. With the in-car system, using GPS, it is possible to change the route whilst in the middle of it, for instance if during a journey the driver becomes aware that a road is blocked, the route can be changed to avoid the road. Some new systems can automatically receive the traffic information and change the route accordingly without driver input. The system must enable the user to:

- specify location you are leaving from and going to
- specify places and roads you want to pass through or avoid
- specify type of journey, for example scenic, fastest or cheapest
- save and print a route in a number of formats, for example text and maps.

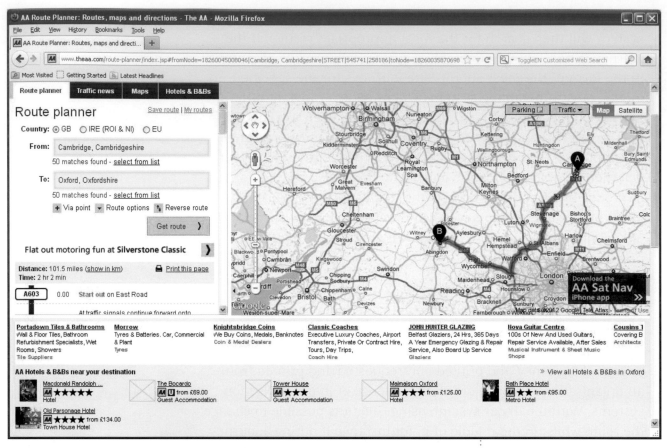

Figure 3.5 A route-finding system

Questions

Compare the use of a software-based route finder with using a map.

Training

Training is the imparting of knowledge and skills to achieve a designated task. A training system is the method by which training is delivered usually through the use of multimedia – the use of sound, video and text.

The training does not have to be for the use of software, it might be on how to create a Lego model. The important point is the use of the computer to deliver the training.

Most training systems are self-paced. This means that it is the person who is doing the training that decides the pace they go through the training system. The system must be able to:

- provide questions at an appropriate level for the user
- provide a positive approach to learning
- incorporate simple and intuitive screens
- enable the user to move from one question to the next based on responses

- allow intervention by the trainer/teacher at any time – this could be done remotely.

In addition to these, a training system should provide some sort of auditory or visual cue to highlight mistakes or correct responses. The system should provide help and further explanations for any part of the training which the user has incorrectly completed – this could be in the form of pop-up boxes or further screens. Feedback on the progress being made and the results of any tests taken should also be given – this could include the signposting of the areas in the training which need to be revisited to increase the user's knowledge and understanding. The users should also be able to go backwards in the training system to revisit sections they are unsure of or skip through sections where they feel confident about their knowledge of that section.

Describe the purpose and characteristics of wizards, style sheets, templates and macros describing the advantages and disadvantages of their use

Most standard/generic applications packages have features that can assist the user. The purpose and characteristics of these features are, generally, the same but the use of the features will vary depending on which package they are in.

Wizards

A wizard facility assists the user to produce the final product, which may be, for example, a document, a presentation master slide or a database. The wizard found in each application will present options to the user which apply to that application.

Figure 3.6 shows the options that can be selected and completed by the user using a wizard to produce a letter using a word-processing package. In new versions of word-processing software the letter wizard is within the mail merge tool.

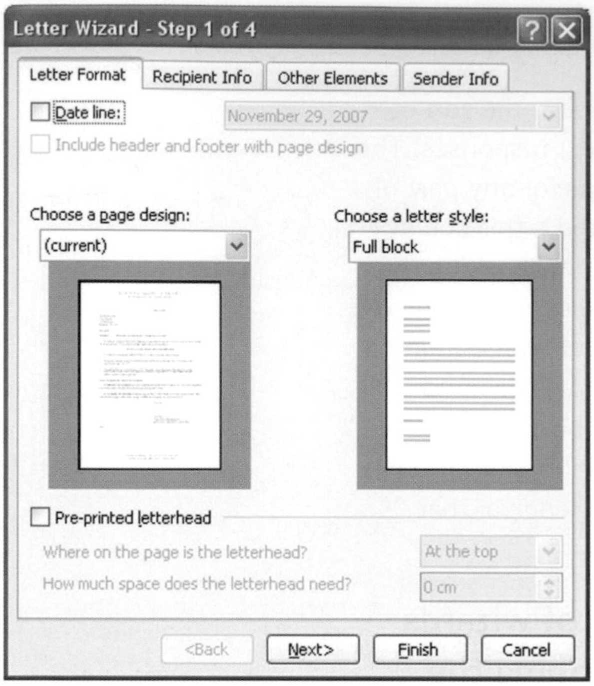

Figure 3.6 Letter wizard

A wizard offers the user a range of screens where a user can make choices and enter information. Having completed all the wizard stages, the user is presented with the completed document (or other requirement) containing the information in a pre-set format. A wizard helps a user who is unfamiliar with a particular task, however there are a limited number of options available in wizards. This may result in the end result produced by the wizard not meeting the exact needs of the user, but it can often be close needing only minor editing/ formatting to get it exactly right.

There are a number of advantages and disadvantages to using wizards.

Activities

Investigate the wizards available in the database, presentation and DTP packages available at your centre. Describe the advantages and disadvantages of using the wizard in each package.

Advantages	Disadvantages
• They save time for the inexperienced user. • They ensure that no important information is forgotten. • Standard formats can be used. • There is an element of user friendliness.	• There is no individuality to the end result. All documents can end up looking exactly the same. • The end result may not fully meet the needs of the user. • It is harder for documents to be tailored to meet the needs of the targeted audience.

Style sheets

Style sheets are similar to templates and are used to set out layouts. Style sheets can also be referred to as master documents. Style sheets usually relate to word-processed documents or those produced using a desktop publishing (DTP) package.

Elements which could be included in a style sheet include:

• font size
• font style (i.e. bold, underline, italic)

- margin size
- alignment

The use of a style sheet ensures that all documents produced conform to a pre-determined layout, usually the house style of a company or business, yet still give the producer of the documents some scope for creativity. For example, a company may decide that its newsletter should be simply styled with:

- headings in Arial, font size 32, bold and centred
- body text in two columns, Arial, font size 13 and justified
- 14pt spacing between a heading and the following text.

The style sheet used for the creation and writing of a book can be extensive ensuring consistency throughout all formatting features.

Here are some advantages and disadvantages of using style sheets.

Advantages	Disadvantages
• There is a lack of confusion from document writers/creators as the different elements required have been clearly defined. • Different people can work on parts of the same documents but because of the use of a style sheet the end results will be consistent and conform to the house style.	• Someone needs to develop the style before it can be set as a template. • Can be restrictive and not fully meet the needs of the document being produced.

Templates

A template provides standard pre-set layouts and formats. For example in a word-processing package a template will determine the basic structure and settings of a document and includes:

- character formatting (font size, colour, type of font etc.)
- page formatting (margins, size, layout etc.)
- text inserts (standard words, date, time etc.)
- graphics inserts (standard logo, position etc.).

Every word-processed document is based on a template; when a new blank document is created the package's pre-set template option is selected by default. Many word-processing packages also have a range of templates which can be selected by the user. The templates cover a range of different documents including memos, reports, letters and faxes. These templates have pre-set formats and the user can simply insert the text required. The screenshot on page 76 shows the pre-set templates available for producing a letter or fax. In recent versions of the software the templates are accessed online.

Figure 3.7 Letter and fax templates

Question

Identify **three** features of a word-processed document that can be set by the template.

In presentation software a template will specify the colour scheme as well as the master slide and master title slide layouts with custom formatting and fonts. These are all designed to create a particular look. When a design template is applied to a presentation, the master slide, master title slide and colour scheme of the new template replace the existing design of the presentation. When a design template is applied each new slide will follow the same custom look.

Most presentation software comes with a wide variety of professionally designed templates but a design template can also be created. If an original design template is created then it can be saved as a template to be used again.

A variety of pre-designed colour schemes are also available in most presentation software packages. These are sets of balanced colours designed for use as the main colours of a slide presentation. They detail the colours to be used for text, background, fill and accents. Each colour in the pre-designed scheme will be used automatically for the appropriate element on the slide. A colour scheme can be selected for an individual slide or for an entire presentation. When a pre-set design template is applied to a presentation then the presentation software will offer a set of pre-designed colour schemes made to go with that design template.

Question

Describe the disadvantages of using design templates in the production of a presentation.

Macros

A macro is a set of stored commands that can be replayed by pressing a combination of keys or by pressing a button. A macro enables the user to automate tasks that are performed on a regular basis. This is done by recording a series of commands to be run whenever that task needs to be performed. The complexity of the macro is only limited by the task requirements and the ability of the programmer.

For example, in a word-processing package a macro may be recorded to add a name as a header to documents.

In a spreadsheet package macros can be used to give additional functionality to the spreadsheet and increase the customisation of the interface. The macro can be attached to a button, for example to open a worksheet or to initiate an event (such as a cell becoming a particular value). Some examples include:

- moving to a different part of the spreadsheet or a different worksheet
- running a calculation
- closing the application
- printing the application
- adding a header and footer to the spreadsheet.

Once the macro has been recorded then it can be run by pressing the keys assigned when it was recorded. Macros can also be activated through the use of a button placed on the toolbar. A macro will only run when the application program to which it is associated is being used. A macro will not run on its own or with a different application program.

Some advantages and disadvantage of macros are given in the next table.

Advantages	Disadvantages
• A repetitive task can be performed using a simple instruction (e.g. key press, button click). • Errors may be reduced as the instructions included in the macro are run automatically and are the same every time. • Inexperienced users can perform complex tasks by using a pre-recorded macro.	• Errors may occur if the conditions when the macro is run are different from those when it was recorded. • Users must know and remember the key combination to run the macro. • Inflexible – the macro may not do precisely what the user wants. • If the macro is run from a different starting point than intended then it may go wrong. • To correct any errors the user must have some knowledge of how the macro was recorded.

Question

What are the advantages of using macros?

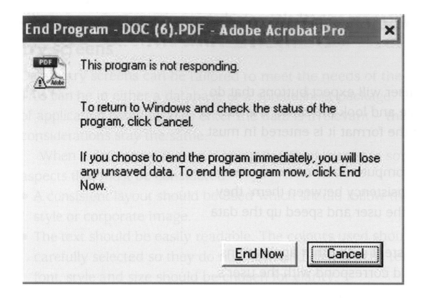

Figure 3.8 An error message

Intuitiveness

It is unlikely that the user will use the system only once, so the interface needs to be designed in such a way that the user can remember what they have done. This is linked to naturalness – the interface must appear appropriate for completing the task and reflect the user's knowledge and understanding. If the user can relate to items within the design, this will help them use the interface.

Describe how standard/generic applications software can be tailored using buttons, forms, form controls, menus and templates and give examples of the use of each

An interface can be tailored to meet a user's needs through the custom use of buttons, forms, menus and macros.

Buttons

These can be used to take the user to a specified page or to run a selected action/command. A macro can be run when the user clicks a button. For example a command button can be added to a database user interface to run a search, or to sort or edit data. A button can also display pictures or text.

Forms

These can be used to assist in the entry of data. A form can give the user help and guidance on what data should be input. Instructions to the user and error messages can be included on forms. It is also possible to include on the form some data validation. A form may include drop-down boxes for data selection, option boxes and automatic fill-in boxes, which can help a user.

An example of an automatic fill-in box might be when a postcode is entered and the street name and town automatically appear on the form. The user would then simply have to input the house number. This is a very common feature in business today.

Menus enable a user to select actions. There are three main types of menu: full-screen, pop-up and pull-down. Each type of menu gives the user choices of actions in a particular context.

Form controls are generally used to increase the interactivity with the user and improve usability. Here are some of the form controls that might be available.

- Button: the user can click the button to start an event. The button can be linked to a macro.

- Check box: the user can tick an option, for example an invoice has been paid.

- Group/Frame: Form controls can be grouped together. For example if you have two related option buttons, by grouping them you can make them into choice buttons so only one can be selected at a time.

- Option button: options can be selected and given values.

- Text box: this allows text to be written and picked up and used in the application.

- Combo box: items can be selected from a drop-down box.

- List box: this gives a list of items – either single or multiple items can be selected.

- Image: a picture can be inserted.

- Label: instruction labels or titles can be added.

Questions

1 Identify three different controls that can be used to customise the user interface.

2 What are the disadvantages of customising a user interface?

3 What are the benefits of using buttons and forms to customise a user interface?

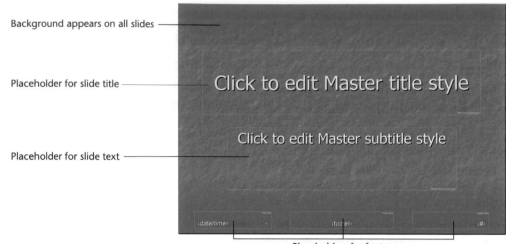

Background appears on all slides ——

Placeholder for slide title ——

Click to edit Master title style

Click to edit Master subtitle style

Placeholder for slide text ——

‹date/time›   ‹footer›   ‹#›

Placeholders for footers

Figure 3.10 A master slide in PowerPoint

It is possible for a team to work on the development of a presentation. By using templates and master slides a team can work individually on different parts of the presentation and then collate their work once it is finished.

Question

What is a master slide?

In a word-processing package, a master document is a collection or set of separate files or sub-documents. A master document can be used to set up and manage a multipart document, such as this book or a company report, that has several sections or chapters. The master document can be used to organise and manage a long document by separating it into smaller manageable sections or chapters. These are known as sub-documents. This enables several different people within an organisation to work on a long document and still maintain a consistent house style.

By using a master document a table of contents, index, references and headers and footers can be created for all sub-documents. Once created, the master document also lets the authors:

- expand or collapse sub-documents or change views to show or hide detail
- quickly change the structure of the document by adding, removing, combining, splitting, renaming, and re-arranging sub-documents.

The template used for the master document can control the styles used when the entire document is being viewed or printed. Different templates, or different settings within the templates, can be used for the master document and for individual sub-documents.

As any changes are made to the sub-documents these are automatically updated in the master document. This means that if any changes have to be made to part of a company report then the specific sub-section can be changed without having to recreate the whole document.

Styles

Styles help a user apply formatting to a document e.g. customised headings, subheadings and bulleted lists. If all text in a document looked the same then it would be difficult to read. Styles enable text to be formatted to both meet the house style of a company and enable the reader to fully understand the message of the document.

A style will be set and can then be used by all document writers and creators. The style will be set so that users do not have to format each different section, or element, of a document but can simply select the style, which has already been set, for that element. For example, a subheading may be set as Arial, bold, font size 14. Once this style has been set on the software it can be selected and the pre-set formatting will be applied by the software.

By creating and setting styles on the software there is a greater chance that all documents created and sent out by the company will conform to the house style.

Style sheets

Style sheets are used to describe the format that should be applied to a document. They include a written description of the style (font size, font type, font colour etc) and general page information (margin sizes, logo positioning). The style sheet is used to create the style. Style sheets can also be referred to as master documents. They can relate to complete word-processed documents or those produced using a desktop publishing (DTP) package. The use of a style sheet ensures that all documents produced conform to a pre-determined layout, the house style, yet still give the producer some scope for creativity. For example a company may decide that a letter sent from the company should be formatted as:

- the company logo at the top right-hand side
- the company contact details will be in the footer, in Arial type face, font size 10, bold and centred
- body text will be Arial, font size 12 and fully justified.

Some benefits and limitations of using style sheets are listed below.

Advantages	Disadvantages
• All company documents are produced to a consistent house style making them recognisable and identifiable to the brand. • Different people can work on parts of the same document but the end results will be consistent and conform to the house style.	• All documents can end up looking exactly the same. • It is harder to tailor documents to meet the needs of the targeted audience. • Designers need to be paid to develop a corporate/house style.

Templates

Templates can be used to produce the different documents that can be used by a company. Templates can be created, and saved, for each document required by a company. For example, templates can be created for reports, letters and memos. By creating a template to be used when a document is being created the company can be sure that each instance of the document will look exactly the same.

The template will define, for example, the layout, font size/type and where any graphics, such as the company logo, will be placed. By using templates, the house style of the company can be applied consistently during document production.

Explain the need for different file types and the advantages and disadvantages of having different file types

Output from different software providers is often saved in different formats. Different software providers can also create their own methods of storing files from their applications. Different applications from the same provider will also save the files in different formats. This is because different file types are suited to different applications. For example Microsoft uses the doc file extension for word-processed documents, the xls extension for spreadsheets, and the mdb extension for databases, but, respectively, OpenOffice uses the odt, ods and odb extensions.

Another reason for having different file types is that operating systems recognise the file extensions and associate them with particular programs, this is usually done automatically on installation. This enables the operating system to know which program to start when a user wishes to open a file.

Knowing the file extension or the type of file can help when searching for files. For example to search for a letter saved in Microsoft Word, the user can start by searching for all files with a doc extension (*.doc).

If data is saved in one application but the user needs to use it in a different application then the data will need to be converted. The applications may be completely different (e.g. from a word-processed document to a spreadsheet file), they may be the same type of application (e.g from Microsoft Word to Corel WordPerfect), or they may be different versions of the same application (e.g from Microsoft Word 2003 to Word 2007). Files can also be converted across different computer systems (e.g. from PC to Apple Mac). Some file types are universally recognised:

- txt and rtf (rich text format) for documents
- CSV (comma separated variable) and TSV (tab separated variable) for spreadsheets or tables of data
- dbf and CSV for databases.

If these file types are used to save the file then it is easier to share the data across similar applications, it is also easier to convert the data.

There are two standard procedures for converting files from one format to another

For example a file saved in Package A needs to be read in Package B.

Option 1: Package A can save the file in Package B's format.

Procedure:

1 Open the file in Package A (Open).

2 Save as or export to the Package B format (Convert).

3 Open in Package B and save (Save).

Option 2: Package A cannot save to Package B's format. In this case the file should be saved to a third format – one that Package A can export to and Package B can import from.

Procedure:

1 Open the file in package A (Open).

2 Save as or export to the third-party format. (Convert).

3 Open the file in Package B (Import).

4 Convert to the format required by Package B (Convert).

5 Save in the new format (Save).

Chapter summary

Standard application/generic software
Word-processing
    Letter writing
    Memos
    Reports
Desktop publishing (DTP)
    Flyers
    Brochures
    Posters
    Business cards
Spreadsheet
    Graphs
    Modelling data – mathematical and objects
    Forecasting

Database
  Handling data – searching and sorting
Web authoring
  Producing web pages
Presentation
  Creating slides – acetates or electronic

Systems

Personnel
Stock control
Invoicing
Booking
Timetabling
Route finding
Training

Characteristics and purposes

Wizards
Style sheets
Templates
Macros

Design considerations

Consistent layout / house style
Font style, font size
Colours
Error messages
Flow of information required
Validation of information
On-screen help (such as pop-ups and clear exits)

Customising applications

Buttons
Forms
Form controls
Macros

House style

Recognition by clients and customers
Pre-defined colours/font style and size
Consistency across all company documentation
Achieved by using:
  Master documents
  Master slides
  Styles
  Style sheets
  Templates

Chapter tests

Test 1

A company has recently introduced a telephone ordering system.

1 Describe **three** design considerations that should be taken into account when designing data-entry screens to input customer's orders. [6]

2 The data-entry screens are to follow the company house style. Explain what is meant by house style. [4]

3 A stock control system is to be linked to the telephone ordering system. Describe the characteristics of a stock control system. [6]

4 Describe how a master document could be used during the production of the user guide for the telephone ordering system [4]

Test 2

A company selling antique furniture is updating the systems they currently use.

1 The company has a style sheet. Identify four elements that could be defined in a style sheet for a document. [4]

2 Explain why it is important to have the company logo on every document produced by the company. [4]

3 Describe how the owner of the company could use a timetabling system to find out the times of trains between London and Cambridge. [6]

4 A template is used to create a brochure for the company. Describe **two** advantages and **one** disadvantage of using a template to create the brochure. [6]

4 Spreadsheet concepts

Introduction

This chapter covers the basic concepts relating to spreadsheets and how spreadsheets can be used. You will need to make sure you understand the use of spreadsheets in a variety of situations and are able to apply this knowledge.

This chapter covers:

- Characteristics of modelling software
- Variables, formulae, functions and rules
- Worksheets, workbooks, rows, columns, cells and ranges
- Absolute and relative referencing

Describe the characteristics of modelling software and give reasons why a model might be used

There are two main types of modelling used in ICT:

- Modelling of objects (rooms, buildings, cars etc.)
- Mathematical modelling (financial, calculations, spreadsheets etc.)

Modelling of objects

Figure 4.1 Computer modelling

Computer models allow you to create a virtual representation of the item within the computer. You can model large items such as buildings and look at the effect on them from different external influences, for example earthquakes, fire or explosions.

It is possible to see different layers: external view, electrical wiring view, basic frame and so on. The model can be rotated so that different aspects can be viewed. It is possible to zoom in on a particular part, for example in a model of a vehicle, individual nuts and bolts can be viewed. How individual components will react to different circumstances can also be seen.

An important characteristic of software used to model objects is the ability to ask questions of the model: to change the components and see how it reacts, to move an item and try a different design. The effects can be gauged at the touch of a button, without having to take the risk of building the real thing.

Mathematical modelling

	A	B	C	D	E	F	G
1							
2							
3							
4		SA income					UK Savings
5	Month 0	ZAR 27,840.00					
6	Month 1	ZAR 3,652.00	ZAR 27,000.00	to UK at	14	ZAR/£	£1,928.57
7	Month 2	ZAR 6,464.00		saving at		5.5%	£1,656.04
8	Month 3	ZAR 9,276.00				5.5%	£1,382.52
9	Month 4	ZAR 12,088.00				5.5%	£1,107.98
10	Month 5	ZAR 14,900.00				5.5%	£832.45
11	Month 6	ZAR 17,712.00				5.5%	£555.90
12	Month 7	ZAR 524.00	ZAR 20,000.00	to UK at	14	5.5%	£1,706.91
13	Month 8	ZAR 3,336.00				5.5%	£1,433.67
14	Month 9	ZAR 6,148.00				5.5%	£1,159.22
15	Month 10	ZAR 8,960.00				5.5%	£883.87
16	Month 11	ZAR 11,772.00				5.5%	£607.52
17	Month 12	ZAR 14,584.00				5.5%	£330.14
18	Month 13	ZAR 396.00	ZAR 17,000.00	to UK at	14	5.5%	£1,266.04
19	Month 14	ZAR 3,208.00				5.5%	£991.08
20	Month 15	ZAR 6,020.00				5.5%	£715.12
21	Month 16	ZAR 8,832.00				5.5%	£438.14
22	Month 17	ZAR 11,644.00				5.5%	£160.14
23	Month 18	ZAR 14,456.00				5.5%	-£118.87
24	Month 19	ZAR 268.00	ZAR 17,000.00	to UK at	14	5.5%	£815.38
25	Month 20	ZAR 3,080.00				5.5%	£538.77
26	Month 21	ZAR 5,892.00				5.5%	£261.15
27	Month 22	ZAR 8,704.00				5.5%	-£17.50
28	Month 23	ZAR 11,516.00				5.5%	-£297.16
29	Month 24	ZAR 14,328.00				5.5%	-£577.85
30							

Figure 4.2 Example spreadsheet

Tasks with mathematical elements, such as finance, are commonly modelled with spreadsheets.

Spreadsheets are based on a layout of rows and columns. This layout assists financial modelling. It allows items to be laid out in a logical and easy-to-follow format. The use of rows and columns leads to the use of sequencing and replication. Replication is the copying of a cell either horizontally or vertically. The value of the cell can be incremented. If the value is an item in a list, the next item in the list can be given in the next cell, for example, days of the week or months of the year. Formulae can also be copied and cell references automatically adjusted.

Spreadsheets have many features to help when modelling. They can be based on functions and formulae, which allow numbers to be input into the spreadsheet and for any changes to be automatically recalculated. This means that many different scenarios can be tried out using a single model.

'What-if?' questions allow a user to change values and see what the effect would be on end results. An alternative method of asking questions is to start with the result and to see what would need to happen for that result to occur – this is known as goal seeking.

Spreadsheets can use variables and constants. A variable is a changeable value that is entered into a cell that is then used in a formula. The variable can be changed by a user when required, and the change will lead to a re-calculation of figures based on that variable. For example, a cell contains a formula to calculate a currency conversion. The conversion will depend on the rate of exchange at a given time. The user will need to enter the rate of change and amount to be converted: these are the variables. The cell containing the conversion formula will be updated depending on the figures entered as the variables. Constants are values that are used in formulae but which cannot be changed by a user. For example, a company finance department uses a spreadsheet to calculate the VAT owing at the end of each quarter. The VAT rate is a constant (currently 20%) and will be used in every purchase or sale figure.

In spreadsheets individual cells or ranges of cells can be given names to make them easier to remember. For example, instead of referring to cell C10, you can give the cell a name relating to its contents, for example VAT_RATE, which can then be used to refer to the cell. This makes formulae easier to understand.

Other features include the use of multiple worksheets and graphical representation of data.

Why is computer modelling used?

There are many reasons why computer modelling is used.

- It is less risky (safer and cheaper) to test a model of a design (financial or an object) than to create it in reality and test it. For example to build an aircraft, test it and have it go wrong could cost human life.
- Only one model needs to be created in a computer. The model can be altered and changed. If a real model or the real thing was to be created, a new one would need to be created for each different alteration. This would cost time and money.

- A computer model can be backed up and shared. Since it is stored electronically, it can be backed up on a disk. It can be emailed or sent to others who can also work on the model.
- Computer models can be accelerated or slowed down to see effects that could not be viewed in reality. For example an explosion happens very quickly. A computer model can slow the process down so that its different stages can be analysed. The creation of the universe happened over a long period of time. A computer model can speed this process up so that it can be used effectively for research purposes.

It should be remembered that ultimately, all modelling is based on mathematics. The creation and manipulation of objects in the model is mathematical, as is the modelling of purely mathematical simulations such as financial models.

Questions

1 Describe **three** characteristics of software used to model objects.

2 Why is software used to model objects?

3 What are the disadvantages of using software to model objects?

4 Describe **three** characteristics of software used to model financial data.

5 What are the advantages of using a software modelling package to model next year's accounts?

6 Describe the similarities between software used to model objects and software used to model financial data.

Describe how variables, formulae, rules and functions are used in modelling software

A model has four main characteristics that allow it to manipulate numbers and text. These features allow the model to recalculate values when a number changes, questions to be asked and answered with the minimum amount of effort, and different scenarios to be tested. These features are:

- variables
- rules
- formulae
- functions.

Variables

A variable is an identifier associated with a particular cell. Within the cell there will be a value. The variable could be a cell reference (e.g. D4) or the cell could have a name (e.g. VAT_RATE). When the variable is used in a spreadsheet, it is the value contained within the variable that is used.

Explain the advantages and disadvantages of using a spreadsheet to create and run simulations

A computer model comprises a set of data about something and a set of rules that control what the data does. You have already seen that there are two main types of modelling:

- mathematical modelling
- object modelling.

A model is an artificial re-creation of an object or event that should behave in the same way as the real thing. For example, a model of a bridge should enable the designers to simulate what will happen to the bridge under different conditions.

There are advantages and disadvantages to using a spreadsheet to create and run simulations/models of both objects and mathematical situations.

Advantages	Disadvantages
• 'What-if?' questions can be asked without rebuilding a model from scratch each time a test is run. • Automatic re-calculation: if a change is made then all related formulae and values change. • Graphs can be produced: these will automatically change as any values change. • Variables and constants can be used: this enables the entire model to be changed by changing one or more values. • The model can be saved and backed up: if the original is lost or corrupted there is a copy. • The model can be shared between different people in different locations. • No additional software is required: spreadsheets are standard business software. Most people are able to use a spreadsheet, so no specialist training is needed. • It might be quicker and cheaper to build a computer model than a physical model. • Only one model needs to be built which can then be changed. If a physical model is built then a different one will be needed each time a change is made. • It can be safer to run a simulation/model under extreme conditions than to build an actual model and test it. For example, testing a ship in storm conditions would risk it sinking. • Computer-based models can be speeded up or slowed down to see effects that are difficult to see in real life.	• The model may not be an accurate representation of the real world. The real world is complex! • If the model relates to people then an accurate result may not be given. For example, if a model is constructed to show the time taken to evacuate a building it might not take into account the fact that people panic. • Many variables may need to be considered and it is easy to miss things out! This may lead to misleading results. • Producing an effective model may be time consuming and running the model may need expensive hardware and software.

Questions

1 Describe what is meant by a 'What-if?' question.

2 Give **three** examples of 'What-if?' questions that could be asked while modelling an aircraft.

3 Describe **two** advantages of using a computer model to answer 'What-if?' questions instead of a physical model.

4 Describe **three** features of models that make them suitable for answering 'What-if?' questions.

Describe and explain the purpose and use of worksheets, workbooks, rows, columns, cells and ranges in spreadsheet software

A spreadsheet is made up of different parts. Each part has a different function and purpose.

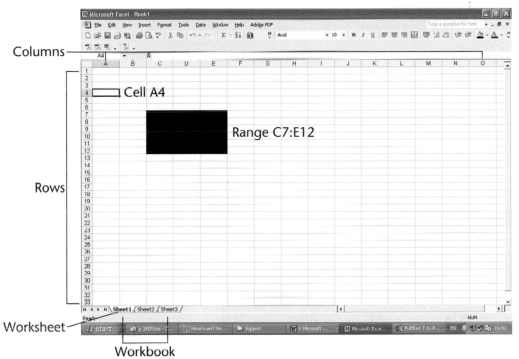

Figure 4.3 Parts of a spreadsheet

Worksheet

A worksheet (called a sheet or spreadsheet in some applications) is a large grid of cells on a single sheet. A worksheet can be used to hold data on a single area of the business. For example, it can hold the sales data, the expenditure or the stock. Worksheets can be given names.

Workbook

A workbook is a collection of more than one worksheet in the same spreadsheet. Separate worksheets could contain financial figures for different areas of a business. Together they comprise a workbook, and contain the figures for the whole business.

For example, a workbook might contain worksheets on income, expenditure, stock and a summary (four worksheets within the workbook).

Workbooks can be used to divide data up into different categories and organise it. For example the owner of a chain of shops might have a workbook on each shop, or a worksheet on each shop and a single workbook for all of them.

One advantage of using workbooks is that data that is changed on one worksheet will be reflected across the whole workbook. Another advantage is that different access rights can be given to different worksheets. For example, if a workbook contained several worksheets and each worksheet contained data relating to a single shop, you could allow the manager of each shop access only to their shop's worksheet.

As a workbook is saved as a single entity, it is easy to backup, copy and send to other people. All the data required is in a single location.

Rows and columns

A row is a range of cells that goes across the spreadsheet. A column is a range of cells that goes down the spreadsheet. In most packages, rows are given numbers and columns are given letters.

Rows and columns are used to organise the data. They can hold headings to show where the data is stored and they can be used to hold the data within a tabular structure.

	A	B	C	D	E
1	Sales by Groups of Item Each Quarter				
2					
3		1st quarter	2nd quarter	3rd quarter	4th quarter
4	Pens	576	454	876	343
5	Pencils	345	232	545	323
6	Pads of paper	54	45	76	43

Figure 4.4 Rows and columns

The width and height of rows and columns can be altered, for example columns can be widened to fit the text.

If necessary, rows and columns can be hidden. If a set of columns contained some calculations that you did not want to be shown, you could hide them from the user.

Cell

A cell is an individual data store identified by a column and row indicator, in that order, for example A4, BJ100 etc. Every cell in the spreadsheet is uniquely identified. Cells can also be given names as unique identifiers.

Cells can be formatted. Each individual cell can be formatted independently of the others, to change, for example, background colour, font, font size, validation, alignment and conditional formatting.

Cells can also be protected to stop the data within them being altered without a password.

Range

A range is a group of cells. The group can be given a name or just be known by their cell references. A range is usually given top left to bottom right and separated by a colon. For example A4:B6, C7:G12 etc.

A range is used when the cells within it contain similar data. They may contain grades, marks for an exam or names of stock items. Ranges are often used in formulae and functions. They make it easier to understand the spreadsheet and how it is working, and allow the same formatting to be applied at the same time (instead of individually to a cell).

Questions

1 Describe how a cell could be used in a financial spreadsheet.

2 What is a range? Give an example of how a range could be used in a sports league spreadsheet.

3 Describe the benefits of using a worksheet for a sweet shop.

4 Describe how a furniture shop could use a workbook.

Describe absolute and relative cell referencing, and give examples of uses of each method

Referencing in spreadsheets is the use of cell identifiers to include the value contained within the cell in a formula or function. For example the formula C2 + D2 uses two cell references and the cell containing the formula would show the result of adding the contents of the cells C2 and D2.

When you copy formulae or functions in a spreadsheet there are two ways the cell reference can be affected. It can move in relation to the direction of the copy (relative referencing) or it can stay the same (absolute referencing).

Relative referencing

Relative cell referencing is when the cell referenced in a spreadsheet formula changes when the formula is copied to other cells. This means that when a formula or function is copied the cell reference within the formula or function will move.

In the example shown in Figure 4.5, the formula in cell A3 has been copied to the right into cells B3, C3 and D3. Each time, relative addressing ensures that the columns referenced in the formula are also changed by the same amount so the correct result is shown in each formula cell.

	A	B	C	D
1	23	43	54	23
2	34	54	2	12
3	=A1+A2	=B1+B2	=C1+C2	=D1+D2

Figure 4.5 Relative addressing

Relative addressing also works to ensure the correct cells are referenced when cells are copied to new rows.

Relative referencing is used when you want the cell reference to change when you copy the cell.

Absolute referencing

Absolute referencing is used when a referenced cell in a spreadsheet formula needs to remain exactly the same when the formula is copied to other cells. For example, a cell might contain a constant value such as the VAT rate, so this cell will always be referred to in calculations that use it, even if the cell containing the calculation is copied. This means that when a formula or function is copied the cell reference within the formula of function will not change.

This is used when you have a value entered into a single cell that the formula of function refers to, for example:

- VAT: all individual figures need to be multiplied by the VAT rate
- postage: all individual sales totals have the same postage added on.

Using the previous example, each value contained in cells A2, B2, C2 and D2 are to be added to the value in cell A1. Relative referencing will give the incorrect answer because it will use the values in cells B1, C1 and D1 in the calculation. Clearly this is wrong as cell A1 needs to be 'locked' so it doesn't move as the formula is copied. This is achieved by putting a dollar sign ($) before the column and row parts of the cell reference as shown.

	A	B	C	D
1	23			
2	34	54	2	12
3	=$A$1+A2	=$A$1+B2	=$A$1+C2	=$A$1+D2

Figure 4.6 Absolute addressing using the $ symbol

Absolute referencing can also be done using the name of a cell.

	A	B	C
1	**P&P (£)**	1.99	
2			
3	**Order number**	**Order total (£)**	**Total with P&P (£)**
4	A123B1	45.33	=B4+Post
5	B432H7	27.54	=B5+Post
6	J345U9	19.99	=B6+Post
7	F342K8	56.87	=B4+Post

Figure 4.7 Absolute addressing using names

In the example, B1 has been given the name of 'Post'. When Post is used in the formula it refers to cell B1 because it is not incremented when copied: the name makes it an absolute reference.

The main advantage of absolute references is that if you want to change the cost of P&P, you only need to change the value in B1 and all formulae that use the value it contains will re-calculate.

Absolute referencing is used when a value is used in the same formula or function many times.

Questions

1 What is meant by referencing?

2 Using an example, describe relative referencing.

3 Give **two** advantages of relative referencing.

4 Using an example, describe absolute referencing.

5 Give **two** advantages of absolute referencing.

Chapter summary

Characteristics of modelling software

Used to model objects

 Virtual representation

 Use of layers

 Questions can be asked

Used for financial modelling

 Based on functions and formulae

 Variables and constants can be used

 'What-if?' questions can be asked

Variables, formulae, rules and functions

In a spreadsheet:

- a variable is an identifier associated with a particular cell and within the cell there will be a value
- a formula is a calculation which uses numbers, addresses of cells and mathematical operators
- rules are a set of procedures that must be followed and can also be the sequence of events required for the calculation to work
- a function represents a complex formula that uses reserved words.

Worksheets, workbooks, rows, columns, cells and ranges

Worksheets consist of all of the cells on a sheet.

A workbook is a collection of worksheets.

A row is a range of cells, denoted by numbers that go across a spreadsheet.

A column is a range of cells, denoted by letters, that go down a spreadsheet.

A range is a group of cells denoted by either a name or cell references.

Absolute and relative referencing

Relative referencing: the cell referenced in a formula changes when the formula is copied to other cells.

Absolute referencing: the cell referenced in a formula remains exactly the same when the formula is copied to other cells.

Chapter tests

Test 1

A car repair garage is considering a move to new premises.

1 It has been advised to use a spreadsheet model to simulate the expansion of the business. Describe **two** advantages of using a spreadsheet model to run the simulations. [4]

2 Using examples related to the garage describe how relative and absolute cell references could be used. [4]

3 Describe **two** differences between a formula and a function. [4]

4 Using examples related to the garage describe how worksheets and ranges could be used. [4]

5 Describe **two** advantages of being able to give a cell a name instead of using the column and row identifier. [4]

Test 2

A sportswear company uses a spreadsheet to model future sales.

1 The company can use formulae and functions within the spreadsheet software to create 'What-if?' calculations. Describe **two** other characteristics of spreadsheet software that the company could use to model future sales. [4]

2 Explain **three** advantages to the company of using spreadsheet software to answer 'What-if?' questions. [6]

3 The sportswear company uses spreadsheet software to store its accounts. Describe the terms cells and ranges and give an example of how each could be used in the accounts software. [4]

4 Using examples related to the sportswear company, describe how absolute and relative cell references could be used. [4]

5 Relational database concepts

Introduction

This chapter covers the database element of ICT. There is a large amount of theory that is required before the practical elements can be attempted.

This chapter covers:

- Terms used when describing databases
- Entity relationship diagrams (ERDs)
- Data dictionaries
- Characteristics of data in first, second and third normal form
- Advantages and disadvantages of normalisation
- Selecting appropriate data types
- Simple and complex queries using static and dynamic parameters

Describe the terms typically used in relational database terminology

Databases involve a large amount of terminology and it is essential that the key terms are understood before progressing to the later sections of this chapter.

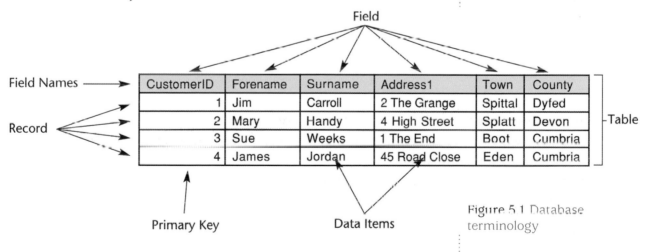

Figure 5.1 Database terminology

A table is made up of records, records are made up of fields and fields are made up of characters.

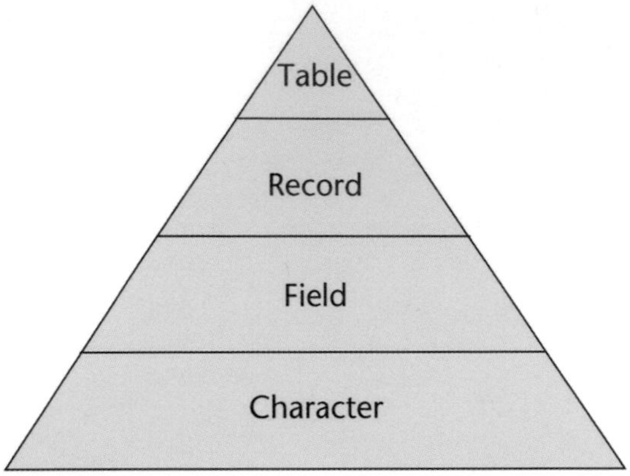

Figure 5.2 Parts of a table

Table

Tables contain data about 'things', for example students, orders, events, purchases, customers, suppliers etc. A table is a data structure made up of rows and columns that contains data about the items.

A table is a very specific and regulated item within a database. The following requirements must be met for the data structure to be called a table:

- The table must have a unique name.
- Each field/column must have a unique name.
- Each record/row must be unique.
- Each data item within a field must contain only a single data item.

The order of the records within the table does not matter. The order of the fields does not matter.

Record

A record is a single row within a table. It is a collection of data about a single item or a single event. For example a record might be about an individual, such as a customer, an order that has been placed, an item in stock or an appointment etc.

Records are made up of fields and can contain different data types. In a table, each record must be unique.

Field

A field is an individual data item within a record. Each field within a record should have a unique name. A field should only contain a single data item.

Fields have individual data types and can have their own validation.

Key

There are several different keys that can be applied to a table. The most important key is the primary key. This is a field, in the table, that allows each record to be uniquely identified. Every value of the primary key must be unique.

Forename	Surname
Charlie	Smith
Lacey	Adams
Charlie	Smith
Jim	Carroll
Jan	Jordan

ID	Forename	Surname
1	Charlie	Smith
2	Lacey	Adams
3	Charlie	Smith
4	Jim	Carroll
5	Jan	Jordan

Wrong.
Neither of these fields is suitable as a primary key as there are duplicate values.

Correct.
ID can be the primary key as it has a unique value in each record.

Figure 5.3 Simple primary key

The primary key can be of two types:

- simple
- compound or composite.

A simple primary key is one which is made up of a single field only, like ID in the example shown in Figure 5.3. A compound primary key is one which combines more than one field to make a unique value.

In the example shown in Figure 5.4, a student can only be in one place at a time. Therefore combining the student name, date and period gives a unique value. These three fields could be combined to make a composite primary key.

Student	Date	Period	Present
H Top	12/12/2008	1	Y
S Small	12/12/2008	1	Y
P Andres	12/12/2008	1	N
H Top	12/12/2008	2	Y

Figure 5.4 Composite primary key

Secondary key

A secondary key is a field that is identified as being suitable for indexing the data. It is used to sort the data in a different order to the primary key. A table can have many secondary keys – every field could be a secondary key.

Foreign key

A foreign key is used to link tables together. A foreign key is a field in one table that is linked to a primary key in another table. The data types of the fields that are linked must be the same.

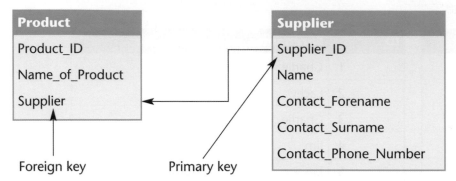

Figure 5.5 Foreign key

Questions

1 Identify the **four** requirements of a table.

2 What is the difference between a field and record?

3 Identify **three** properties of a field.

4 What is the role of the primary key?

5 Describe the difference between a simple primary key and a composite/compound primary key.

6 What is the role of a secondary key?

7 Using an example, describe how a foreign key works.

Relationships between entities

Entities are difficult to define. Chen, who introduced the entity relationship model, defined an entity as 'a thing that can be distinctly identified'. The idea of an entity is central to understanding entity relationship models. There are some general observations we can make about entities that can help.

- The world is made up of entities.
- Entities can be classified into entity types. For example, we can identify EMPLOYEE as an entity and instances (records) of the entity EMPLOYEE would be individual employees.
- Each entity of the same type has a set of properties that can be applied to the entity type. For example, each instance of the entity EMPLOYEE has a salary and a department where they work. This applies to every entity type.
- Entities can be linked to each other by means of a relationship.

Relationships

There are three types of relationship that can be identified as existing between entities.

Relationship	Symbol used
One-to-one	
One-to-many	
Many-to-many	

One-to-one relationship

If it is true that any instance of the entity X can be associated with only one instance of entity Y, then the relationship is one-to-one.

When determining one-to-one relationships you need to consider the timescale and not be concerned with historical values.

For example:

```
┌──────────┐              ┌──────────────┐
│  School  │──┤────────┤──│ Headteacher  │
└──────────┘              └──────────────┘
```

A school can only have one headteacher and a headteacher can only be a headteacher of one school.

Historically, a school is likely to have had many headteachers and a headteacher may have held a post as a headteacher at a previous school. It is therefore easier to discount what can happen historically when considering relationships.

Here are some other examples of one-to-one relationships.

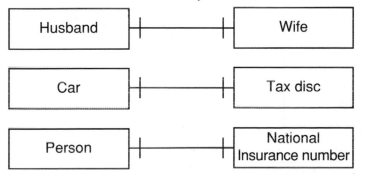

In database design it is uncommon to find a one-to-one relationship. If there is a one-to-one relationship then it is likely (but not always so) that the tables would be combined.

One-to-many relationship

This is the most common type of relationship between entities. A single instance of an entity can be associated with many instances of

Figure 5.6 One-to-one relationship

Figure 5.7 One-to-one relationships

another entity. Within the relationship it is true that many instances of an entity are associated with only a single instance of another entity.

When looking at entities and relationships it is necessary to look in detail at the situation as the relationship between similar entities could be different in different situations.

Here are some examples of one-to-many relationships.

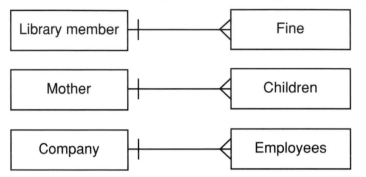

Figure 5.8 One-to-many relationships

A library member could have several fines at the same time for different books. However, each fine is only owed by a single member.

A mother can have several children, but every child has only one mother.

A company has many employees but (in this situation at least) each employee is only employed by one company.

Many-to-many relationship

Many instances of an entity can be associated with many instances of another entity.

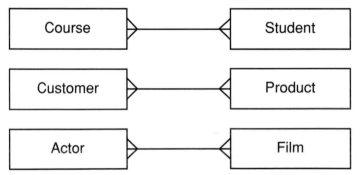

Figure 5.9 Many-to-many relationships

A student in a school takes many courses. A course has many students registered on it.

A customer can purchase many products and a product can be purchased by many customers.

An actor has been in many films and a film has many actors.

Many-to-many relationships break the rules of normalisation. There should be no many-to-many relationships in a normalised database.

If you have a many-to-many relationship a link entity needs to be added. This is an entity that sits between the two current entities and has a one-to-many relationship with each.

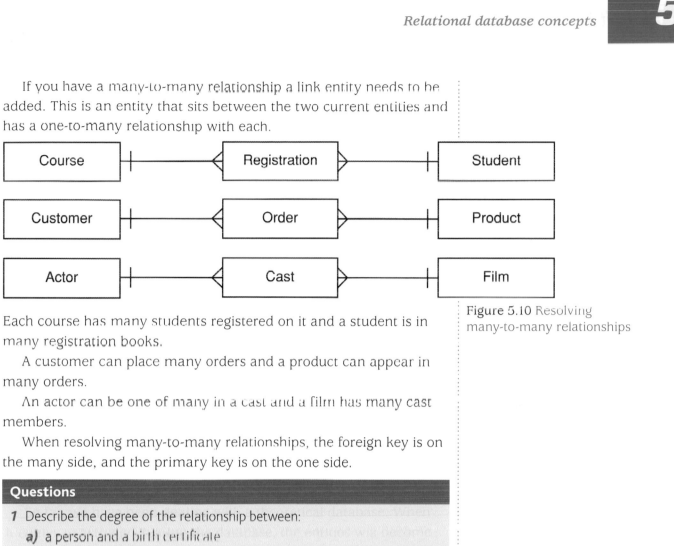

Figure 5.10 Resolving many-to-many relationships

Each course has many students registered on it and a student is in many registration books.

A customer can place many orders and a product can appear in many orders.

An actor can be one of many in a cast and a film has many cast members.

When resolving many-to-many relationships, the foreign key is on the many side, and the primary key is on the one side.

Questions

1 Describe the degree of the relationship between:
   a) a person and a birth certificate
   b) a film and an Academy Award
   c) a car and an owner
   d) a teacher and a school.

Explain your reasoning for each.

2 Resolve the following many-to-many relationships:
   a) additives to plants
   b) books to authors
   c) library members to books.

Explain your reasoning for each.

3 Describe the characteristics of an entity.

4 Describe the **three** types of relationship.

Databases require a good understanding of the technical aspects and language. It is important to learn the terms used, so the following revisits the definitions and places them within a practical context.

Records, keys and relationships

In order to see how the table works, it is necessary to look at the table with data in it.

Forename	Surname	Address Line 1	Town	County	Postcode	Phone
John	Green	43 The Grove	Chatham	Kent	ME1 2AB	01634 12345
Harry	Blue	18 Hilltop	Chatham	Kent	ME1 3AB	01634 22345
Susan	White	23 The Street	Chatham	Kent	ME1 4AB	01634 32345
John	Green	43 The Grove	Chatham	Kent	ME1 2AB	01634 12345

Each line is known as a record. The example above has four records in it. (The top line containing the headings is not a record.) A record is a collection of fields that all relate to the same topic.

There are rules for tables. In order for the table to conform to the rules, every row needs to be unique.

In the example above, every row is not unique: the first and last have the same details. These may refer to the same customer, but they may refer to different customers (two people who live at the same address with the same name).

To make the records unique, we need to have a primary key. The primary key is a field that makes each record uniquely identifiable. (Note that the primary key does not make the table unique, only the records.)

Primary keys are usually numeric and, in many database systems, the data type can be set to Autonumber. This is a number field that the database will start at 1 and automatically increment for each new record.

Customer ID	Forename	Surname	Address Line 1	Town	County	Postcode	Phone
1	John	Green	43 The Grove	Chatham	Kent	ME1 2AB	01634 12345
2	Harry	Blue	18 Hilltop	Chatham	Kent	ME1 3AB	01634 22345
3	Susan	White	23 The Street	Chatham	Kent	ME1 4AB	01634 32345
4	John	Green	43 The Grove	Chatham	Kent	ME1 2AB	01634 12345

As you can see, the primary key is just a number, but it now makes every record unique: no two records will have the same primary key.

One of the advantages of a relational database is that it removes duplicate data. Imagine if you had to write out the customer's name and address every time they placed an order. If they placed 50 orders that is a lot of data that is duplicated. Would it not be better to store their name and address once and link it to their orders?

Activities

For the library example used earlier, write out the tables and field names.

If we go back to the original scenario it will help find the links between tables:

- Each paint has a supplier.
- Each customer orders a paint.

Look at the tables and field names. The following field names are repeated in different tables.

- In the PAINT table there is **SupplierID** (also in the SUPPLIER table).
- In the ORDER table there is **CustomerID** (from CUSTOMER table) and **PaintID** (from PAINT table).

CUSTOMER		ORDER		PAINT		SUPPLIER
CustomerID Forename Surname Address Line 1 Town County Postcode Phone		OrderID CustomerID PaintID Date		PaintID Colour Name SupplierID Type Cost		SupplierID Name Contact Name Phone

Figure 5.12 Entity diagram with attributes and links

Notice how one of the sides of the link is always a primary key and the other is just a field. This is important. The one that is just a field but is part of the link is called a foreign key.

A foreign key is a field in one table that is also a primary key in another table and is used to create a link between the two.

Look at the tables below showing the PAINT and SUPPLIER tables. The value of the primary key of SUPPLIER matches the value of the foreign key in PAINT allowing a link between the two tables and the data to be matched between them.

PaintID	Colour	Name	SupplierID	Cost	Type
1	Blue	Sky During Day	1	£14.99	Gloss
2	Green	Rough Sea	1	£12.99	Matt
3	Yellow	Jaundice	2	£12.99	Matt
4	White	Bright Light	2	£15.99	Gloss

SupplierID	Name	Contact Name	Phone
1	Natural Colours	Jordan Carroll	012 345
2	Radiant Paints	Sylvia Farrant	012 346

Figure 5.13 Entity with data showing links

The only way to get comfortable with entity relationship diagrams (ERDs) is by practising. There are a few rules that will help you.

- An ERD should not contain any many-to-many relationships. If it does, then a link entity needs to be put between them, the relationships for this link entity will be one-to-many and many-to-one.

For example, a supplier provides products. The supplier can provide more than one product and a product can be provided by different (more than one) suppliers.

Activities

Complete the tables and attributes for the library and draw out a diagram showing the links between tables.

This gives us an ERD of:

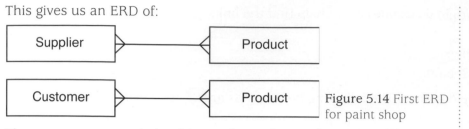

Figure 5.14 First ERD for paint shop

The many-to-many relationship needs resolving. This is done by the addition of a link table. In this case, the link table is the list of products from the PRODUCT entity that an individual SUPPLIER can provide:

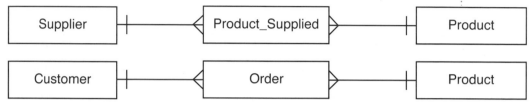

Figure 5.15 Resolving many-to-many relationships for paint shop

Notice how the link table contains the 'many' and the original table contains the 'one'.

Steps in creating an ERD

The following steps can help in creating an ERD:

- Read and re-read the narrative
- Make assumptions
- Identify the entities
- Define the relationships between the entities

The Seed Shack is a new shop in Westwood Way. They have a new system that stores the product details and manages stock levels. A customer walks down the aisles and places items in their basket. At the checkout a cashier will scan the item where it is added to a checkout transaction and the stock level of the item is reduced. In order to keep the system efficient the items are stored in categories.

Having read the above scenario, re-read it and make assumptions (about what is being stored):

The Seed Shack is a new shop in Westwood Way. They have a new system that stores the product details and manages stock levels. A customerwalks down the aisles and places items in their basket. At the checkout a cashier will scan the item where it is added to a checkout transaction and the stock level of the item is reduced. In order to keep the system efficient the items are stored in categories.

This gives us entities of:

Product (Item)

Checkout (Checkout Transaction)

Category

Customer

Cashier

As the system does not deal with employees, cashier is not strictly necessary, neither is customer.

Questions

1 What assumption has been made about product? (Think expansion of the system and suppliers)

2 What details will appear in the checkout entity?

Having identified the entities, the next step is to define the relationship between the entities:

CATEGORY – this is linked to PRODUCT in a 1:M relationship, one category can be in several PRODUCT details.

PRODUCT – as above, linked to CATEGORY but also PRODUCT details (name, price, quantity sold) will appear on the receipt – in this case, the CHECKOUT in a 1:M relationship.

Referential integrity

Looking at the paint shop example, it is possible to have a supplier in the database who did not supply the company with any paints. They may have done so in the past but you do not stock any of their paints now. However, it is impossible to have paints in the database which do not have any supplier. Referential integrity makes sure that it is impossible to enter a reference to a link which does not exist.

Activities

Expand the above ERD to cope with online ordering by customers and suppliers for the products.

Activities

Using a database program, create the paint shop database, enforce referential integrity and see what happens.

PaintID	Colour	Name	Cost	SupplierID	Type
1	Blue	Sky During Day	£14.99	1	Gloss
2	Green	Rough Sea	£12.99	1	Matt
3	Yellow	Jaundice	£12.99	2	Matt
4	White	Bright Light	£15.99	2	Gloss
5	Purple	Plum Island	£18.99	3	Gloss

Supplier:

SupplierID	Name	Contact Name	Phone
1	Natural Colours	Jordan Carroll	012 345
2	Radiant Paints	Sylvia Farrant	012 346

Figure 5.16 Referential integrity working and not working

Referential integrity as SupplierID in PAINT table has a corresponding record in SupplierID in SUPPLIER table

No corresponding record for Paint 5 (supplier 3) – therefore referential integrity has been broken

Questions

1 Describe the following database terms:
   a) database
   b) record
   c) field.

2 Describe the difference between an entity and a table.

3 Using an example, describe the primary key and explain why it is needed.

4 Using an example, describe the foreign key and explain why it is needed.

5 What is referential integrity and why is it important?

First, second and third normal form

Normalisation

Data is normalised in order to reduce redundancy and inconsistency, and to make it easier to use and maintain. There are specific rules attached to each normal form.

Before a table gets to 'first normal' form it is in 'unnormalised' form – UNF or 0NF.

The next example is based on a local a`uthority requiring exam results from all students within its area.

Tip

You will not be required you to carry out the actual process of normalisation during the examination. However, you will be required to know the rules of normalisation and be able to identify which normal form data is in, with reasons. This section does not, therefore, cover how to normalise data but it does describe what to look for in each normal form.

Student No	Student Name	School Code	School Name	School Location	ExamID	Exam Name	Exam Date	Exam Result
AB12	Joe May	PT1	Prior Taylor	Chatham	HI1	History GCSE	24/05/07	A*
AB12	Joe May	PT1	Prior Taylor	Chatham	MA1	Maths GCSE	20/05/07	A
AC15	Phil Sept	HT1	Hall Taylor	Rainham	FR2	French AS	13/05/07	B
AC15	Phil Sept	HT1	Hall Taylor	Rainham	IT2	IT AS	10/05/07	C

First normal form (1NF)

A table is in 1NF if every data value in a field is atomic and each record does not contain repeating data.

Atomic means that the data value cannot be broken down any further. The **Student Name** and **Exam Name** fields are not atomic as they both contain two data items each. **Student Name** contains 'forename' and 'surname' and **Exam Name** contains 'subject' and 'level'.

To make a start on normalising this table we need to make each field contain only atomic data.

Student No	Student Forename	Student Surname	School Code	School Name	School Location	Exam ID	Exam Name	Exam Level	Exam Date	Exam Result
AB12	Joe	May	PT1	Prior Taylor	Chatham	HI1	History	GCSE	24/05/07	A*
AB12	Joe	May	PT1	Prior Taylor	Chatham	MA1	Maths	GCSE	20/05/07	A
AC15	Phil	Sept	HT1	Hall Taylor	Rainham	FR2	French	AS	13/05/07	B
AC15	Phil	Sept	HT1	Hall Taylor	Rainham	IT2	IT	AS	10/05/07	C

As defined earlier, a table has its own set of characteristics:

- Each row must be uniquely identifiable.
- Each field name must be unique.

For each row to be uniquely identifiable it needs a primary key. (When showing a table with data in it, the primary key is identified by putting an * next to the field name.)

All the field names used in a table must be unique: they cannot be duplicated.

Student No*	Student Forename	Student Surname	School Code	School Name	School Location	Exam ID*	Exam Name	Exam Level	Exam Date	Exam Result
AB12	Joe	May	PT1	Prior Taylor	Chatham	HI1	History	GCSE	24/05/07	A*
AB12	Joe	May	PT1	Prior Taylor	Chatham	MA1	Maths	GCSE	20/05/07	A
AC15	Phil	Sept	HT1	Hall Taylor	Rainham	FR2	French	AS	13/05/07	B
AC15	Phil	Sept	HT1	Hall Taylor	Rainham	IT2	IT	AS	10/05/07	C

Note the use of the composite primary key, **StudentNo** and **ExamID**. This uniquely identifies each record because a student only takes each exam once (in this scenario).

Checks for 1NF:

- Does the table have a primary key?
- Is each field name unique?
- Are there any repeating fields in a single record?
- Is all the data within a field atomic?

Second normal form (2NF)

A table is in 2NF if it is 1NF and all its non-key attributes are dependent on the entire primary key (or there are no partial key dependencies).

We therefore need to create a school table.

StudentNo*	Student Forename	Student Surname	School Code
AB12	Joe	May	PT1
AC15	Phil	Sept	HT1

School Code*	School Name	School Location
PT1	Prior Taylor	Chatham
HT1	Hall Taylor	Rainham

All non-key items are now fully dependent on the primary key, so all tables are now in 3NF.

The rule here is that a new table needs to be created for each new dependency.

Checks for 3NF:

- Is the table in 2NF (and also, therefore, in 1NF)?
- Are all non-key items fully dependent on the primary key?

The correct notation for table structures

When writing data structures there is a notation that is universally understood and should be used.

The table name should be in capitals and the attributes (field names) in brackets separated by a comma. The primary key is underlined and foreign keys are overlined.

For example:

STUDENT(StudentNo, StudentForename, StudentSurname, SchoolCode)

SCHOOL(SchoolCode, SchoolName, SchoolLocation)

EXAM(ExamID, ExamName, ExamLevel)

STUDENTEXAM(StudentNo, ExamID, ExamDate, ExamResult)

Questions

1 Describe first normal form.

2 Explain why the following data structure is not in first normal form.

Student Name	Year	Classes	Games	Games
Fred Smith	11	11ICT 10Ma2	Football	Rugby
Heather Phipps	11	11MA4, 11Mu	Netball	Lacrosse
Alex Oliver	10	11En1, 11Ma1	Hockey	Rugby

3 Describe second normal form.

4 Explain why the following data structure is not in second normal form.

Seat Number*	Performance	Date*	Time*	Customer Forename	Customer Surname
A1	We Will Rock You	27/12/2004	2.30	John	May
B1	We Will Rock You	27/12/2004	2.30	Fred	Deacon
C1	We Will Rock You	27/12/2004	2.30	Brian	Taylor
A1	We Will Rock You	27/12/2004	7.30	Roger	Mercury

(The primary key is a compound key: Seat Number, Date and Time.)

5 Describe third normal form.

6 Explain why the following data structure is not in third normal form.

ID*	Forename	Surname	House Name/Number	Town	County	Postcode
1	John	Davies	18 Bright Road	Nottingham	Notts	NG8 5EP
2	Alice	Hall	24 Halls Avenue	Nottingham	Notts	NG8 5ET
3	Joan	Stevenson	19 Walbrook Close	Nottingham	Notts	NG8 5EZ

7 Explain why it is an advantage to have a standard notation for tables.

Advantages of normalisation

The normalisation process gives many advantages to the database that emerges at the end.

The final tables will have no redundant data within them as normalisation removes redundant data from the tables. The process also removes duplicate data. This saves on storage space and makes the data consistent. If you are holding multiple copies of the data and only update one of them, they will become unsynchronised. If this happens the data has lost consistency and it has lost integrity. You will not know which data is the right data.

A normalised data structure is easier to maintain than one that has not been normalised. If the data is not duplicated then an update on a single piece of data will mean that any process that uses the data can be relied upon.

The data that is stored at the end of the process is stored in an efficient structure. This means that, as every data item is atomic, it is possible to combine the data in any desired format. If multiple data items were stored in a single field and only part of the field was required, a lot of programming would have to be done to extract the item required.

The database structure is very flexible. This means that if the requirements of the organisation using the data alter, the database can adapt without a major redesign of the structure.

The advantages of normalisation can be summarised as follows:

- removes redundancy
- increases consistency
- increases integrity
- easier maintenance
- flexibility for future expansion.

Disadvantages of normalisation

There are some disadvantages to normalising a database. The main one is reduced database performance. When a query of an action is sent to the database, there are a large number of factors involved. These include CPU usage, memory and input/output. A normalised database requires greater use of those resources as it must locate the requested information from across different tables, join the data from the tables and even from within the same table. This takes more time than from an unnormalised database.

How the database will be used will affect whether it is necessary to have a normalised or unnormalised database. Databases have two main purposes: transactions and reporting. Transaction databases require a lot of inserting, editing and deleting of data, whereas reporting presents data but rarely changes it. Unnormalised data is better for reporting systems because it is likely that the data is in a structure suitable for the reports required and can be presented quicker and with less processing and memory requirements. Normalisation is vital for transactional databases to ensure data integrity and to increase the speed with which records can be added, edited, and deleted.

Databases that are required to store historical data need to break the rules of normalisation. In a normalised database, the price of a purchase (invoice), for example, is calculated. In the future, if the price of an item changes then the invoice total will change. If you needed to go back and look at a historical invoice, it would be based on today's values, not the ones at the time. It is therefore, in certain circumstances, necessary to store calculated values.

Components of a data dictionary

A data dictionary is often called a database about a database. It contains metadata (data about data). Different database packages will contain slightly different information in the data dictionary. The list below is the basic data that would be expected in them all.

The data dictionary holds:

Data	Description
Table name	The name of the table. A unique name for each table in the database.
Field name	Each field is identified.
Field data type	The data type allocated to each field: text/string/date/Boolean etc.
Field length	The number of characters allocated for the contents of the field.
Field default value	If a field has a default value that automatically appears on the creation of a new record.
Field validation	Any validation applied to the field.
Table security	Who has access to write, update, edit, delete etc. values to and from the table.
Keys	Primary and foreign keys are identified.
Indexes	Any field which is indexed.
Relationships	Relationships between tables identified: one-to-one etc.

Questions

1 Describe **three** items found in a data dictionary that relate to fields.

2 Describe **three** items found in a data dictionary that relate to tables.

3 How would a designer use the data dictionary?

Select appropriate data types for a given set of data

The main data types available are:

- Text/string – Any key on the keyboard. It can be used to store text (Mr Jones), text and numbers (TN18 7PU), or just numbers (54).

  Numbers are only stored as text if they are not to be manipulated as numbers (i.e. if no addition, subtraction etc. is to be done). Telephone numbers do not have mathematical functions applied to them so they are stored as text. Telephone numbers also have spaces within them and start with a 0 (e.g. 01234 56789), which makes them text based not numeric.

- Integer/real – Numbers. Integer without decimal places and real with decimal places. When assessing the data to be stored it is necessary to look at examples of data and decide the data type.

  Currency is usually stored as a real number (e.g. £43.00). The symbol, although text, is stored separately. However, consider the appropriateness of storing house prices as real.

- Boolean – Boolean fields can store one of only two possible values (e.g. yes/no, true/false) that can be used to represent any question with two possible outcomes (male/female, video/dvd etc.).

- Date/Time

The advantages and disadvantages of using the data types are related to their use within a given scenario and what the data will be used for. For example, if the data for a field 'Does the house have a garden?' has only two possible options (yes or no), this is appropriate for a Boolean data type, because it takes up the minimal amount of memory space and can be validated to ensure the data stored is one of those two values. It also enables easier searching of the data.

> **Questions**
>
> *1* Describe the **five** main data types.
>
> *2* When should numbers be used?
>
> *3* What are the advantage of using the Boolean data type?

Simple and complex queries using static and dynamic parameters

The ability of databases to run queries is what makes them particularly useful.

Parameter queries return fields from tables where the value of the parameter is matched.

The parameter is the value that is used by the query to select records. The next table shows a selection of records from the PRODUCT table. Each product has a supplier. Some suppliers supply more than one product.

Product_ID	Name_of_Product	Supplier
1	Red pens	Jones the PenMaker
2	Red pens	No Frill Quills
3	Lined A4	The PaperMaker
4	Blue pens	Jones the PenMaker
5	Purple pens	Jones the PenMaker
6	Plain A4	The PaperMaker
7	A4 book covers	The Paper Place
8	Green pens	Jones the PenMaker
9	Spiral notebook	The PaperMaker
10	Propelling pencils	Pencils 4 All
11	Blue pens	No Frill Quills
12	HB pencils	Pencils 4 All
0		

Figure 5.17 The PRODUCT table

Simple query

Using a parameter query all the suppliers of a particular product could be shown.

To find all the suppliers of blue pens, the Name_of_Product column needs to be searched to match the text 'Blue pens'. The other fields to be displayed also need to be selected.

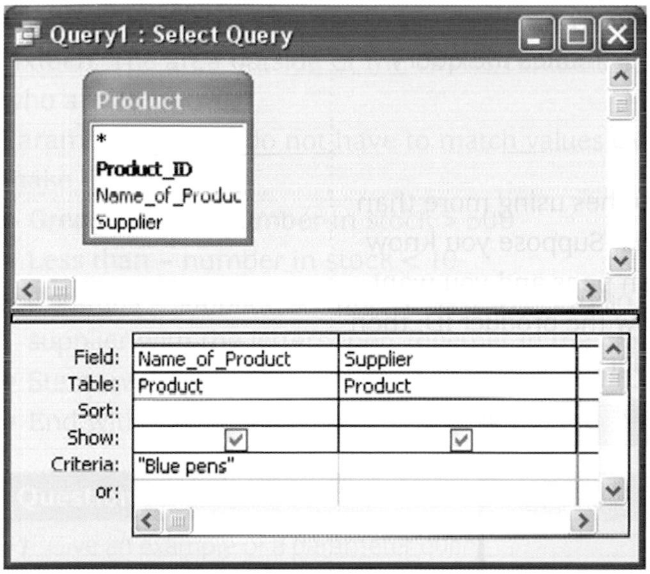

Figure 5.18 Simple query

The results of the query will display two fields and two records.

Name_of_Product	Supplier
Blue pens	Jones the PenMaker
Blue pens	No Frill Quills

Figure 5.19 Results of query in Figure 5.18

In the query above, the parameter has been 'hard coded'. This means that the query cannot be changed: whenever it is run it will always and only search for blue pens. This is known as a static parameter query. There will be occasions where the user will want to search for different products. It would not be efficient to have separate queries for every product because not every product is likely to be known when the database is being designed.

Parameter queries can be created which ask the user for the value to search for. These are known as dynamic parameter queries. A dialogue box can be created that takes a value from the user and uses that value in the query.

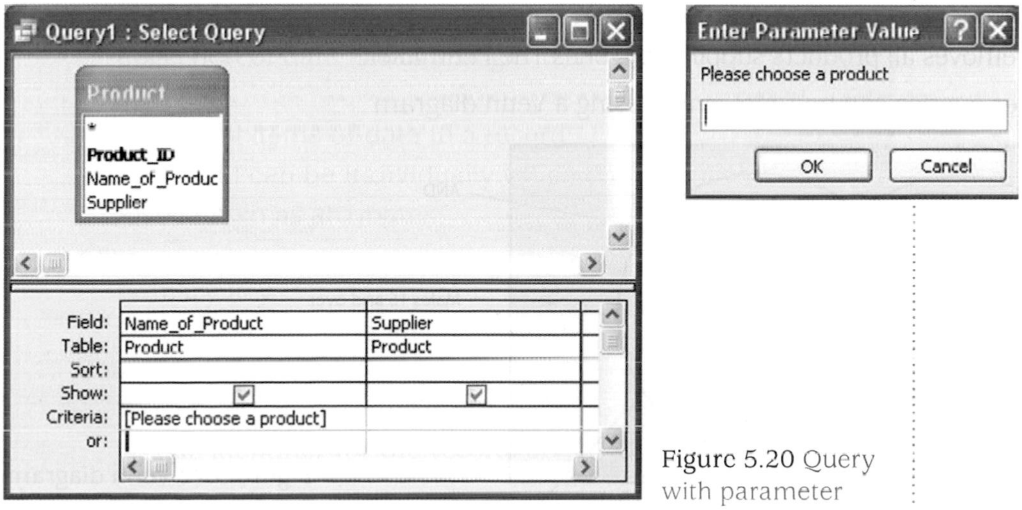

Figure 5.20 Query with parameter

Foreign key
> Primary key in one table, field in another table, used to join tables together

Secondary key
> Used to index a field

Entities

Single objects or processes
Information about things
Each entity becomes a table
Entities linked by relationships

Relationships

Links between entities/tables
> One-to-one – where one record in a table is linked to only one record in another table
> One-to-many – one record in a table is linked to many records in a second table
> Many-to-many – the many link goes both ways between two tables

Referential integrity

Ensuring that for every record in a table with a foreign key, there is a record in the corresponding table with the primary key

Normalisation

Process applied to data structures
Decreases redundancy
Increases integrity
First normal form
> Every data value is atomic
> No repeating data
> Primary key

Second normal form
> Must be in 1NF
> Non-key attributes are dependent on the entire primary key

Third normal form
> Must be in 2NF
> No functional dependency between non-key items

Advantages of normalisation
> Removes redundancy
> Increases consistency
> Increases integrity
> Easier maintenance
> Flexibility for future expansion

Disadvantages of normalisation
> Reduced database performance
> Problems with historical calculations

Data dictionary

Database about a database
Contains design details about the database
Includes table name, field name, data type, length, validation relationships, security

Data types

Text/string – anything not requiring a calculation
Integer – whole numbers only, NOT telephone number
Real – numbers with decimal places
Boolean – one of two values
Date/Time – store age, dates, times
Look to see what the data is going to be used for

Parameter

Simple query
> A query where there is only one parameter

Complex query
> A query with more than one parameter
> Makes use of AND, OR and NOT to join parameters

Static
> Parameter is hard coded into the query and cannot be changed by the end user

Dynamic
> Request for the parameter given to the end user at run time, usually by a dialogue box.

Chapter tests

Test 1

A small corner shop runs a newspaper round. Until now, the details about the newspaper round have been stored manually. The shop wants to computerise its records. The shop will require a database.

1 Describe the following database terms:

a) table

b) record

c) field. [6]

Application software used for presentation and communication of data

6

Introduction

This chapter covers the basic concepts relating to presentations and the communication of data. You will need to make sure you understand the features of application software used for presentations and communicating data and are able to apply this knowledge to a variety of situations.

This chapter covers:

- Characteristics of documents
- Mail merge
- Reformatting documents to meet the needs of an application
- Clipart and thumbnail images
- Vector and bitmap graphics
- Graphic libraries
- Features of presentation software

Describe the characteristics of documents and how they should be used

All documents have common characteristics that can be used in their production. The characteristics used may be dictated by the house style of the organisation they are being produced for or to meet the needs of the target audience.

The main characteristics of documents are:

- characters
- paragraphs
- sections
- frames
- headers
- footers
- footnotes
- pages.

Character

A character is any letter, number or symbol used in a document.

Paragraph

Paragraphs are generally used when a long document is being created. They are generally defined by the use of a carriage return at the end of the text.

The paragraph may have a style that could be pre-defined through the use of a corporate or house style or they may be defined by the user. A paragraph style defines the features of the text. These features may include the paragraph alignment (left, right, centred or justified), indentations, line spacing, font size and style and bullets or numbering. Styles are generally applied to paragraphs and headings but may also be applied to frames and tables. Here is an example paragraph style definition:

Style: Paragraph 3
Font: Verdana, 20 pt
Format: Bold
Paragraph alignment: Centred
Spacing before: 12 pt
Spacing after: 6 pt

Section

A section is a portion of a document in which page-formatting options can be set. A new section can be created when properties such as line numbering, number of columns, or headers and footers need to be changed. Until section breaks are inserted, the word-processing package will treat a document as a single section. Sections can be used to allow the layout of a document to be varied within a page or between pages. Section breaks are inserted to divide the document into sections, and then each section can be formatted to meet the needs of the user.

Frame

A frame is an area of a page that can contain text or graphics. The frames can be positioned anywhere on the page. Changes to the content of one frame will not affect the content of another. A DTP package usually makes use of frames.

Word-processing packages can use frames but are not exclusively frame based. Therefore, the position of each object on the page depends on the position of everything else. For example, if a paragraph or sentence is deleted, everything else moves to take its place.

Word-processing packages are not frame based.

The position of each object on the page depends on the position of everything else.

For example if a paragraph or sentence is deleted then everything else moves to take its place.

← If this paragraph is deleted then everything else moves up to take its place.

Word-processing packages are not frame based.

For example if a paragraph or sentence is deleted then everything else move to take its place.

← This paragraph has now moved up to fill the space.

In a DTP package each individual frame can be easily moved or resized. This means that a page in a DTP publication can be edited by changing the size or position of the frames. A frame can also be moved from one page to another.

Figure 6.1 Deleting a paragraph in a word-processed document.

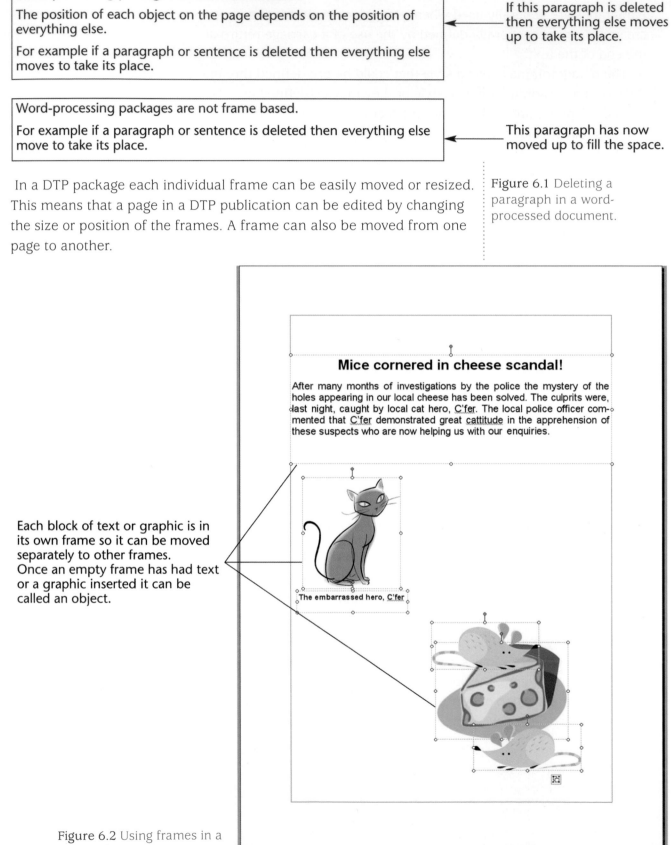

Each block of text or graphic is in its own frame so it can be moved separately to other frames.
Once an empty frame has had text or a graphic inserted it can be called an object.

Mice cornered in cheese scandal!

After many months of investigations by the police the mystery of the holes appearing in our local cheese has been solved. The culprits were, last night, caught by local cat hero, C'fer. The local police officer commented that C'fer demonstrated great cattitude in the apprehension of these suspects who are now helping us with our enquiries.

The embarrassed hero, C'fer

Figure 6.2 Using frames in a DTP package

Text, as well as graphics, can be positioned in a frame. Once a text frame has been created, it can be positioned and resized. Text is typed or imported into the frame. Ususally, frames can be linked so if all the text does not fit in the original frame, the excess text flows into the next. The DTP package may do this automatically. Alternatively, the text may need to be edited to fit the original frame.

> **Question**
>
> Describe, giving an example of its use, what is meant by a frame.

Header and footer

A header is text which appears on a document in the top margin of every page. A header may include the creator's name, title and date. A footer is text which appears on a document in the bottom margin of every page. The general rule is that the footer contains the page numbering, date or file name.

You can use the same header and footer throughout a document or change the header and footer for part of the document. For example, you can use a unique header or footer on the first page, or leave the header or footer off the first page. You can also use different headers and footers on odd and even pages or for part of a document.

> **Question**
>
> Describe, giving an example of its use, what is meant by a header.

Footnote

Footnotes are used to briefly explain a word or phrase without including the explanation in the body of the text. A reference number is placed next to the word or phrase and the explanation is placed at the 'foot' of the page which is identified by the same reference number. Here is an example to explain the word footnote.[1]

> **Question**
>
> Describe, giving an example of its use, what is meant by a footnote.

Page

Pages are each printed side of paper containing the components of a document. The components may include, for example, text, graphics, tables or the contents page. (A website also contains pages.) Each page contains a pre-defined amount of content. This may be defined by the use of a house style or by the user. Pages can also be used to break a long document, such as this book, into chapters with each page being numbered.

Activities

Collect a range of business documents. Describe the characteristics which have been used and whether they make the document 'fit for purpose'.

---

[1] *A footnote is found at the foot of the page.*

Describe how word-processing and desktop publishing (DTP) software can be used with data from a spreadsheet or database for mail merge, and describe the advantages and disadvantages of using this technique

A standard document created in a word-processing or DTP package can be combined with information from a spreadsheet or database. Mail merging allows the user to create and send a personalised version of the same document to many different people or organisations (recipients).

A data source is created containing all the information to be included in the document. The data source may be created specifically for the mail merge process or it may be an existing data source, for example customer records or student records.

The standard document/template is then produced including merge fields. These are based on the fields in the spreadsheet or database that is being used as the data source. An example would be **Dear <title> <lastname>** where title and lastname are fields in the data source. The standard document can be a letter, address label or envelope.

The data source and the standard document/template are then linked and merged. The software merges the data by inserting the appropriate fields from the data source to produce the personalised documents.

The personalised documents can be sent to a printer or used to create a new file.

If there are 100 customer records held in the data source then the mail merge process would produce 100 documents. The advantages of using the mail merge process include:

- Only one letter needs to be actually created. The rest of the letters required will be automatically generated so it is faster to produce a mass mailing.
- Only one copy of the document needs to be proofread/checked for errors so there are less chances of mistakes being included.
- The data source can be used for many different mail merge and other processes so saving time not having to recreate the data source each time a mail merge needs to be completed.
- The data source only needs checking for accuracy once. The letters produced during the mail merge process should be sent to the correct person and address.
- The standard letter/template can be saved and reused.

The disadvantages of using the mail merge process include:

- The data file – moving the data file, renaming fields etc. can cause the merge to fail as the word processor program cannot find the data sources it needs.
- The database that provides the information for the mail merge letter must be kept up to date if it is going to be useful.
- It is unlikely that every single letter produced will be checked for errors and with a large mail merge run it is possible that some errors will creep in, having a negative impact on the reputation of the organisation.
- Whilst a simple mail merge is easy to do and novice/inexperienced users can complete it, a complex merge involving word fields can be complex and require training. The mail merge wizard does not have the options available to complete a complex merge and an understanding of field codes is required.
- Mail merging makes it very easy to create vast amounts of junk mail – it is more difficult to personalise each letter for each individual so they may feel like they are receiving a bulk letter rather than one tailored to them specifically.
- Mail merged letters can lack a personal touch because the only individual part in a mail merged document is the data merged from the database.

Questions

1 What is mail merge?

2 What are the disadvantages of mail merge?

Describe how a document can be reformatted to suit the needs of a given application

Word-processing packages have many features that can help users format the documents being produced to exactly meet their needs. Users can format the attributes of documents including:

- page size, settings and orientation
- text position, size and style.

Page size, settings and orientation

The size of the page and the size of the paper to be printed on can be selected by the user to meet their needs. The next figure shows the A5 page size selected in Microsoft Word.

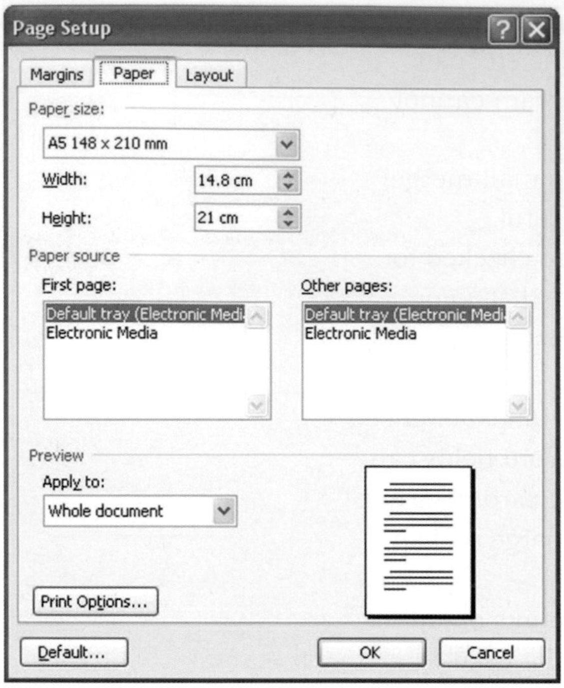

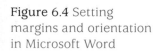

Figure 6.3 Setting page size in Microsoft Word

Page margins are the blank space around the edges of the page. In general, text and graphics are positioned in the printable area surrounded by the margins. However, some items can be positioned in the margins, for example headers, footers and page numbers.

The user can also select the orientation of the page: either portrait or landscape. The next figure shows the landscape orientation selected.

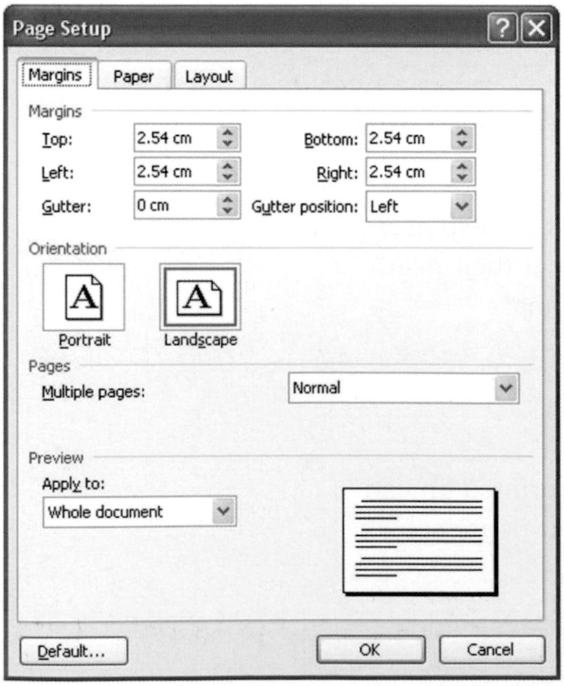

Figure 6.4 Setting margins and orientation in Microsoft Word

Text position, size and style

Text position is also known as alignment. The user can select the most appropriate alignment to meet their needs. Headings are often centred, but the user may also choose left, right or justified alignment.

A user may also select the font to use. There are many different fonts to choose from. Some fonts are easy to read such as **Verdana**, **Arial** and Times New Roman. Other fonts are very difficult to read such as *Pristina*, *Palace Script MT* and **Mistral**. A user may also choose to highlight some words or phrases through the use of bold, italic or underline features. The style of font selected must be appropriate to the document being produced and the needs of the end users.

The size of the font may also be selected. The size of the font must also be appropriate to the document being produced and the needs of the end user. It would be very difficult to read a business report in 'size 8 font' because the end user would have to strain their eyes. The font size used for this text is size 11.

Describe the advantages and disadvantages of using clip art images and collections of thumbnail images

Clip art images are either supplied 'free' with software packages or at a cost from a software manufacturer. Clip art images can be edited or used as they are.

Advantages	Disadvantages
<ul><li>Images are readily available.</li><li>Images are available immediately.</li><li>The use of clip art can reduce the cost of the design process, for example when designing a logo a designer does not have to be employed.</li><li>Extra equipment, such as scanners and digital cameras, does not have to be purchased.</li></ul>	<ul><li>Choice of images is limited to what is available.</li><li>The quality of the images ranges from very poor to good.</li><li>Clip art is not original or unique.</li><li>Clip art images, especially from internet sources, may be subject to copyright.</li></ul>

Collections of small images, thumbnails, are generally based around a topic showing a preview or a representation of the actual image. When the image is clicked then the actual image is shown.

Using collections of thumbnail images enables many images to be shown in one go, although the quality of the images may be poor. Images that are alike (categories) can be grouped together which enables a user to search for the images required. If the user finds a thumbnail image which may be the image required, then this can be enlarged. This means that individual images, taken from the library, can be opened rather than having all the images open. This will reduce the processing / memory needed on the computer. Several thumbnail images can be selected to compare the images so that the user can select the most appropriate one for their needs. It is also possible to add descriptions to the images so that they can then be searched.

It is not always possible to tell whether the actual image is of a better quality or a larger size than the preview or thumbnail image. Some thumbnail image collections can hold vast amounts of images. This means that the user can spend a long time selecting the image they require as there is so much choice. If the thumbnail image collection holds a large number of images then it can take a long time to download.

Activities

List the advantages and disadvantages of using a collection of thumbnail images.

Advantages	Disadvantages

Describe the differences between vector and bitmap graphics and evaluate their suitability for given applications

There are two main ways in which graphics can be stored: as bitmap graphics and as vector graphics.

Bitmap graphics

These are also known as raster graphics. A bitmap graphic is made up of pixels. In a true black and white graphic each pixel is represented by one bit which is either switched on or off (1 or 0). The more bits representing each pixel, then the more colours can be displayed. If a pixel is represented by four bits in a black and white graphic then 16 different shades of grey are available, whilst eight bits per pixel means that 256 different shades of grey can be used.

Most graphics are stored in colour. These graphics combine the primary colours of red, green and blue to produce a palette of different shades. Each primary colour, if represented by eight bits, can have a value between 0 and 256. When combined this gives $256 \times 256 \times 256 = 16\,777\,216$ (i.e. more than 16 million) possible shades.

The table below shows how the values of red, green and blue could be allocated to a specific pixel.

Primary colour	Value
Red	190
Green	55
Blue	137

Each pixel has two key properties associated with it: a position on the grid which makes up the image and a colour value. These properties are stored as data in the computer's memory. When the graphic needs to be displayed the data held in the bitmapped file is used to reconstruct the graphic.

A bitmap graphic is produced when an image is taken from a scanner or a digital camera.

Bitmapped files appear in a number of different formats. Some of these are shown in the table.

Format	Description
BMP	Windows bitmap. The standard file format used with Windows applications.
GIF	Graphics Interchange Format. These files are often used on websites especially as animated GIFs. They have a 256 colour limit (8 bits per pixel) and use a lossless compression algorithm to save on the amount of memory used.
JPEG	Joint Photographic Experts Group. These are also frequently used on websites. JPEGs are often used when good-quality photographic images need to be stored as they can store 24 bits per pixel and have the capability to store 16 million colours. There are different JPEG formats, which relate to the level of compression used.
TIF/TIFF	Tagged Image File Format. The file structure is more complex than some of the other formats but this format can be used on several different platforms.

Vector graphics

Vector-based graphics are also known as object-orientated graphics and work in a different way to bitmap graphics. Rather than being stored as data relating to a grid of pixels, this type of graphic is stored as geometric-based data. The file for a vector-based graphic contains mathematical data that defines the key properties of every element in the graphic. Instead of individual pixels storing the required data, vector graphics work on the basis of lines, where drawing starts from a certain point which is central to the image.

If, for example, there is a straight line in the graphic then the data in the file will define its starting point, length, thickness, location within the graphic etc. The file data, also known as the display list, will also specify the order in which each component will be displayed. This is also known as the hierarchy of the objects.

approach also means that all software relating to the production of maps uses the same symbols with the same meaning.

The main problem with graphics libraries is keeping them up to date. For example, the continual advances in the IT industry means that sometimes the graphic of a new component may not be included or components are included that are no longer used or available. Also, as interior design changes with new concepts, materials and ideas, it could be very difficult for the users of the graphic library to include these as the components required may nor be available in the library.

However, through the use of graphics libraries the diagrams and designs which are constructed will follow an industry standard and will be recognisable in all parts of the world.

Compare image libraries, clipart libraries and graphic libraries.

An image library can be defined as 'a large collection of images (either owned by a photographer or an organisation), available for sale, or free, to anyone wanting to use or publish the image'.

A clipart library can be defined as 'a collection of cartoon like or drawn images'.

A graphics library can be defined as 'a collection of graphics, usually related to a specific topic such as network design, which are used in related applications'.

	Image library	Clipart library	Graphic library
Originality	Usually contains photographs so high probability of originality of images	Shipped with products so likely to be used by many people	Contains industry standard symbols
Copyright	Some images can be copyright and royalty free. Some images, usually those of high resolution, may need to be purchased	Can be free to use if library is integrated with a software package	Can be with the manufacturer of the product (e.g. CISCO router) or with the software producer
Quality	Can be high or low resolution images: images are defined as such in the image description	Usually cartoon-like and bitmap so cannot be enlarged without pixelation	Industry standard symbols so quality appropriate for professional, such as designers, use. Usually vector-based images.
Availability	Large number of image libraries available on the internet	Integrated with the package that has been purchased. Also available as collections on the internet	Available as an add-on within the package
Use	Where specific images are required such as advertising or websites. Personal use – collections of own photographs	In documents such as posters	In specialist applications such as interior design, network design and cartography

Describe the features of presentation software: text, images, sound, video, animation, slide transition, hyperlinks, hotspots and buttons

Text

The text used on a presentation slide must meet the needs of the audience. The text style and size should be selected with the audience in mind and should enable the audience to clearly read the text on each slide. The rules, given at the end of this chapter, must be considered at all times. Fancy text, *like this*, should be avoided and the amount of text on each slide should also be considered.

Images

The use of images and graphics on a presentation slide can help to convey a message relating to the presentation or as an aide-memoire for the presenter. Again, it is important that the number of images and graphics used on each slide is kept to a minimum and are of a size that can be clearly seen by the audience. If images and graphics are used then any copyright must also be considered.

Sound

Sound can be used in many different ways within a presentation. Sound effects can be set with animation effects, for example they can be used to signify the 'arrival' of a piece of text on the screen. Examples of available sound effects are:

- clapping
- drum roll
- chime.

If used appropriately these sounds can be used to emphasise an important piece of information and add impact to the slide. Sound effects should be used sparingly as they can detract from the information contained on the slide.

Sound can also be used in other forms, such as speech and music. Sound files can be a pre-existing file, such as a company jingle, or downloaded from the internet. It is also possible to record sound files to meet the specific needs of a particular presentation.

Video

Video clips can be inserted into a presentation, for example part of a company's advertising commercial. The video clip can be set to play automatically when the slide is shown or can be started by the presenter, (e.g. by clicking a button or pressing a key). Do not use too many video clips in a presentation; like other special effects, they can draw attention away from the content of the presentation.

Animation

Animation effects are visual effects that can be added to text or other objects, such as a chart or picture. All the elements of a presentation, including text, graphics, movies, charts and other objects, can be animated. By using animation it is possible to control the way that objects appear on each slide. For example, the presenter may want to introduce a bulleted list one item at a time. Each bullet point can be made to appear when the presenter performs an action, for example a mouse click. Text can also be animated to appear one letter, word or paragraph at a time.

Animation emphasises important points, controls the flow of information within a slide and adds interest to a presentation.

Another example of the use of animation may be to change the side that text first appears on the slide. English text is read from left to right, and the animation on bullet points is set up so that they appear from the left, but to emphasise a bullet point, it could be animated to appear from the right. The change will grab the audience's attention thereby reinforcing the text in that bullet point.

Other effects might be to dim text or objects, or to change an object's colour when a new element appears on the slide.

The order and timing of animations can also be changed. If the presentation is to be shown without a presenter then it is possible to set the animations to occur automatically without any human intervention.

When the animations for a presentation have been set up it is possible to preview the presentation to ensure that all the effects are appropriate and that they do not detract from the content of the presentation.

Slide transition

Transition effects can be applied to a slide to make the presentation more interesting. Transition effects govern how the presentation software moves from slide to slide. The transition effect can be changed to indicate a new section of a presentation or to emphasise a particular slide.

Presentation software offers a range of transition effects. Some of the effects that may be available are:

- cut
- dissolve
- wipe left.

It is also possible to set the speed at which the transition occurs.

A transition effect can be applied to one particular slide or to the whole presentation. They can also have a sound associated with them. The sound effects connected to each slide transition can be set to occur with one specific transition or within the whole presentation. Sound effects should be used sparingly as they can detract from the presentation and its contents.

Hyperlinks

A hyperlink is coloured and underlined text, or a graphic, which, when clicked, takes the user to a file, a location in a file, or an HTML page on the web or an intranet. Hyperlinks can also link to newsgroups and to Gopher, Telnet and FTP sites.

Hyperlinks can be included on presentation slides and used to move to a variety of locations, for example a specific slide within the presentation, a different presentation, a document or spreadsheet, or an internet, intranet or email address. Any object, including text, shapes, tables, graphs, and pictures, can be configured as a hyperlink.

Hotspots

A hotspot is an area on a screen display which responds to a mouse click. This may be a piece of text or a graphic which will take the user to another page or screen. A hotspot is normally used in a multimedia presentation.

Buttons

An on-screen button can be used to move from one slide to the next. When this method of navigation is used the presentation is interactive. This means that the presenter or user is interacting with the presentation by using it to meet their needs. By using this method the user can select the slides viewed and sometimes select the order of viewing. This method is useful where the user needs to jump to another part of the presentation to view the information they need.

Activities

Investigate the different slide transition effects that are available on the presentation software you have access to. Identify the advantages and disadvantages of using transition effects.

Questions

1 Explain the advantages of using video in a presentation.

2 What is meant by slide transition?

3 Explain the disadvantages of using sound in a presentation.

4 How could hyperlinks be used in a presentation?

Compare delivering a presentation using printed acetate and using a computer and projector, describing the advantages and disadvantages of each

Printed acetate versus computer and projector

Presentations can be given using a computer and projector or by using printed acetate slides on an overhead projector. Presentation software can also be used to create and print acetate slides.

Computer and projector presentations	
Advantages	**Disadvantages**
• The full range of features (e.g. special effects, hyperlinks, interactivity etc.) are available. A presentation does not have to be followed in the slide sequence. • Once a presentation has been developed and saved then it is relatively easy to edit the presentation, and the slides are immediately ready to be shown. • The slides do not deteriorate with repeated use.	• There is a temptation to overuse special features. • Requires a computer and a projector. Both are relatively expensive and not all places have a projector (which are not very portable). • Special software is required to allow the presenter to annotate slides in real time. • Unless the presenter has kept a paper copy of the presentation, then it cannot be given in the event of a power cut.

Printed acetate presentations	
Advantages	**Disadvantages**
• It is easy to write on the slides to annotate them and explain/highlight items. • An overhead projector (OHP) is the only equipment needed. OHPs are relatively cheap and most places have access to one. They are simple and robust so they seldom go wrong. • In the event of a power cut, the presenter is able to read from the acetate slides.	• Special effects and interactivity cannot be used (e.g. bullet items in a list will have to be covered and revealed one at a time). • It can be difficult to jump to a slide that is out of sequence to revisit it or if a different route through a presentation is required. • When a change is made new acetate slides will have to be printed. • Slides can deteriorate with repeated handling, possibly becoming unreadable. • Blank acetate slides have to be bought and then printed on. A high use of colour (e.g. for backgrounds) can quickly use up ink/toner.

Compare and give advantages and disadvantages of different modes of navigation (automatic and manual transition) and identify and give examples of when the use of each method is more suitable

A route through a slide show may be navigated using manual or automatic transition methods.

Manual transition

Manual transition involves some form of action from the presenter/viewer to move on to the next slide. If the slide contains a number of items then each item can be displayed manually. For example, if the slide contains a bulleted list, using the manual method, the presenter can perform an action to display each bullet point in turn. Manual navigation allows the presentation to run at a speed determined by the presenter or viewer. For example, a speaker to an audience can control when each slide, or item, is displayed, and can tailor the navigation to meet the needs of the audience. A viewer can move to another slide when they are ready by clicking a button, or they can navigate to somewhere else in the presentation by selecting an item in a menu list.

Automatic transition

A presentation can be set up to run automatically with no intervention required to move on to the next slide. Timings can be set up so that the next slide is displayed automatically after a specified time period. The timings must be set to give the audience sufficient time to read the information contained on a slide before the presentation moves on to the next one. The presentation can also be set to re-start as soon as it has finished. This navigation method is suitable for presentations where no presenter is involved, such as at an exhibition. Automatic navigation is not suitable for verbal presentations as the presenter may struggle to keep pace with the presentation.

Activities

Using the table headings below, identify the advantages and disadvantages of using manual and automatic navigation methods.

	Advantages	Disadvantages
Manual transition		
Automatic transition		

Questions

1 Identify an appropriate situation where manual slide transition might be used.

2 Identify an appropriate situation where automatic slide transition might be used.

Activities

Investigate how and where presentations are given and, using the advantages and disadvantages described above, and any others your might think of, describe situations where one presentation method might be chosen in preference to the other.

Tip

You may need to be able to identify which method of transition is more suitable for a given situation. The method you identify in the examination must be relevant to the situation in the question.

Describe non-linear and hierarchical presentations giving the advantages and disadvantages of each. Identify and give examples of when each may be more suitable

A presentation is made up of a number of slides. When designing a presentation the structure of the presentation should be developed carefully. The three main structures which a presentation can take are:

- linear
- non-linear
- hierarchical.

The structure of the presentation should be chosen to meet the needs of its content and the target audience. The structure of the presentation will provide the routes that can be taken through the presentation.

A linear presentation is one in which slides are shown in a pre-determined order and in which any jump out of this sequence is not allowed, that is the slides follow an ordered line from beginning to end of the presentation.

A non-linear structure is where slides can be accessed in any order. This structure gives the presenter the option to jump over slides to specific groups or individual slides. It can be represented by a mesh diagram. The user can move through a presentation by going forward to any other slide or by jumping back to any previous slide in the presentation. This structure can become very complicated but can provide a presentation that meets the needs of either the individual user or of a presenter who wishes to use the same presentation for different audiences. Buttons and hyperlinks can be used to jump backwards and forwards to different slides in the presentation.

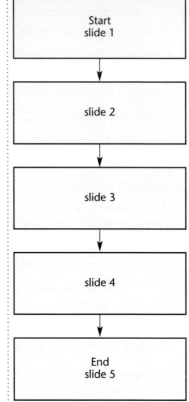

Figure 6.6 Linear presentation

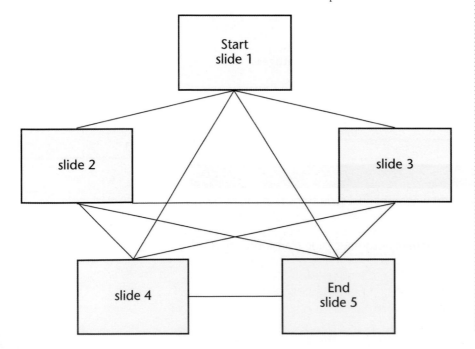

Figure 6.7 Non-linear presentation

A hierarchical structure allows different, but pre-determined, slides to be jumped to from a slide depending on an option selected (e.g. a menu item or similar), but movement through the slides will follow a pre-determined route and the user cannot jump to any slide, only to those in the path.

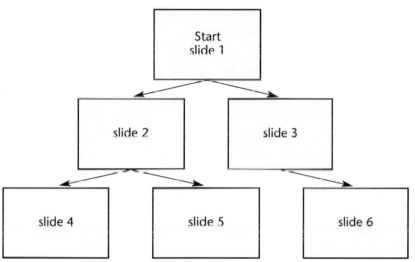

Figure 6.8 Hierarchical presentation

Activities

Using the table headings below, identify the advantages and disadvantages of the non-linear and hierarchical structures. Provide an example of when each structure could be used.

	Non-linear	Hierarchical
Advantages		
Disadvantages		
Example of use		

Rules!

If a presentation is carefully designed then it can be an effective tool to communicate information. There are some rules that must be considered when designing a presentation to ensure that the presentation is effective and meets the needs of the presenter and audience.

- The style and size of any font used should meet the needs of the presentation and the audience. There should be no more than three different font styles on each slide in the presentation. More than this and the slides will be difficult to read.
- The size of the text should be large enough for an audience to be able to read from a distance.
- When an on-screen presentation is being developed the slide background should contrast with the text colour. Consideration should be given to avoid clashing, garish colour schemes, for

example bright green and bright pink, as these can cause eyestrain for the audience and the presenter.

- The text on the slides should be kept to a minimum. The text contained within the slides should be a summary with the presenter expanding these points in their talk.
- Graphics should be very carefully selected. A graphic can add impact to the points being made but if too many graphics are used then they will distract the audience.
- Animation, sound and transition effects should also be carefully considered. As with graphics these features can add to the impact of the presentation but if too many are used then they can detract from the content of the presentation.

Chapter summary

Characteristics of documents
Characters

Paragraphs

Sections

Frames

Headers

Footers

Footnotes

Pages

Mail merge
Create data source.

Create template document.

Insert merge fields from data source.

Check merge fields with data.

Complete merge.

Formatting documents
Page size, settings and orientation

Text position, size and style

Images and graphics
Bitmap graphic

    Made up of pixels

    Quality is lost on re-sizing

    File sizes very large

    Deal well with complex highly detailed images such as photographs

    Subtle changes can be made to the properties of a graphic

    Files can be compressed

Vector graphic
    Components described by their features (length, colour, thickness etc)
    Can be grouped
    Files cannot be compressed
    Individual elements can be edited independently
Clip art
    Readily available
    Available immediately
    Little, if any, extra cost required (e.g. designer or extra equipment, such as scanners)
Thumbnail images/libraries
    Based around a topic
    When preview clicked image shown
    Lots of thumbnail images can be shown in one go
    Quality of actual image may be poor
    If image library is large may take a long time to load
Graphics libraries
    Interior design
    Landscaping
    Network design
    Cartography

Features of a presentation
Text
Images
Sound
Video
Animation
Slide transition
Hyperlinks
Hotspots
Buttons

Presentation delivery
Printed acetates
Computer and projector

Presentation navigation methods
Manual
Automatic

Structure of presentation
Non-linear
Hierarchical

Chapter tests

Test 1

Answer the following questions in the context of producing a flyer which will be sent with a mail-merged letter to all its customers.

1 Describe **two** advantages of using mail merge. [4]

2 Clip art images will be used in the flyer. Describe **two** advantages and **one** disadvantage of using clipart in the flyer. [6]

3 The clip art image is a bitmap graphic. Describe bitmap graphics. [4]

4 The letter includes a header and paragraphs. Describe headers and paragraphs giving an example of when each could be used. [6]

5 Describe how the page size and orientation could be used to format the letter. [4]

Test 2

Answer the following in the context of a school that is setting up a 'healthy eating' snack bar.

1 A logo needs to be created for the snack bar. Describe **two** advantages and **one** disadvantage of using an image library to select the logo. [6]

2 The logo selected is a vector graphic. Describe vector graphics. [4]

3 A presentation will be shown advertising the snack bar. Sound and animation will be used in the presentation. Describe sound and animation, giving an example of when each could be used. [6]

4 The presentation is to be shown using a computer and projector. Explain **two** advantages and **one** disadvantage of using a computer and projector to show the presentation. [6]

5 The presentation has a linear structure. Describe a linear structure. [2]

7 The role and impact of ICT

Introduction

This chapter covers the discussion elements of ICT. A large proportion concerns the legal position and Acts of Parliament relating to ICT. You will need to ensure you understand the implications of the laws. This chapter covers the topics you need to know for the discussion question at the end of every examination paper.

This chapter covers:

- The main aspects, purpose and implications of the
  - Data Protection Act
  - Computer Misuse Act
  - Copyright, Designs and Patents Act
  - Regulation of Investigatory Powers Act
  - Electronic Communications Act
  - Freedom of Information Act
- Methods for combating a range of ICT crimes
- The advantages and disadvantages of networking computers
- The required standards and the impact of different standards
- A range of health and safety problems related to working with ICT and measures for avoiding them
- The social impact of ICT upon individuals, organisations and society
- Possible future developments in ICT

The Data Protection Act (1998)

The Data Protection Act was passed to protect individuals from organisations. There is a lot of information available on individuals and this is collected by many different organisations and government agencies.

The Data Protection Act limits the data held by individual organisations to only that which they need. It was meant to stop organisations holding excessive quantities of data on individuals for which they do not have an immediate purpose.

There are a number of terms related to the Data Protection Act.

- **Personal data** – Any data which relates to a living, identifiable individual.
- **Data** – Anything that is held that can be said to be part of a record. This covers both manual and computer data. If you store data on people, such as their health or education records, whether it is on paper or on computer, it is classed as data. Data is also anything stored that is processed by a computer.

Activities

List **three** organisations and **three** government agencies. For each, list all the information on individuals you can think of that might be stored by them.

- **Processing** – Obtaining, recording or holding the information or data. It also covers any operation performed on the information or data. Operations on the data include organising it (sorting, indexing), changing it, retrieving it (searching) and using it in some way. Operations on the data also include disclosing it (telling someone else or passing it on) and destroying it.

There are several people who are specifically mentioned by the Act and have different rights and responsibilities.

- **Data subject** – The data subject is the living identifiable human being about whom the data is being held.
- **Data controller** – This is the individual within the company who is responsible for making sure that all the provisions of the Data Protection Act are being complied with. This is also the person that you would contact if you had any queries with a company about the Data Protection Act.
- **Data processor** – This is any person (other than an employee of the data controller) who processes the data on behalf of the data controller. This is for companies that hire third parties to process their data for them. Even if the processing is done by a third party the data controller retains responsibility for making sure the Data Protection Act is not contravened.
- **Recipient** – These are individuals who are given the data in order to do some form of processing on it. They are usually employees of the data controller or are data processors.
- **Third party** – This is the person who receives the data for processing. A company may need to pass on its data to certain people in order to do its job, for example schools give references and information to the Government. These people are known as recipients.
- **Information Commissioner** – This is the individual who is responsible for ensuring that the Data Protection Act is being adhered to, by giving advice, running training sessions and investigating complaints.

As an individual, you have certain rights under the Data Protection Act. There are six main rights that you possess.

- **Right to subject access** – You are allowed to see what information is being held on you by a company. You need to write to the data controller and request a copy. You will need to pay an administrative charge. The company must provide the information within a reasonable time of receiving the request (credit agencies 7 days, schools 15 days, other organisations 40 days).
- **Right to prevent processing likely to cause damage or distress** – If the processing of the data is going to cause you damage and

distress, you can ask the company to stop. The level of damage and distress needs to be very high and, if the company does not think it is causing damage and distress, it is up to the courts to decide.

- **Right to prevent processing for the purposes of direct marketing** – Direct marketing is mail that is sent to you advertising goods and services. You can request that it be stopped.
- **Rights in relation to automated decision making** – Some decisions are taken by a computer. Credit checks are an example – points are awarded for things such as time in work, owning your own home etc. and, based on the number of points you get, a decision is made as to whether you can have a credit card or not. You can request that a person takes the decision, not a computer.
- **Right to compensation if damage and distress is suffered by the Act being contravened** – If you can prove that the data controller did not follow the requirements of the Act and, by not doing so, you suffered both damage and distress, then you are entitled to compensation. Damage can be physical or financial loss. You cannot be compensated for distress on its own
- **Right to rectify, block or erase incorrect data** – If the data that is held is wrong, then you can get it changed.

The Data Protection Act is very long and complicated. The above discussion is a very simplified version of the main points.

There are some reasons for exemption from the Act. A few of them include:
- national security
- crime and taxation – you cannot see your records
- health, education and social work – if giving the subject access will cause them harm
- domestic purposes – data held on your own computer for your own use, such as a mailing list for Christmas cards.

Questions

1 Describe what is meant by data controller.

2 What is the difference between a recipient and a third party.

3 What are the implications for a company under the Data Protection Act?

4 What does the Data Protection Act mean by data?

5 Who does the Data Protection Act apply to?

6 Describe the rights of the individual under the Data Protection Act.

7 Describe **four** exemptions under the Data Protection Act.

Activities

Investigate and summarise the main exemptions from the Data Protection Act.

The main aspects of the Data Protection Act (1998)

The Data Protection Act has eight principles that must be followed.

1 Personal data shall be processed fairly and lawfully

This means that there should be consent for the processing to occur.

2 Personal data shall be obtained only for one or more specified and lawful purposes, and shall not be further processed in any manner incompatible with that purpose or those purposes

When a company wants to collect and hold personal data, it must let the Information Commissioner know what it is going to hold and what it is going to do with it. The company can only collect and process data that meets those requirements.

3 Personal data shall be adequate, relevant and not excessive in relation to the purpose or purposes for which they are processed

Holding more information than is necessary is not allowed. For example, there is no need for a school to hold information on the pets that your parents had as children. It would not be relevant.

4 Personal data shall be accurate and, where necessary, kept up to date

The company must endeavour to ensure that it only has accurate information on you. This may entail them sending out the information they hold for you to check. If they find any inaccurate information, they must correct it.

5 Personal data processed for any purpose or purposes shall not be kept for longer than is necessary for that purpose or those purposes

You cannot hold data indefinitely. Eventually it will no longer meet the purpose. For example, a school does not have a need to keep records on detentions from five years ago – it is not needed or consistent with the current purpose. However, schools are required to hold student records for seven years in case of requests for a reference.

6 Personal data shall be processed in accordance with the rights of data subjects under this Act

The data subject has certain rights. These include access to the data, the right to correct data if it is wrong, the right to compensation if the processing has caused damage and distress and the right to prevent processing from causing damage and distress.

7 Appropriate technical and organisational measures shall be taken against unauthorised or unlawful processing of personal data and against accidental loss or destruction of, or damage to, personal data

The company must ensure that there is sufficient security in place to prevent the data being deleted or being stolen. Backups should be taken to restore deleted data.

8 Personal data shall not be transferred to a country or territory outside the European Economic Area, unless that country or territory ensures an adequate level of protection for the rights and freedoms of data subjects in relation to the processing of personal data

This is to ensure that data is only given to companies in other countries where there is a similar law to the UK's Data Protection Act. This protects the rights of the data subject. However, if the data subject gives their consent for a transfer then the data can be transferred anywhere.

Questions

1 Describe the implications for companies of the seventh principle listed above.

2 What do companies need to do to ensure they comply with the second and third principles listed above?

3 Why is a Data Protection Act necessary?

4 Is the Data Protection Act a workable Act? Describe any problems you can think of with the Data Protection Act.

The Computer Misuse Act (1990)

Main provision

The Computer Misuse Act was introduced to protect data held by companies from hackers. It was reinforced by the Police and Justice Act (2006). It has four main provisions:

- **Unauthorised access to computer material** – This covers entering a computer system without permission by guessing or discovering an individual's password. This is 'hacking' into a computer.
- **Unauthorised access with intent to commit or facilitate the commission of further offences** – This is in addition to entering the computer system. This could be to gain access to a user account and use it to transmit illegal material.
- **Unauthorised acts with intent to impair, or with recklessness as to impairing, operation of a computer** – This is making changes to the contents of a computer or denying access to the computer through Denial of Service attacks.
- **Making, supplying or obtaining articles for use in computer misuse offences (known as Section 3A)** – This involves malicious scripts or software that will modify original code (e.g. in set top boxes).

Benefits

Until the introduction of the Computer Misuse Act, theft of electricity was the only crime a hacker could be charged with. The Act allows companies a legal recourse if their security has been compromised.

Problems

There has to be intent. Accidental intrusion is not a crime. There is also the problem of finding out who is responsible. Just because you can track a computer that is being used for hacking to a property, it does not mean that you know who was responsible. You then need to prove who within the property was using the computer at the point in time that the crime was committed. As with all laws, the Computer Misuse Act is only enforced once the crime has been committed. If a hacker does gain access and obtains confidential information, they could have disseminated it before they are caught. Another problem is that the organisation is the body that determines what is authorised and what is not. This applies in education. If a code of practice for a school indicates that only you are allowed to use your account, if you give your password to your friend and they use your account, technically they have broken the law.

The Copyright, Designs and Patents Act (1988)

Main provision

Among many items, the Act makes it illegal to steal or create unauthorised copies of software. It also covers manuals, books, CDs and music.

Benefits

A lot of time and effort goes into the production of software, books and music. The people who put in that effort deserve to be rewarded. The reward is in royalties. If the items are copied and distributed then they will not receive any money. The Act allows the individuals and corporations who invest time and money to reap their rewards.

Problems

When you buy software, you haven't bought the software itself, only a licence to use it. The company who wrote the software continues to own it and allows you to use it under licence on certain conditions. There are many different types of software licence, and these conditions vary depending on the software and the company. Some do not allow the software to be installed and run on more than one machine. Some allow it to be installed on a desktop PC and a laptop so long as they are not used at the same time. Other types of licences include site and network licences, which specify a maximum number

Activities

1 Discuss the problems for a school and a company of users sharing passwords.

2 Investigate the number of cases of contravention of the Computer Misuse Act that have been brought against people. Why do you think this number is so low?

of users who can run the software at any given time. Understanding the licences can be difficult and many people wrongly think that because nobody can see then it isn't a crime to copy and distribute software freely. Similarly, copying a CD or downloading copyright music from the internet is also a crime and the practice damages people's livelihoods and hinders future developments at the end of the chain. 'Microsoft already has too much money, they won't miss me not paying' is a common defence for copying software, but it is still illegal. 'If I had to pay for it I would not buy it' is not an excuse, nor is arguing that everyone does it.

The Regulation of Investigatory Powers Act (2000)

Main provision

Nicknamed the 'snoopers' charter', the Regulation of Investigatory Powers Act was introduced to address concerns about the use and misuse of communication interception techniques by public and private organisations. The Act allows for the lawful interception of postal, telecommunications and digital communications. The Act came about because of a court case (Malone vs UK) where the defendant was acquitted and subsequently sued the police for intercepting his phone calls. The case was thrown out and taken to the European Court of Human Rights. They declared that the practice of interception was insufficiently grounded in law. This led to a 1985 Act that was subsequently updated as it did not cover private networks.

The Act makes it a criminal offence to monitor communications without lawful authority. Communications include telephone calls, emails, post etc.

To be lawful, 'the interception has to be by or with the consent of a person carrying on a business, for purposes relevant to that person's business, and using that business's own telecommunications system.' Organisations may monitor and record communications:

- to establish the existence of facts to ascertain compliance with regulatory or self-regulatory practices or procedures or to ascertain or demonstrate standards which are or ought to be achieved
- in the interests of national security
- to prevent or detect crime
- to investigate or detect unauthorised use of telecommunications systems
- to secure, or as an inherent part of, effective system operation.

There are some circumstances where the organisation may monitor but not record:

- received communications to determine whether they are business or personal communications
- communications made to anonymous telephone help lines. Public interceptions can also be made with 'lawful authority'.

Benefits

The benefits to the company are that it can monitor what its employees are doing. This in turn can ensure that the facilities are only being used for legitimate work and that company secrets are not being revealed or time wasted.

Problems

Any form of monitoring may be seen as a breach of trust. Some people may say, if we have nothing to hide, we should not be afraid of being monitored, but there is a desire by many to cling to their privacy. The Regulation of Investigatory Powers Act could be seen as going against that desire. Some people may also be concerned about what controls there may be on organisations that monitor communications.

The Electronic Communications Act (2000)

Main provision

The Government wanted 'to make the UK the best place in the world for e-commerce' and 'to create a legal framework so that people can be sure about the origin and integrity of communications'. In order to achieve this, the Electronic Communications Act was passed.

The legislation is in two main parts:

- **Cryptography service providers** – This allows the Government to set up a register of 'approved cryptography suppliers'.
- **Facilitation of electronic commerce, data storage** – This recognises digital signatures, which are now admissible in law.

There is a lot of legislation that is in conflict with digital signatures. The Electronic Communications Act gives Ministers the power to make delegated legislation to remove any restrictions in other legislation which prevent use of electronic communications in place of paper.

Benefits

Contracts that are signed over the internet have the same legality as those signed by hand. This increases the security with which individuals can engage in e-commerce and the contracts entered into have legal backing.

Activities

Research the Regulation of Investigatory Powers Act. Discuss the benefits to companies and what they need to do before they can monitor communications. What is your attitude to someone looking at all your post and emails?

Problems

Although there is legislation in place to remove many of the laws that prevent digital signatures being accepted, this will take time. Conveyancing (buying and selling a house) and wills are two areas where digital signatures will take a long time to be introduced.

There is always a security risk. The first digital signature made by a Cabinet Minister was effectively hijacked within 24 hours of its creation. A document digitally signed by the Trade and Industry Minister had an additional statement opposing the Government's cryptographic policy inserted into it.

The Freedom of Information Act (2000)

Main provision

The Freedom of Information Act came into force at the beginning of 2005. The Act deals with access to official information, that is being able to find out information on any topic from any public authority.

The Act applies to all public authorities, this includes government, health service (hospitals and doctors' surgeries), schools and police.

The Act allows anyone to make a request – there are no restrictions on age. A letter to the public authority that you think has the information you want, along with your name, address for them to send the information to and a description of what you want is all that is required. Most requests will be free, however a small charge may be requested to cover photocopying and postage.

Public authorities have 20 working days to comply with your request.

Benefits

The main benefit is that information that was not accessible to the general public is now available. This increases accountability – the pubic authority cannot take decisions and then hide those decisions. The information is now available to those that request it.

Problems

It is possible to ask for any information at all. However, this does not mean that you will receive it. Some information might be withheld to protect various interests or it may come under some of the other exemptions.

The Act is part of a set and requesting information under the wrong Act will delay the information being received. For example, information about yourself needs to be requested under the Data Protection Act.

The public authority does not have to confirm or deny the existence of the information you have requested. It does not have

Activities

Research what is meant by 'public authority'. Apart from the ones mentioned above, what other organisations are covered by the Act?

to provide it if an exemption applies, if the request is too vague for information to be found, if it is similar to a request previously received, or if the cost of collating and producing the information exceeds an appropriate limit.

Activities

Investigate and report on the exemptions to the Freedom of Information Act.

Questions

1 What are the main provisions of the Computer Misuse Act?

2 Explain the disadvantages of implementing the Computer Misuse Act.

3 Explain the problems of enforcing the Copyright, Designs and Patents Act.

4 Describe the main provisions of the Regulation of Investigatory Powers Act.

5 Why do you think there is opposition to the Regulation of Investigatory Powers Act? Explain your reasons.

6 What are the benefits of having a Regulation of Investigatory Powers Act?

7 Who benefits the most from the Electronic Communications Act and why?

8 Explain the problems with the Electronic Communications Act.

9 Describe the main provisions of the Freedom of Information Act.

10 Explain why you may not be given the information you have requested under the Freedom of Information Act.

Describe methods for combating a range of ICT crime

ICT crime is crime involving a computer or related technology. It could be the physical theft of the computer or of components from a computer, or using one computer to attempt to gain access to another computer system and commit a crime.

The computer crimes that are seen in films are not usually possible in the real world. Stopping a time clock and stealing money, collecting all the fractions of money and getting them paid to you or hacking into a bank and transferring money to your account all sound easy enough but are extremely rare if not impossible to achieve.

However, crimes involving computers do exist. It can be industrial espionage (finding out what a business competitor is doing), breaking into a computer system or trying to find personal data.

There are two main groups of methods for combating computer crime:

● physical methods

● logical methods.

Tip

The specification requires you to be aware of any updates and changes to the above Acts. Make sure that you are aware of any changes.

Physical methods

Physical methods prevent a person from gaining access to a computer in person. Instead of getting access across the internet, physical access means actually walking in and sitting at a computer yourself.

Ways to protect against physical access include having security guards on the door and giving each employee a pass that the guard checks. You could have an automatic door that responds to a pass given to each employee. The computers could be kept in locked rooms with only specific people given access to them. Security cameras could monitor corridors and rooms.

Physical methods also include the positioning of the screen and keyboard. If the machine is in an open access area, like a reception area, then having the screen so it cannot be seen by the public or the keyboard so they cannot see a password being typed in are sensible precautions.

The use of wireless networks has increased the difficulty of ensuring physical security.

Increasingly biometric measures, such as scanning a person's iris or fingerprint, are being used to provide physical security.

There are two types of physical security, those that by themselves prevent access and those that will sound an alarm but not prevent. For example, security cameras on their own do not prevent, but in conjunction with guards, who are monitoring the cameras and can react, do prevent.

Logical methods

These are computer-based methods that can be applied to the computer by a system administrator. They include usernames and passwords, access rights and user groups. Other logical methods include screensaver passwords so if you leave your desk for any length of time no one else can use the machine, firewalls and anti-virus software as well as logging actions and analysing these logs.

When you log on to a computer system or network you are asked for two pieces of information:
- a username or user ID (authorisation)
- a password (authentication).

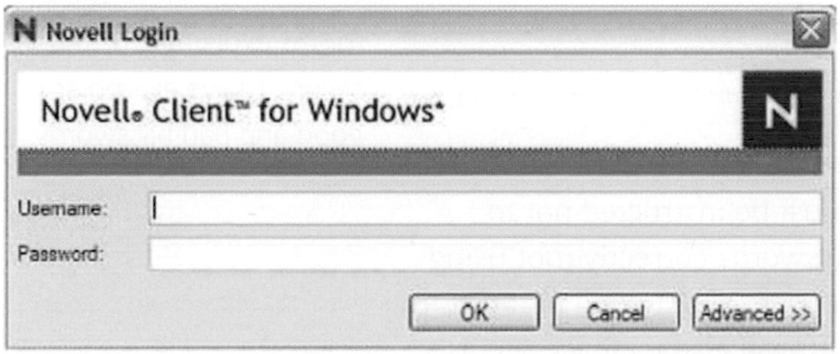

Figure 7.1 A network log-on dialogue box

Activities

Give the disadvantages for each of the physical methods described above. For example, how might someone determined to get into a building overcome the physical methods?

The user ID:

- is a unique identifier for a user, identifying who the user is to the system
- can be allocated to groups and those groups can have access rights and programs allocated to them (e.g. according to which user group they belong to, a user might be only allowed to read a file, while other groups might have edit or delete access)
- can also restrict the user to only logging onto certain machines or at certain times of the day
- can also be used to log what the user is doing.

A password is a method of restricting access. Unless you know the password you cannot perform tasks. When used in conjunction with a user ID, the password authenticates who the user is – that they are who the user ID says they are. This assumes that only the user knows the password.

Passwords are the weak link in any system. User IDs tend not be kept secret, but passwords need to be.

Authentication takes many different forms: they can be textual (passwords) or biometric (fingerprint, voice, retina). They are all a method of confirming the identity of the user to allow them access.

The network manager can apply controls to the password to make them harder for other people to find out. Such controls might include:

- using a minimum number of characters
- using a combination of numbers and letters
- not using a word in the dictionary
- changing passwords regularly (e.g. monthly)
- keeping a record of passwords so you cannot reuse one you have already had
- restricting the number of attempts (e.g. three wrong passwords and the account is locked)
- making the password impersonal.

Questions

1 Why are user IDs required?

2 What is a password?

3 What is authentication?

4 Why are user IDs not kept secret?

5 Describe **three** measures the network manager can undertake to ensure passwords remain secure.

Activities

Create a poster for the ICT rooms explaining password security. Give examples of good and bad passwords.

Password security is important so users must be instructed not to give out passwords and how to choose passwords correctly (not using dictionary words, for example). Educating users about good practice in computer use, such as ensuring they log off, will also increase security.

Preventative methods for combating ICT crime include the threat of legal action. As seen previously, there are several laws that can be broken when using a computer and many of these carry fines or imprisonment as a punishment.

Software releases ensure that the software is kept up to date and can prevent people getting into the computer through a software vulnerability. Keeping anti-spyware, anti-spam and anti-virus software up to date is just as important.

Questions

1 Describe **three** physical methods of preventing a computer crime.

2 How can using access rights combat computer crime?

3 Describe **three** laws that would be broken by hacking.

4 Describe **five** different ICT crimes.

Other methods that can be employed to make it more difficult for data to be stolen and used include auditing, firewalls and encryption.

Auditing is a method of looking over logs. Logs can be created for events that occur on the network: users logging in, applications run, websites visited, emails sent etc. A log can be used to build up a profile of a user.

Software can be used to look at logs to spot patterns of change, for example maybe a user starts logging in at different times or accessing different data. A change in habits might set alarm bells ringing and warrant further investigation in case the username and password are being used by a different person.

A firewall is a hardware and/or software gate between two networks or between a system and a network that filters the data transferred based on security policies. Firewalls are used on computers that connect to the internet to prevent unauthorised access to the system or network the computer is part of.

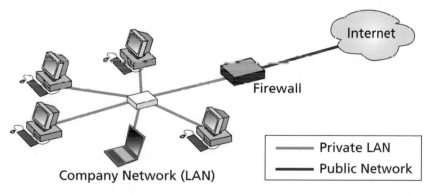

Figure 7.2 Use of a firewall

Encryption does not prevent the data being stolen. It aims to prevent anyone who has the data being able to understand it without the appropriate key.

Encryption is the process of taking the plain text and applying an algorithm to it to turn it into encrypted text. Only someone with a key should be able to convert the encrypted text back into plain text.

Alphabet ⟶ | A | B | C | D | E | F | G | H | I | J | K | L | M | N | O | P | Q | R | S | T | U | V | W | X | Y | Z |

Alphabet – shifted four places right ⟶ | W | X | Y | Z | A | B | C | D | E | F | G | H | I | J | K | L | M | N | O | P | Q | R | S | T | U | V |

Figure 7.3 Simple encryption

CAESAR CIPHER becomes YWAOWN YELDAN

Encryption has been around for a long time: the advent of computers has just made the ciphers more complicated.

Questions

1 Describe how a network manager might use a log to find a hacker on the system.

2 Give **two** ways a firewall can be used to protect data.

3 What is the difference between encoding and encryption?

4 Describe the disadvantages of using encryption as a method of securing data.

Activities

Research Pretty Good Privacy (PGP) encryption. Discuss why the US Government did not want it widely used. Do you think they were correct?

Describe the advantages and disadvantages of networking

A computer that is not connected to any other computer (i.e. it is not networked), is said to be stand-alone. A network exists when two or more computers are connected together. The next table gives some of the advantages and disadvantages of networking. The advantages of stand-alone computers are the disadvantages of a network and vice versa.

Advantages	Disadvantages
• Peripherals, such as printers and scanners, can be shared by several workstations, reducing the cost (as you do not have to buy one for each). The quality of the device purchased can be better than the quality of the individual devices (as more money can be spent on a better device). • Data can be shared. This allows standard files, such as templates, to be available from a central source. Data can also be shared by several people in a team allowing them to work on the same document. • Access to data is controlled by usernames, passwords and associated access rights. The network manager can also log who has used what file and ensure that security is not being breached. • Access to applications can be controlled from a central area. This can ensure that the use of licences is legal. • The resources used by individuals can be monitored and logged, allowing access to the resources to be charged to the appropriate department. • Backups and virus checking can be controlled from a central location. • Users can communicate with email systems and an intranet can disseminate useful information.	• All the services a network provides become unavailable if the network fails without adequate contingency in place (which can be expensive). • The devices that are required to build the network depend on the different topologies. • If a virus is introduced into a single workstation, then it can use the network to spread to the rest. • If the network is particularly busy, it may have a detrimental effect on the work that the user can do.

There are different groups of individuals within an organisation and the advantages and disadvantages of networking are not the same to all groups. The main groups are:

- users/employees
- network manager/technicians
- management
- customers.

Professional bodies

A professional body is a formal group that is set up to oversee a particular area of industry. The two main professional bodies that oversee the ICT industry are BCS, The Chartered Institute for IT (in the UK) and the Institute of Electrical and Electronics Engineers (worldwide).

Professional bodies perform a variety of roles and offer their members many benefits. For example, BCS:

- promotes education and training, liaising with universities to ensure that the skills required in the industry are being provided by the universities
- sets standards for the employees within the industry – this involves a code of conduct that its members must uphold
- provides examinations – by setting a standard and maintaining it, a qualification from BCS is valued worldwide and recognised by similar bodies in other countries
- provides publications and discussion papers on a variety of topics, enabling members to keep up to date
- holds conferences, where members can meet like-minded individuals and ensure that they are current with any new developments
- provides input into legislation and the industry

Professional bodies are not the same as trades unions, which are more directly involved in pay and conditions of service negotiations. They are not likely to offer specific technical advice to individuals outside of their publications and conferences.

The purpose of a professional body

The purpose of a professional body, such as BCS, is explained best in its own words:

As a professional body, BCS represents its members and the IT Profession as a whole on issues of importance, and liaises with other professional bodies, the government, industry and academics to initiate and inform debate on IT strategic issues.

BCS maintains relationships and affiliations with an extensive range of professional and government organisations.

As a Learned Society, BCS is governed by a Royal Charter, which defines our purpose: to promote the study and practice of Computing and to advance knowledge and education for the benefit of the public.

Our Charter enables us to admit qualified members. Without our members, we would be unable to undertake many of our charitable activities to promote IT at all levels.

www.bcs.org/category/6988

The advantages, for a network manager, of joining BCS are:

- career recognition – membership gives them an accredited qualification that present and future employees recognise and understand. BCS also provides career progression for the network manager, allowing them to develop and improve their qualifications, taking them to the next level;
- networking – this allows the network manager to meet with specialists in different areas, to meet local people in the same line of work;
- knowledge and best practice – the IT industry moves very quickly and covers a wide area. A professional body will give the network manager access to the latest industry news and access to online libraries that will help them research any issues or just read around the topic to improve the understanding.

The disadvantages of belonging to a professional body include:

- you will need to follow their code of conduct, this may contain elements that you do not believe in or subscribe to;
- there is a cost implication in joining a professional body and maintaining the subscription;
- it may be only one professional organisation and this could be seen as a 'club' and self serving rather than for the benefit of its members.

Activities

Investigate other professional bodies that a network manager could join and compare the different activities and benefits.

Questions

1 Describe **three** activities that BCS, The Chartered Institute for IT provides for a network manager.

2 Explain the advantages to a network manager of joining BCS.

3 What are the advantages to the management of having their network manager being a member of BCS?

Describe a range of health problems related to working with ICT and measures to avoid them

Working with ICT can be a dangerous activity. There are several problems that can be caused by using computers for long periods of time.

The problems can be divided into two groups: those relating to health and those that cover safety.

Health problems are those based on activities that can cause physical damage to the body due to prolonged use of the computers. Some examples are given below. The causes given are not the only causes.

Heath problem	Description	Cause	Prevention
Deep vein thrombosis (DVT)	Blood clot, usually in the leg	Sitting in a chair that puts pressure on the back of the knees	Stand up and move around. Ensure correct posture when sitting in a chair.
Repetitive strain injury (RSI)	Chronic pain experienced in the arms, shoulder or back	Repetitive actions, poor posture while working, maintaining a fixed forced position	Use correct workstation, keyboard rests, foot stools, adjustable chairs and frequent breaks from continuous activity.
Carpal tunnel syndrome	Pressure on the median nerve in the wrist	Repeated wrist movements such as typing	Avoid the repetitive actions. Frequent breaks between the actions.
Ulnar neuritis (cubital tunnel syndrome)	Compression of the ulnar nerve in the elbow	Leaning on the elbow for prolonged periods of time	Use of wrist rests, adjustable height of chairs and correct desk height.
Eye strain	Hazy vision, tired eyes	Looking at a monitor for long periods of time, dehydration of the eyes	Take plenty of fluids and frequent breaks. Use correctly adjusted, flicker-free monitor.
Back pain/ache	Muscle spasms	Poor posture, sitting in the same position, forced position	Use correct posture and adjustable chair.
Fatigue	Tiredness and lethargy	Caused by continued periods of mental work	Take a five-minute break every hour. Vary the type of work.
Stress	State of mental strain	Overwork or software/hardware not doing what you expect	Take a five-minute break every hour. Train in the software.

Many health problems are caused by incorrect posture.

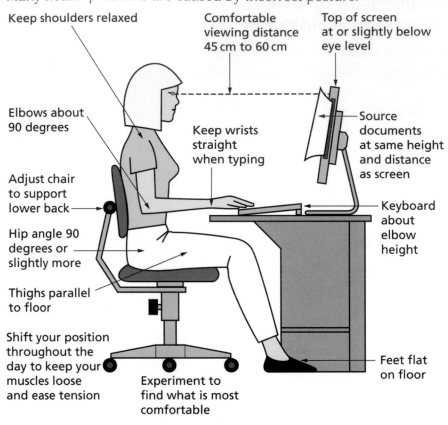

Keep shoulders relaxed

Comfortable viewing distance 45 cm to 60 cm

Top of screen at or slightly below eye level

Elbows about 90 degrees

Keep wrists straight when typing

Source documents at same height and distance as screen

Adjust chair to support lower back

Hip angle 90 degrees or slightly more

Thighs parallel to floor

Shift your position throughout the day to keep your muscles loose and ease tension

Experiment to find what is most comfortable

Keyboard about elbow height

Feet flat on floor

Figure 7.4 Correct posture at a workstation

Activities

Investigate the Health and Safety Regulations for the use of computers. Make a list of the equipment that could be provided by a company to prevent health problems and for each explain the problem that it prevents.

Describe a range of safety problems related to working with ICT and measures to avoid them

Safety hazards are items which can cause injury or damage. They are likely to be immediate rather than built up over time. Some examples are given in the table.

Safety hazard	Description	Prevention
Trailing wires	Wires from computers trailing from desks and along floors	Cable management systems to cover wires
Fire	Overheating of computers can cause them to catch fire Overloading of plug sockets can cause fire	Adequate ventilation, and clear space around equipment Not overloading plug sockets Correct number of sockets on a breaker Using the correct type of fire extinguisher (CO_2) for electrical fire.
Electric shock	Water and electricity can cause an electric shock (possibly fatal) Bare wires, when touched, can cause electric shock	No drinking near computers No water near computers All wires to be frequently checked and repaired
Unstable surfaces and chairs	Desks and surfaces that wobble can cause computer equipment to fall off	All surfaces to be stable before computer equipment is placed on them
Food and drink	Liquids can cause shorting and lead to fire Crumbs from food are a fire hazard	No eating and drinking near computers

Discuss the impact of ICT on individuals, organizations and society

Capabilities and limitations of ICT systems

ICT is often put forward as the solution to many problems. It is certainly true that ICT has helped in many areas but it should always be seen as a tool: a tool that we control and we decide when to use. The use of ICT is not always appropriate and there are occasions where its use should be discouraged.

Here are some advantages and disadvantages to the use of ICT systems.

Advantages

Computers can perform the same actions over and over again, and they can do this very quickly and reliably. For example, calculating interest on bank accounts or working out electricity bills – the same processing is performed on every single account and because of the number of accounts it needs to be done very quickly.

Computers can search large volumes of data and they can do it very quickly. At an ATM the computer needs to search through vast numbers of customer accounts to find yours. You do not want to be standing waiting so it needs to do it quickly. Consider the amount of data being stored by a company like a bank: every single transaction on every single account – and not just for this year, for previous years as well. It is no good storing the data if you cannot find your way around it and access the required data. Their storage needs to be structured and accessible.

Computers can perform tasks that are impossible or dangerous to humans, for example control systems.

Disadvantages

There are limitations on the use of ICT, one of the main being the hardware. The speed of hardware development is phenomenal. In 1975, Gordon Moore finalised his prediction for the increase of processing power: the number of components on semiconductor chips with the lowest per-component cost doubles roughly every two years. This has also been applied to storage. Put simply, the same amount of money will purchase twice the speed or twice the storage it did two years previously. For the most part, this has proved, until recently, to be true.

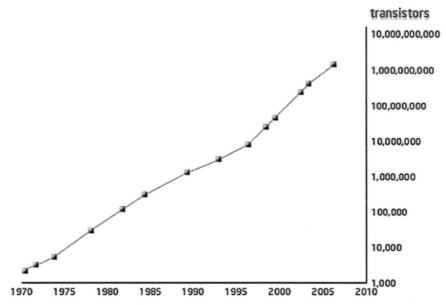

Figure 7.5 Moore's Law

However, hardware limitations are beginning to have an impact on future developments. People want things done now, not in a few seconds' time. The interface to the computer, such as the keyboard, is archaic and not useful for entering vast quantities of data quickly.

The software that is used limits what can be done. It can still be cumbersome to use and often requires training. The design and development of software itself can limit what can be done with it.

As we utilise the communications available within computers more and more so we demand more and more bandwidth. We want video on demand, faster downloads of software, music and movies, and interactive conversations with people on the other side of the world. At the moment this is restricted because of limitations in bandwidth.

Communications systems

One of the biggest improvements brought about by technology is in the field of communications. Communications have shrunk the planet: we can send messages in seconds to countries anywhere in the world.

Activities

Describe the ICT and technology that you have seen in films and television programmes recently, for example the ability to manipulate images on a computer screen by hand in *Minority Report*. How realistic is the technology that was used? Do you think that it will eventually be introduced? What are the advantages and disadvantages?

One effect of this is to increase the globalisation of companies. They can retain control over offices and employees from anywhere in the world.

Communications covers a variety of areas: the internet, intranet, mobile phones, telephone systems and interactive television, to name a few.

Telephone systems

Telephony is a relatively old method of communication, but it has had a digital upgrade over the last few years. The telephone systems available today allow you to contact other individuals quickly and have an element of personal contact (even if it is only by voice). It is now possible to have conference calls, answer phones, mobile phones, remote access, different ring tones, call forwarding, SMS messaging and many other features. The systems allow you to send documents (either as faxes or as attachments to emails) and emails, and many computers connect to the internet using telephone systems.

The internet

The internet is a vast collection of interconnected computers for the purpose of sharing data. One of the biggest benefits and problems of the internet is that it is outside of any government's control. (Governments can attempt to filter or restrict access but they cannot control the content of websites. Attempts to do so have resulted in the content being relocated to countries with laws that allow that content.) The advantage is that the internet cannot be turned on or off, or controlled. The disadvantage is that it has security problems, problems with pornography, and it can used by criminals and terrorists.

The internet is used to find information. This can be by using websites (which, when taken together, contain the largest encyclopaedia available) or downloading files. The internet gives access to a large repository of information through the web. The web is useful for technical support: almost every topic has a help page. Drivers for computers can be located as well as software updates. It is possible to use the internet to chat with friends and relatives and take part in discussions.

With all the unregulated information on the web it is sometimes impossible to tell what is true and what is not. Anyone can create a website and put their views and opinions on it. It is necessary to consider carefully all the information posted on the web and not leap in and believe it all.

The internet is also an efficient means of transmitting viruses. Downloading files and opening them could infect your machine. It is important that when using the internet you have an appropriate firewall and virus checker.

Activities

The use of mobile phones has increased over the last few years. What features are available on a mobile phone and what new features do you want? Describe the advantages and disadvantages of mobile phones.

Activities

What are the charges relating to the Internet for a user and for someone wishing to set up a website?

Identification of individuals is difficult on the internet. When chatting, how do you know who you are talking to? The person may say they are sixteen and a pupil at a local school but how can you verify this?

Breach of copyright is a problem on the internet. The ease of posting and availability of files (movies, music and software) makes it difficult to apprehend people who break copyright laws). The location of the server being used to disseminate the data can also cause problems. Governments have little control globally because the laws of one country are different from those of another: crimes in one country may not be crimes in another. The location of the web server may be in a country where it is legal to post certain content that would be illegal elsewhere.

Laws regarding tax and purchases using the internet are difficult to enforce. If you purchase items from websites and you are getting them from another country then they are subject to taxation and import regulations when they come into the country. Enforcing this is difficult.

Email

An email is an electronic message sent using the internet from one person to another located anywhere in the world. Documents, spreadsheets and other files can be attached to an email. Digitally signed emails can be accepted as a contract (see Electronic Communications Act).

Activities

There are now many communication methods available to us. Have they shrunk the world or increased physical isolation?

Copy out and fill in the table. Give examples of the advantages and disadvantages of the different communication methods, giving reasons why. Add in other means of communications that have not been covered above.

Method	Advantages	Disadvantages
Telephone		
Mobile phone		
Email		
Internet		

How ICT has changed society

The introduction of ICT into society has brought about some major changes, particularly in the areas of shopping, medicine and health care, disabled people, education and entertainment.

Shopping

Most high street stores have a web presence. Today, there are some shops you can only buy from online because they do not have a physical presence so you cannot walk into them to make a purchase. Amazon is perhaps the most well known of this new generation of retailers.

The advantages of internet shopping for the customer include availability (a website is open 24 hours a day, 365 days a year). It does not matter where the 'shop' is: it could be in this country or on the other side of the world. Currency is not an issue: if you possess a credit or debit card then the conversion is done automatically. There are sites that will compare prices for you to enable you to get the best deal. This is particularly useful for those people who are housebound (the elderly and disabled) or those in remote areas.

However, there are disadvantages to online shopping. How do you know that a website is genuine? How do you know that the site has not been set up purely to get credit card details? You may never see the goods. At least when you go to a shop you come out with the goods at the end of the transaction. You also need to be at home when the item is delivered or arrange to collect it from the delivery company. A buyer also needs a computer and internet connection to shop online: this can be expensive.

There will be a tendency for people to become lazy and unhealthy. If you can shop without leaving your home this will reduce the amount of exercise you take and this in turn leads to an unhealthy lifestyle.

Online food shopping has increased in popularity and websites offering this service allow you to keep a weekly shopping list of staple items that you need every week. However, you are reliant on someone else picking your food and sometimes items you don't want might be substituted for those out of stock.

Companies that have only an online presence do not have to maintain premises and large numbers of staff, however, they will need to be employ website designers, technical support and packers.

Delivery firms have benefited from the increase in posted goods, and there are fewer journeys made: one delivery vehicle can take the place of several car journeys. This decreases congestion and pollution.

Activities

Summarise the advantages and disadvantages of online shopping for both a customer and a company.

Medicine

Medical improvements are occurring all the time. The impact of ICT in medicine has been in two main areas: treatment and administration. The use of computers in administration has enabled medical staff to have access to patients' notes, treatment records and information on treatments, as well as latest research. The medical staff can now create care plans, drug administration records and monitor the patient more effectively.

Computers are used to help people with hearing and sight disabilities, they have improved the manufacture of artificial components such as limbs and they have allowed three-dimensional images to be created of the body for surgeons to examine.

Not everywhere has access to medical computing facilities. It is important not to become over reliant on the technology to the extent that medicine cannot be practised without it.

ICT and the internet have also made it easier to share research. Universities can pool their findings and collaborate more effectively.

Many people, non-experts, now use medical websites as a first port of call for information on medical conditions, but a little knowledge can be a dangerous thing and information, whether from a book or online, cannot replace a fully-trained medical practitioner. There are medical expert systems that you can consult. They will ask you questions and, based on your answers, recommend treatment or a further consultation with a doctor.

Education

There are three aspects where ICT has affected education: administration, teachers and students.

Electronic registration is common in many schools. This allows schools to immediately contact parents if their child is absent unexpectedly. Details on students (e.g. exam results, detentions, medical conditions etc.) can be stored and accessed, and the information gained can be used to give appropriate help and support. Performance can be monitored and any problems picked up before they become serious.

Students benefit from internet access to a wide range of information, the use of computers to write up and share work given to them, and the use of presentation software and handouts to liven up the lessons! Virtual Learning Environments (VLEs) allow teachers to structure topics and provide all the lesson and testing materials.

Many schools have a facility that lets students access their work stored on the school's computer system from home. This eliminates the need to use portable devices to transfer the work or to forget the work!

Activities

Research and produce a report on all the different parts of the body that can be replaced by an artificial component.

Teachers benefit from ICT in lessons by being able to pre-prepare presentation material with handouts. They can also make use of electronic administration aids for registering and recording marks.

Websites give students greater access to material that can be used to support their projects, but plagiarism and submission of ready-made material have become problems.

The effect of ICT on organisations

Organisations, as well as individuals, are affected by ICT. There was a fear that introducing ICT into offices would mean unemployment. It was argued that with computers, fewer people could do the same job, which meant that fewer people would be required. The actual effect has been to increase employment. ICT has an industry that surrounds it: network managers, technicians, website designers, ICT trainers etc. Organisations have had to employ more people to install and maintain the ICT equipment. There has been a redistribution of employment.

In retail, if a shop closes to become an online-only shop, it will need website designers, packers and delivery people. These are different to the jobs required when it needed shop assistants and shelf stackers.

Those employees that use ICT in their work have benefited from the advantages of electronic filing systems, the ability to edit a document rather than retype it every time it is needed, and email.

The effect on the organisation has been to increase communication. Email, fax, video conferencing and shared diaries have meant that it is easier to track down and get in touch with people. The workload has not decreased. More work is being done in the same amount of time.

Structure of the organisation

The structure of organisations has altered. With electronic communications there is no longer the need for a company's headquarters to be in a major city. It can be located anywhere. The company does not even have to have all its departments in the same location: decentralisation of the organisation is partly a result of ICT.

New departments and directors have been created with the advent of ICT. ICT directors, network managers and training departments have all had to be incorporated in the organisational structure.

Teleworking

One major change in recent years has been teleworking. This is working from home. Employees can spend some or all of their time working from home instead of at a company's premises. Teleworking

> **Activities**
>
> Only a few aspects of education have been touched on. Think about how students, teachers and administration staff use ICT in your school. What are the advantages and disadvantages of using ICT?

has also allowed many individuals to set up successful home-based companies.

The advantages of teleworking for an organisation are that a central location for employees to travel to is not required. An organisation can move out of town to places where the rent is cheaper. The size of building required is smaller as there are fewer employees permanently based at the premises.

An organisation keeps control of its workforce, making sure that employees are working effectively, by using email and tracking set targets. Not every person has the right temperament for working from home: it requires self-discipline and the ability to work alone.

The advantages to the employee are that they do not have to commute to work. They can get up later as there is no travel and be back 'at home' earlier. There are no travel costs and less pollution because of the reduction in traffic. More time can be spent with the family, maybe less child care is required (although this has a knock-on effect on the economy).

Disadvantages might include a lack of motivation: if there is no boss it is very easy to put some work off until tomorrow. There may be a lack of social contact: part of working is not about the job itself but the social interaction with colleagues. Additional equipment may be required: high-speed internet connection, fax etc., but this is often provided by the company. A company and its employees also need to be aware of the issues related to keeping commercial and staff information secure, of protecting equipment from theft, and of protecting staff from potential safety hazards.

Dependence on ICT

We rely on ICT a lot more than might first be apparent. Banking, engine management systems in vehicles, alarm clocks, heating systems etc., all rely on ICT to some degree.

We have become deskilled as a population. This means losing the skills that we did have, but not replacing them with skills that are equally useful. We may have acquired skills in software use, but we have lost some basic survival skills. The majority of us could not survive without ICT. We take ICT for granted, placing our trust in it and getting frustrated when it fails. Consider a supermarket during a power cut: freezers stop working, lighting goes out and the tills cannot be used (no one knows the prices of anything, and even if they did they cannot accept your debit or credit card), and stock control systems fail.

The advent of mobile phone text messages has brought about a new language. Communication is going on but are the traditional language and people skills being lost?

Activities

Would teleworking suit you? How would you cope with only having deadlines and no imposed structure? As a boss, what would you do to try and make sure your employees were working when at home?

ICT has its advantages. There are places where it has made a large difference, but it is not the solution to all our problems. There are areas where it has caused problems and our reliance on it is an issue that will come to the fore over the next few decades.

Questions

1 ICT is used in hospitals. Discuss the effect that ICT has had on patients and medical staff.

2 Explain the advantages to students of teachers using ICT in their lessons.

3 Describe the advantages and disadvantages of teleworking.

4 How can the introduction of ICT affect organisation change?

5 Discuss the impact of ICT on the elderly and the disabled.

6 Explain the advantages for a shop in moving to be an internet-only shop.

7 Discuss the implications for customers of shopping online.

8 Our reliance on ICT will eventually lead to a decline in our standard of living and a return to an existence similar to that of nineteenth-century Britain. Discuss this statement.

Future developments in ICT

There have been many predictions about what the future may hold. There have been some ridiculous predictions in the past and it is likely there will be more in the future. A good place to keep up to date about ICT developments and predictions is the BBC's weekly *Click* programme and supporting website.

Chapter summary

Describe the main aspects, purpose and implications of the
Data Protection Act
  Set up to protect individuals from organisations
  Allows individuals access to information stored on them
  Eight principles organisation must follow
  Rights of individuals including access and correction
  Several exemptions
Computer Misuse Act
  Protect computer systems from individuals
  Four crimes: unauthorised access, unauthorised access with modification, unauthorised access with intent to commit crime, creating materials that could be used for hacking
  Problems: proving an individual is committing the crime

Activities

Describe a typical day from the moment you get up. List all the ways that ICT directly or indirectly affects your life. If ICT was not available what impact would it have on the way you do things?

Activities

Produce a presentation about possible future technologies including driverless cars, tracking devices, neural interfaces and others.

Copyright, Designs and Patents Act
 Illegal to steal music, books, CDs etc. (permission must be given for use)
 Complex licensing rules (difficult to follow)
 ICT equipment makes copying easy
Regulation of Investigatory Powers Act
 Allows the interception of communications
 Interpretation of 'lawful authority'
 Some things can be monitored and recorded, others just monitored
Electronic Communications Act
 Register of cryptography providers
 Digital signatures admissible in law
Freedom of Information Act
 Information held by public authorities is accessible
 Many exemptions

Describe methods for combating a range of ICT crimes

Physical
 Locked rooms
 Cameras
 Biometric (fingerprint, iris scanners etc.)
Logical
 Firewalls
 Passwords
 User IDs
 Up-to-date software
 Education of users

Understand the advantages and disadvantages of networking computers

Advantages
 Work sharing
 Resource sharing
 Centralised control/backup
 Hot-desking
 Uniformity of machines
Disadvantages
 Reliance on centralised components
 Increased costs
 Increased technical support
 Slow down of network due to other users

Professional body
> Provides exams
> Sets standards
> Liaises with other groups
> Advantages: allows knowledge to be shared (knowledge base); accredits knowledge; career recognition
> Disadvantages: cost of membership; code of conduct

Describe a range of health and safety problems related to working with ICT and measures for avoiding them
Health hazards
> Deep vein thrombosis (DVT)
> Repetitive strain injury (RSI)
> Carpal tunnel syndrome
> Ulnar neuritis
> Eye strain
> Back pain/ache
Safety hazards
> Trailing wires
> Fire
> Electric shock
> Unstable surfaces and chairs
> Food and drink

Discuss the implications and consequences of ICT
Positive and negative factors
Reasoned conclusion

Chapter tests

Test 1

Answer the following in the context of a cinema that has created a membership scheme for its regular customers.

1 Describe **two** responsibilities of management in complying with the Data Protection Act (1998). [4]

2 The cinema must make sure that the data is secure. Describe **two** logical security methods the cinema can implement to ensure that the data is not accessible by unauthorised users. [4]

3 The cinema has networked its box office and main office computers. Describe **two** advantages to the cinema management of networking the computers. [4]

4 The cinema broadcasts a copyright notice at the beginning of each film. Describe the main aspects of the Copyright, Designs and Patents Act (1988) [4]

5 The network manager of the cinema is a member of BCS, The Chartered Institute for IT. Describe the purposes of BCS. [4]

6 Identify **two** safety hazards associated with working with computers in the cinema. [2]

7 There are many health hazards associated with working with computers. Two of these are ulnar neuritis and deep vein thrombosis. Describe these **two** health problems. [4]

8 Discuss the impact of ICT on cinemas. [7]

Test 2

Mrs Phipps works for a large insurance company. She is nervous about the amount of information on her stored by the company.

1 Describe **three** of the legal rights Mrs Phipps has under the Data Protection Act (1998). [6]

2 Describe the impact of the Regulation of Investigatory Powers Act (2000) on Mrs Phipps. [4]

3 The insurance company is concerned that employees copy software illegally. Describe **two** measures they could introduce to prevent employees copying software. [4]

4 Describe **two** disadvantages of networking computers together. [4]

5 The company is concerned about data security so they have introduced passwords. Identify **two** methods that can be introduced to force the user to choose passwords that will be difficult to break. For each method, explain why it makes the password harder to break. [4]

6 Explain, with examples, why ICT is not always the answer to every problem. [5]

7 Mrs Phipps is currently looking at increasing the amount of work she does from home. Discuss the effect that ICT has had on teleworking. [7]

8 Examination technique

Introduction

After reading this chapter you will be able to:
- understand how to learn the material
- understand the requirements of a question
- be familiar with the examination papers
- understand the keywords associated with the specification
- know how to interpret the keyword and understand the type of response to give.

The examination papers

There are two modules making up the AS award. The grade you are awarded depends on a combination of your mark for the structured tasks and your examination result. The technical phrase is 'aggregation'. You can take your time over completing the structured tasks but you will have just two hours to do yourself justice in the written paper.

The examiners looking at your paper will have a set of acceptable answers, called 'marking points', and you need to provide sufficient evidence in your answers to be awarded the allocated marks. You need to focus on hitting the requisite number of marking points in each of your answers.

Each question has a keyword within it (describe or explain, for example) and this keyword will determine how you answer the question and the depth you need to give.

Here are some general points for you to bear in mind in examinations

Handwriting

Make it neat to ensure the examiner can read your handwriting. Only use black or blue ink. Other colours cause confusion or are difficult to read.

Long answer questions

Answers must be in continuous prose. Avoid using bullet points. You may limit your marks if you do.

Doodling

This gives a bad impression, so if you have time to spare, spend it going back over the paper to add more detail.

Crossing out your answers

Use a single line through what you want to cross out. Do not obliterate it because you could still get some marks if it is actually correct and you have not written a new answer. Think carefully before you cross out a large section of text – is it really wrong or are you starting to panic and not think clearly? If you cross out an answer and replace it, the crossed out text will not be looked at. If you cross out an answer and do not replace it, then the crossed out text, if it can be read, will be marked. Unless there is direct contradiction in the new answer, you are advised to leave the old answer in place and not to cross it out.

Marks for written content

There are marks for the quality of written communication in your answers. These marks will be awarded for the essay type of answers. You will be told before each question that contains marks for the quality of your answer. Make sure, therefore, that you use punctuation and capital letters where necessary and that you spell the technical terms correctly, especially those that are given in the question.

The examination

This will probably be your first AS ICT examination, you will not have a previous grade to worry you, but it will still be a trial. It will look similar to some of the GCSE papers you will have taken. Do not be fooled into expecting the AS paper to be as easy.

This paper may have between 10 and 15 questions for you to answer to the best of your ability, and they will use a context to help you write suitable answers. The paper covers a lot of material and you need to prepare thoroughly for it – using this book is a good start!

Here are some reasons for poor performance.

The shock of an AS paper

You need to realise that AS is harder than GCSE. The length of the paper sometimes comes as a shock – two hours is a long time to write for.

Candidates are not prepared

Too many written answers show the candidate does not know the topic in the question. You will not have this problem will you? You need to know the basic theory before you can understand and apply it.

Failing to answer adequately

Some answers require a higher level of response: not just a list of points. Later we will discuss the types of questions set.

Answering the questions

The question paper has lines for you to write your answers. You may find that you can write a good answer, in your view, in half the space. If this is so, do not worry. The papers are designed to allow plenty of space for your answers but do not feel that you have to fill the lines, as some candidates do, usually by repeating an answer.

This paper requires a lot of technical knowledge in the seven areas set out in Chapters 1 to 7 of this book.

If you need to plan your answer then please do use a list of points, a diagram or any other device.

BUT do not use:

● the space outside of the box on the paper
● any colour ink other than blue or black – this is important.

You will be asked questions on very different points. Do not assume that one question leads into the next. In this module, all the questions are separate. A difficult consideration is just how much detail you need to go into in your answers. Do think about this and match your response to the marks allocated: a two-paragraph essay for two marks is not sensible. If you do this sort of thing you will leave yourself short of time at the end.

When you have finished a question, look carefully through your answer, while it is fresh in your mind. Ask yourself these questions:

● Does the answer make sense as you read it?
● Have you repeated an answer?
● Can you understand what you have written? Is it what you meant to write?
● Have you identified an item and then described or explained it when asked to do so?
● Have you given enough marking points for the marks available?
● Can your handwriting be read?
● Does the examiner have to add anything or make any assumptions in order to give you the mark?

Now move on to the next question.

Developing an understanding of the required material

Before you can be successful in an examination you must understand the theory (or those topics set out in the specification). There are various ways of doing this, which we will look at now.

Making notes

Some students find it difficult, or feel it is pointless, to make notes in their lessons. Please avoid this attitude. The act of writing notes helps your brain to remember the facts your teacher or the text book is making. Try to find useful models for difficult topics. For example, use lists with points and explanations in a table. Use diagrams if they help you understand. Drawing a similar diagram in the examination may also be a useful prompt to help you answer a question.

Looking over notes

Now that you have some notes you must use them, for example:
- the night after the lesson to make sure you understand them
- when friends ask you questions
- when revising.

Asking questions in lessons

This is a personal matter. Some students like to hide in a class to avoid being asked questions. Don't be shy. Ask if you do not understand. In this way you will gain confidence in providing answers. Examiners appreciate a candidate who exhibits confidence in their answers. It takes time and effort to become confident in a topic, but the effort is worthwhile. However, there is also the converse of being over confident and going over the top in your answers.

Try explaining queries to friends

This is a great way of making sure you know the topics. You will have to think of different ways of answering if your friend does not understand. If you do not know the answer then it is better to find out now rather than in the examination room.

Try practice questions

Write many answers to questions and have them checked against the marking scheme.

How you react to examination papers

This is something that needs careful consideration before you, the candidate, go into the examination. Either you can cope with examinations or you cannot, though some fall in between these extremes. The better you are prepared the more likely you are to be in the former group. Take your time in the examination room. The questions have been tested to ensure that most candidates will have sufficient time to complete all of the paper in the time allowed. Read the question paper through first, planning how you will

Activities

Collect a group of friends.

1 Take your copy of the specification for the theory module and work through section 1.2 making sure that everyone knows what is meant by each section. For example, can you all 'describe common storage devices, indicating typical uses'?

2 Highlight the topics that you don't understand.

3 Ask for help.

answer each question. Do not worry that you have not been taught a particular scenario, look for the understanding required in each question then picture your answer. Try not to leave any questions unanswered.

You must read the question carefully and make sure that what you think the question is asking is accurate. It is a good idea to read the question twice. Recognise, from your knowledge and recall, what is being asked from the specification. Use your knowledge and the structure of the marks allocated to put together a set of information that you think will meet the needs of the question. This is the basis of your mental answer. You now have the task of setting this out clearly in words. Some candidates find this quite difficult so make sure you have plenty of practice.

One common error is to rephrase the same answer and imagine it is a second response. Examiners recognise this and will not award marks. You need to give different answers to earn more than one marking point.

Types of examination questions and how to answer them

If you look at some past exam papers, you will see that the questions all include a keyword such as 'identify' or 'describe'. You must recognise these and respond correctly. These words determine what you are required to do to be awarded the allocated marks.

There is a hierarchy to these keywords, each one requiring more than the one before and building on the one before:

- State/Identify
- Give
- Describe
- Compare
- Explain
- Justify
- Evaluate
- Discuss

State or identify

This is a low-level question. It is aimed at the D and E grades and you should try and make sure that you get all of these types of question right. They are knowledge-based questions – have you learnt the material and can you remember it in the exam. 'State/identify' questions are single marks – one mark for each correct word/phrase.

The examiner is expecting a single word or phrase.

Example

A database package holds data in fields. Forename would be stored as a text data type.

*State **three** data types, other than text, commonly used in databases.* [3]

The answer should be three from: Boolean, numeric, date, memo, object (such as a photograph or sound). Note how the word 'three' is in bold emphasis to make you aware of how many answers are required.

A single word from this list is all that is required. Other correct answers are possible and you would gain marks from these.

Give

You have to provide the examiner with more information than a single-word statement. 'Give' is worth a single mark for each phrase.

Example

The owner of a shop is worried about unauthorised users accessing his computer database if he goes online.

Give **two** examples of illegal actions using ICT.   [2]

Your answers should include two phrases from:

● Illegal use of data.
● Copying data.
● Hacking into restricted files.
● Intercepting credit card details.

Here you need to use a phrase. A single word such as 'hacking' (seen too frequently) will not be given marks. Make sure you provide enough detail. For example 'hacking into confidential data' is a much better answer and will be awarded marks.

Describe

This is moving to a higher level of difficulty. These answers offer you the chance to earn usually two marks for each complete description, but sometimes more. You need to provide an answer that matches the question asked using the given context. As a rule of thumb, always give an example of use related to the scenario for 'describe' answers. Remember a good description might earn extra marks in some questions. Take your time in thinking about these questions and preparing what you will write.

There are two ways that a 'describe' question is asked. You will either be asked a 'describe' question that requires you to identify what you will be describing, or you will be given the item and asked to add a description to it.

● Describe the following types of validation: Range and Type.   [4]
● Describe **two** different types of validation.   [4]

In the first, you have been given the types of validation to describe. In the second, you need to identify the types of validation.

A full description is made up of three elements:

● identify – what you are going to describe (can be given)
● amplify – further information about the identify
● exemplify – applying the identify and amplify to the context of the question.

Depending on the type of 'describe' question, you will either give the 'identify' and 'amplify' or the 'amplify' and 'exemplify'. It also is possible to gain full marks for giving two different amplifications.

When learning how to answer 'describe' questions, a framework can be used.

Example

*Describe **two** design considerations for a tailored data-entry screen for a cinema ticket ordering system.*

Firstly, identify the two design considerations that you are going to talk about. Then, for each consideration, give some more information about it – amplify the design consideration. The exemplification, in this example, is to cover all the basics – it is not actually necessary but makes sure that you obtain the marks.

Identify	Amplify	Exemplify
Background colour	This is the colour that sits behind the text and images on the page.	A pale blue colour could be used because this is gentle on the eye.
Volume of information	This is how much information is put on a page at a time for the user to read.	Each of the ticket booking pages should contain enough text to fit on the page without scrolling.

Having used a grid to plan the answer, take each row and write about it as continuous prose to end up with an answer that is worth full marks.

Example

A word-processing package and a desktop publishing package are used by a secretary in an employment agency.

a) *Describe **two** features of the word processing package that could be used by the secretary to write letters.* [4]

b) *Describe how the secretary could make use of autoflow and border art when creating a newsletter.* [4]

In part (a), the marks are for identifying the feature and giving more information about it. The features could include any two of:
- spellcheck
- auto insert of date
- left alignment
- footers.

This is identification. For full marks, each feature would need additional information given about it, and to make extra sure you have the marks, how the feature could be used by the secretary when writing a letter.

In part (b), you have been given the features so you need to look at amplifying – giving more information about that feature and contextualising (exemplification) the feature in the example given by the question.

Example

Spreadsheets are used for modelling situations. Describe the features of spreadsheet applications that enable them to be used for modelling a move of business premises.

Your answers should include a description such as, how variables can be changed [1] and the application automatically re-calculates values [1]. Other features, such as formatting column widths, will not earn marks, as they do not relate specifically to modelling.

Identify	Amplify	Exemplify
Autoflow		
Border art		

Compare

Here you will need to identify a feature and then say how each of the items to be compared deals with that feature. This can be a comparison or a contrast. A 'compare' question is worth four marks.

Example

Compare the use of a spreadsheet and a database application for holding data on customers for a garage. [3]

Your answer will need to identify a feature/item and give an explanation of how each application would cope. One method you can use to help you is a writing frame as shown here.

Item/feature	Spreadsheet	Database
Search for a customer.	Can use a filter.	Can use parameter queries.
Sort records.	Can sort only a single column or all the columns.	Can sort all of the columns.
Create a file for mail merge of selected customers.	Need to ensure compatibility with program being used. May need to export to CSV format.	Can use built-in features and mail merge from within database.
Create a report on selected customers.	May need to export the data to create a functional report.	Can create and store reports internally.
Carry out and save queries.	Can carry out a query but cannot store them.	Built-in feature.

You then need to write your answer in continuous prose. Make sure it is clear that you have made comparisons. Use words such as: 'whereas', 'and', 'but'.

You only need to make **two** comparisons to get all four marks.

When thinking about comparisons, make sure that the features you select for comparison are easy to write about for both sides. Some of the features will lead to more writing than others – do not just pick the first two you think of, but consider a range and then decide on the two that will give you the best comparison.

A 'compare' question is marked using a grid called a banded response. It is not marked on a point-marking basis.

The grid for 'compare' marking is given below:

4	Two complete comparisons
3	One complete comparison and one individual point
2	One complete comparison
0–1	One individual point about either side.

Just because you make what you think is a comparison, does not make it a comparison. For example, when comparing text and sound as a means to convey information, to identify a feature such as physicality is the first step. To then go on to say you need eyes to read the text and ears to hear the sound is not a comparison of both sides against a single feature. It is two separate descriptions. The comparison would be that you need eyes to read the text but you do not need eyes to hear the sound. (These would need to be descriptions (identify, amplify, exemplify) to get the credit.)

When giving both sides of a comparison you must expand both sides. You will not get the credit for giving 'one side does this, the other does not'. For example, if comparing an image library and a clipart library, one of the features could be type of image – a clipart library contains pre-drawn images, while an image library does not. This does not get the credit for a comparison – both sides needs to be of equal weighting.

Example

Compare the purposes of the Data Protection Act and Computer Misuse Act.

Use the following writing frame to have a go at answering the question.

Item/feature/purpose	Data Protection Act	Computer Misuse Act

Explain

This type of question usually requires you to provide a reason. The question will ask for either advantages or disadvantages and you must give your answer within the context of the question. Your answers must be continuous prose. Using a list will only score low marks. These are fine for planning the structure of a short essay, but are not at the same high level as prose. Do not think that because the marking schemes are listed points your answers must be the same.

When answering an 'explain' question, you need to think about the building blocks of the previous types of questions. An 'explain' question is a 'describe' question with reasons. A 'describe' question is an 'identify' question followed by 'amplify' and 'exemplify'.

This means that in order to successfully explain something, you need to identify what you are going to talk about, amplify it so that you add some substance, then give a reason (either an advantage or disadvantage for its use), then finish with an exemplify (i.e. why it is an advantage/disadvantage in the context set?).

Example

A doctor at a medical practice encodes patient data before sending it home. Explain two advantages of encoding data to the medical practice. [4]

Answers could include:

Points:

- Legal requirement to keep data secure.
- Stops anyone finding out personal information if intercepted.

Each of these points can be expanded and a reason given as to why it is an advantage to encode the data for the medical practice.

So, breaking the answer down:

Identify	Describe	Explain
Legal requirement to keep data secure	The Data Protection Act (1998) requires all data about individual to be secure. The medical practice holds personal information so it needs to conform to the Act.	By encoding the data the medical practice is conforming to the requirements of the law, making sure that it does not get sued.

The identification is the point that you are going to talk about. The description is an amplification of the point and a contextualisation. The explanation is the reason why it is an advantage.

An 'explain' question might ask for a number of explanations (as in the above example where two were asked for) or it may be an open-ended explanation, where a single description may lead to more than one explanation.

Example

Explain the advantages of using a wizard to create a mail merge [4]

This does not ask for a number of explanations. This means that it can be answered using two explanations (four marks total, two marks for each explanation) or it can be answered with a single explanation in enough detail to gain all the marks. Here is an example answer that flows from a single point:

Any user, whether novice or advanced, can make use of a wizard. A novice can follow the step-by-step instructions and produce the mail merge without any training, reducing the need for specialists. The advanced user might find it quicker to run the wizard than perform the task manually because it presents the most commonly used options and

they can be accessed in a single click. This means that they can spend more time on the complex aspects of the mail merge. If an advanced user has not used mail merge for some time they might have forgotten the sequence and the wizard will quickly remind them.

Justify

This is a positive explanation. If you are justifying something, you need to give the reasons **why** it should be used – these are positive reasons. Your answers should be in continuous prose and relate directly to the context given in the question.

In the AS specification, there are very few places where 'justify' questions can be asked. The majority of them are based around justifying the use of specific hardware and software for a given situation, for example.

- Identify an appropriate input, output or storage device for a given situation and justify the choice made.
- Describe specialist hardware devices for physically disabled users: puff-suck switch, foot mouse, eye-typer, Braille printers, keyboards, speakers and microphones; and justify their use for given situations.
- Describe specialist software for physically disabled users: predictive text, sticky keys, zoom and voice recognition; and justify their use for given situations.

You will need to look at the scenario and come up with reasons why the hardware/software is the best to use. The reasons need to be specific and related to the scenario. Some questions will give you the hardware/software and ask you to justify it, other questions may give you the choice of hardware/software. You will need to give it and then justify it.

Example

A homeowner wants to back up their photo collection, which is in excess of 50 GB. Identify and justify an appropriate storage device for this task. [6]

A homeowner wants to back up their photo collection which is in excess of 50 GB. They have chosen to use an external hard disk drive. Justify the choice of an external hard disk drive for this task. [6]

Because of the hierarchy of keywords, any bullet point in the specification that starts with 'discuss' can also be used to ask a 'justify' question:

- Discuss the impact of ICT on society, organisations and individuals.
- Discuss possible future developments in ICT and their impact on the following areas: transport, medicine, the disabled, education, entertainment, digital piracy, shopping, marketing and communication.

- Discuss the main aspects, purpose and implications of the Data Protection Act (1998), Computer Misuse Act (1990), Copyright, Designs and Patents Act (1988), Regulation of Investigatory Powers Act (2000), Electronic Communications Act (2000) and Freedom of Information Act (2000) and subsequent changes/updates.

A 'justify' question is not 'point marked', but marked according to a banded response. The response that you give is looked at as a whole answer and decided into which band it fits. For a 'justify' question, there are three bands:

High	5–6	Candidate has given detailed reasons why XYZ should be used for the given situation.
Medium	3–4	Candidate has described advantages of using XYZ for the given situation.
Low	0–2	Candidate has identified advantages of using XYZ for the given situation.

These bands are targeted at different grade levels. The first two marks (low) are E grade, marks 3–4 (medium) are C/D and marks 5–6 (high) are grade B. This means that the depth of the answer needs to be appropriate to the grade level. The amount you need to write needs to be more to gain higher marks. A response needs to contain more than one of each to gain full marks in each band.

A 'justify' response should be based on identification, description, explanation.

Example

Justify the use of a puff–suck switch for a disabled user who has lost the use of their arms.

The answer below looks at one possible response, moving through the different levels. For a full mark answer, you would need to give more than one.

Identify	Describe	Explain
Don't need any arms	A puff–suck switch is operated by the mouth, blowing into a tube and sucking air from a tube, turning a computer on or off and this can be used without arms	A puff–suck switch can be used to control on/off switches and keys, pressing a key in response to a blow. It can also be used to control the direction of the cursor on the screen, for example, and then select an icon. This allows the puff–suck switch to replace the keyboard and the mouse which require arms to operate.

You need to make sure that the reasons are positive: **why** they should be used. You need to give depth to the answer, making sure that an explanation is built on a 'describe', which is built on an 'identify'.

Evaluate

This is a positive **and** negative explanation. If you are evaluating something, you need to give the reasons why it should be used (these are positive reasons) **and** the reasons why it should not be used (these are the negative reasons). Your answers should be in continuous prose and relate directly to the context given in the question. This is similar to a 'justify' question but you need to balance your answers.

In the AS specification, there are very few places where 'evaluate' questions can be asked.

- Describe the differences between vector and bitmap graphics and evaluate their suitability for given applications.

You will need to look at the scenario and come up with reasons why the vector or the bitmap graphic is the best to use. The reasons need to be specific and related to the scenario.

The hierarchy of keywords means that any bullet point in the specification that starts with 'discuss' can also be used to ask an 'evaluate' question:

- Discuss the impact of ICT on society, organisations and individuals.
- Discuss possible future developments in ICT and their impact on the following areas: transport, medicine, the disabled, education, entertainment, digital piracy, shopping, marketing and communication.
- Discuss the main aspects, purpose and implications of the Data Protection Act (1998), Computer Misuse Act (1990), Copyright, Designs and Patents Act (1988), Regulation of Investigatory Powers Act (2000), Electronic Communications Act (2000) and Freedom of Information Act (2000) and subsequent changes/updates.

Example

Evaluate the success of the Computer Misuse Act (1990) in preventing hacking. [6]

As with a 'justify' question, an 'evaluate' question is not 'point marked' but marked according to a banded response. The response that you give is looked at as a whole answer and decided into which band it fits.

There are three bands:

High	5–6	Candidate has given detailed positive and negative reasons for using XYZ. There is a reasoned conclusion.
Medium	3–4	Candidate has described positive and negative reasons for using XYZ. There may be an implied conclusion.
Low	0–2	Candidate has identified positive or negative points for using XYZ.

The grading, and length and depth, of the answer for each band are the same as for a justification.

An evaluation should be based on identification, description and explanation for both sides. It should finish with a reasoned conclusion, coming to a decision.

Example

Evaluate the suitability of using a bitmap graphic for the logo of a company to be used in different media. [6]

The following answer looks at one response, moving through the different levels. For a full mark response, you would need to give more than one negative and two positive answers.

+ or −	Identify	Describe	Explain
Negative	When made larger it will pixelate	If the bitmap image is to be used on a large poster, the image will pixellate – each pixel will be able to be seen as a large single block	The pixels in a bitmap are a fixed size. If the image is made larger, then the pixels become large and appear as blocks. If the image is to be used on a large A3 poster, for example, it will not have the quality of a smaller image and it will have a negative effect on the corporate identity because it will look cheap and nasty.

You need to make sure that the reasons are positive and negative – **why** they should and should not be used. You need to give depth to your answer, making sure that an explanation is built on a 'describe', which is built on an 'identify'.

Discuss

This requires both sides of an argument. The argument is based on impacts and consequences for each side. There is likely to be at least one and no more than two essays in each G061 paper.

To gain high marks for a discussion question, you need to follow the rules given earlier for building an answer:
- Identify the point being made.
- Describe the point (amplify and exemplify the identifications).
- Explain the point (positive/negative reason why), for impacts and associated consequences.

An easy way of looking at this is that impacts are short term and consequences are the long-term effects of the impacts. For example, an impact of an increased use of social media is that it is easy to send a message that can be misinterpreted. This is short term. The consequence is the long-term significance of sending a text message that can be misinterpreted related to an increased use of social media; for example the consequence might be an increase in unintentional bullying.

It is not enough to list the impacts and consequences (as in the preceding example), but the rules for building a response must be used: identify, amplify, exemplify, reason why. This takes a lot of work. A full mark answer only needs one positive and one negative impact and associated consequences.

The specification talks about discussing the impacts. A discussion of the impacts results in the consequences, hence it is easier to look at essays from the logical flow of point, impacts and consequences.

The marking grid for a 'discuss' question is given below. You need to make sure that your answers are in continuous prose. A rule of thumb is that one side of an argument should be about three quarters of a side of the answer sheet.

9–11	4	• The candidate is able to discuss clearly the impact and consequences. Candidates will show a detailed level of understanding and be able to explain in detail both the impacts **and** consequences of more than one position. • Logical arguments are produced to demonstrate a clear understanding of the question. • Ideas will be expressed clearly and fluently using specific knowledge to support and inform the discussion. • There may be a reasoned conclusion. • Subject-specific terminology will be used accurately and appropriately.
6–8	3	• The candidate is able to discuss the impact(s) and consequence(s). • Candidates will show a limited understanding and be able to explain at least one impact **and** associated consequence of a given position, however explanations may lack specific detail and/or concentrate on either an impact or consequence with a limited explanation of the other. • Subject-specific terminology will be used accurately and appropriately.
3–5	2	• The candidate is able to explain the impact(s) or consequence(s). • Candidates will show a limited understanding and be able to explain at least one impact **or** consequence of a given position, however explanations may lack specific detail. • The explanation, though informed, may stray from the point but specific knowledge will be evident. • Some subject-specific terminology will be used.
0–2	1	• The candidate is able to describe superficially the impact **or** consequences. The information may be poorly expressed and may be in the form of a list of points. • Subject-specific terminology may be limited or missing.

Discussions are marked out of 11 and broken into four bands. As with 'justify' and 'evaluate' questions, it is not 'point marked' but the response is looked at and put into the band where there is the best fit.

'Discuss' questions also include an element of written communication in the marking. This is not used to determine the band the response is in, but is one of the tools used to determine where within the band the response goes. This is spelling, grammar and use of technical terminology.

- Marks in band 1 of the grid are for superficial descriptions. In other words, barely more than a list of points.
- Marks in band 2 are for an explanation, although it will lack specific detail (so description with weak reasons) of an impact or consequence.
- The progression to band 3 is to take the weak reasons of an impact or consequence from band two and to turn it into a logical flow from point, to impact, to consequences with some reasoning. This is done from one point of view (i.e. positive or negative).
- For band 4, the content from band three needs to be completed from two points of view (i.e positive **and** negative) and the explanations should be detailed.

Although it is easy to talk in terms of positive and negative, the marks scheme refers to points of view. For example, an essay such as 'Discuss the impact of ICT on education' could be written as:
- the positive and negative impact of ICT on education
- the impact of ICT on education from the point of view of the teacher and the student.

Either of these methods of writing an essay is acceptable.

When planning an essay, the following grid may be of use:

+ or –	Identify	Describe	Explain impact	Explain consequences of impact

While there may only be one point and impact for each positive and negative argument, there should be more than one consequence given.

One of the main problems when writing the essay is that the depth of the answer given needs to be equally balanced for positive and negative aspects. It is very easy to put the effort into one side of the argument only and not to bother too much about the other. Take the following essay.

Example

Many readers of newspapers have access to the Internet. This allows them to read a wide range of online newspapers and magazines. Discuss the increasing availability of online newspapers and magazines. [11]

The answers expected include a discussion of both the advantages and disadvantages. Items for discussion are:
- up-to-date news
- global news not just national news
- less chance of bias, e.g. state control of media

- legal considerations
- less capital tied up in printing
- variety of reading
- greater access to marketplace
- copyright of images/texts harder to police
- multimedia and other HTML features
- cannot be read as easily on the move
- effects on newsagent
- customised newspapers.

This is not a complete range of answers. The 'discuss' questions are worded so that there are no definitive answers and it is down to you to choose the point and the argument you make.

Any of the statements would need to be described and then the reason why it has a positive or negative impact on the availability of online news. Having given the reason, the answer would then go on to give at least two consequences of the impact.

The same needs to be repeated for the opposite view. A conclusion is **not** required to gain full marks in a discussion essay.

Activities

1 Look through past papers and find questions using 'compare' and 'explain' as keywords. Produce writing frames to structure your answer.

2 Now write answers in continuous prose.

3 Do a number of these because they are where you can gain a good number of marks.

How to practise answering questions

You really must spend time working on questions.

At the end of a topic

Here you will have the opportunity to find out what you have learned in the topic. Your teachers may well give you tests at this point.

Before school tests

It makes sense to do well in school tests. Your applications for further education are based on the outcomes of these tests. It is another opportunity to measure your knowledge and understanding under examination conditions.

According to your revision plan

You will draw up a schedule for revision! Then over this period you should answer questions to ensure you know the style to use and the subject matter.

Past papers

Use them. They are the best guide to the style of question to be set. Your centre will have copies. They are not available online. Do be aware that each examination board uses the same subject material in their specifications, but expect different marking points in the answers to their AS examinations. That is why you need specialist books like this one.

Identify likely topics

You should have built up a table of the topics and past questions from over the past few years of papers and looked for a pattern. The specification uses letters of the alphabet as code to identify each section.

In the examination

This is the end point that all the preparation has been leading up to. You really do need to be prepared. You then stand much more chance of giving answers that will be awarded marks. There are some techniques that you could use in the examination room that might help you do the best you can.

- Focus on the question you are answering – Forget the last question and the next section. Concentrate on reading the current question and structuring the best answer you can to match the keyword and the marking scheme. Some candidates go wrong in a question and this disturbs their concentration for several more questions. Try to focus and forget!

- One mark per minute – If a question is worth two marks then do not spend more than two minutes writing the answer. Sometimes candidates' essay answers are too long and detailed. This means that later answers are rushed and marks are lost because time has been wasted.

- Find a relax point – During the examination you will need to give your brain, back and eyes a brief rest. Look at the clock or a point at some distance just to relax for 30 seconds or so. Do not look around the room as this will distract others. It will also interrupt your thought processes. Take two different pens with different shapes to help rest your hand when you write for a sustained period.

- No crossing out – If you do need to cross out anything, then be organised. Use a single line and then calmly write a second answer.

- Always read carefully what you have written – Is it exactly what you need to say? The words used and their order can make a difference, so take care. You need every mark.

- Just a bit extra – Just add one more example in your response if it is appropriate. Just take that bit of extra time to think about your answer before you start to write. Take care reading your answer.

- Last few words – Remember that examiners really would like to give you the marks, but they need to see that you can write a clear answer to the question set. Examiners are nice people, but they cannot read your mind! As you write your answers think about what the examiners will read from your response.

9 Introduction to coursework

Introduction

The coursework for the AS in ICT is worth 40% of the qualification. Whether your skills lie in coursework or exams, you should be putting as much time and effort as you can into the coursework to get as many marks as you can. The tasks are out of 80 marks. Although the number of marks for an A grade changes each year, you need to try to get at least 66.

The *Structured ICT Tasks* (G062) are set every year – a different set of tasks for each year. The final version is released in September and they need to be completed, submitted to your teacher for marking and marks passed onto OCR by 15 May the following year. Your teachers will set an internal deadline that will give them time to mark the work.

The tasks are based around a scenario. This is not a difficult scenario and you will be given time to research it. In the past, these scenarios have included a carpet measuring company, a bike hire company, a theme park and a cyber café.

The tasks will cover the following areas:

- design
- software development
- testing
- documentation.

The tasks might involve:

- the design of part of a system
- the production of a testing strategy
- the use of software for development
- the production of documentation to show the user how to use/ amend/update the system.

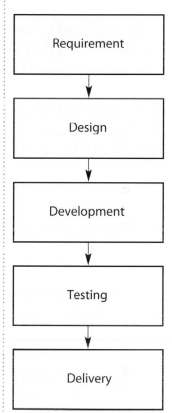

Figure 9.1 System development work flow

Key words

Design – drawing how the system will look and work so that a third party could interpret the designs and develop the solution.

Software development – using software to create a solution that meets the customer's requirements.

Testing – creating a plan that tests the system to make sure that it works – this is done with valid, invalid and extreme data.

Documentation – producing user guides and help sheets to assist the user with using, amending and updating the system that has been created.

Generic advice

The following advice is generic advice to be applied to all the tasks. Look through this before starting the tasks.

Do only what is required by the tasks.

Look carefully at the requirements of the task. It is very easy to get carried away and do a lot more than the task requires. This will not only take you longer to do but it will also make the production of the evidence more difficult and you may miss some marks.

It can be very easy to go over the top and get too involved in the project. For example, if you are asked to create an animation or a logo, you could spend a long time making it perfect, however the marks will be only for meeting the requirements.

No need to show all stages of development of the tasks

Look carefully at the tasks and the evidence that it is asking you to produce. It is very unlikely that the task will ask you to show every step of the development. It is more likely that you will be asked either to show the final result or how the final result was achieved.

Always look at the marks available

With the exception of the database and the spreadsheet requirements, the tasks generally have a small number of marks. These marks are for relatively straightforward tasks and do not require a lot of work to gain the marks.

The spreadsheet and the database requirements often need a lot of work for very few marks. When preparing for a task, look at the marks available, the type of task that it is and the type of evidence that you are being asked to produce. This will give you some idea of how much work is expected.

Choice of software

You will have been taught the skills that you need to complete the tasks. You will have been taught these skills using specific software. Unless you have a **very** good reason, you should use this software to complete the task. It is possible to use a range of different software and get the same result. For example a mail merge can be completed using a database, spreadsheet or word processor, however, using the correct software makes the task easier. If the software you are using cannot fulfil all the requirements, you will lose marks.

Advice and help from your teacher

Your teacher can give you only limited help on the actual tasks. Excess help can be punished by having the marks reduced, forfeiting the entire paper or even having all your papers for that particular session withdrawn.

Your teacher can	Your teacher cannot
• teach you generic skills that you will need for the coursework • help you on similar, but different tasks, and show you how to apply the skills (see the comment on cloned tasks) • go through previous tasks and mark schemes with you, including sample work from previous tasks • go over how to interpret a task – on previous tasks, not live tasks • go over the meaning of key words that you will find in the tasks and the evidence requirements.	• give you verbal or written help on the actual tasks – this means your teacher cannot comment on what you are doing, point out mistakes or show you how to do something on the task. • provide a tick sheet for you to go through to make sure you have covered everything in the task • go through the task with you or give you a sample mark scheme • hand back the task to you once it has been submitted • give you cloned tasks for practice – a cloned task is one that is very similar to the live task with a few words changed.

When completing your work:

Do	Do not
• make sure each task has a cover sheet with your name, candidate number, centre name and centre number on it • present your work in a manila folder with a treasury tag in the top left-hand corner (loosely tied) • make sure you have read and signed the Candidate Authentication Form before submitting your coursework • try to make sure the work is sequential – each part of the task is labelled and follows in order.	• submit your work in ring binders or with each page in a plastic wallet • use colour printing – there is no need for the work to be printed out in colour • hand in your work without checking it – make sure that every part of the task has been answered and the evidence provided is as required • miss out parts of the task – have a go at everything – if you get stuck, move on to the next part of the task.

10 Design

Introduction

Design comes before development. It is what the finished system will look like, how it will store data, how it will process data, how it outputs data and how the system is linked together. It should be possible to hand a design to a third party, who, without any other questions, can create it exactly as the designer intended.

The important part of any design is annotation. Make sure that you have written on the design.

Layout design

A layout design is the design that underpins the content. It is **not** the content itself, but how the content is saved and displayed. For example, on a web page, the layout design will show how the page is laid out, that is the positions of the headings, the navigation bar, the main page content and the pictures.

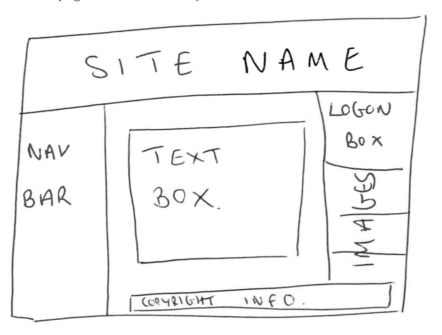

You can see that it does not tell you what the content is or what the page will look like and the colours to use; it focuses on where the page elements go. A presentation layout design would look similar to one for web pages.

There are many different designs for a database. A layout design, however, focuses only on two areas: input and output. In the case of databases these are forms and reports, respectively.

Figure 10.1 Layout sketch

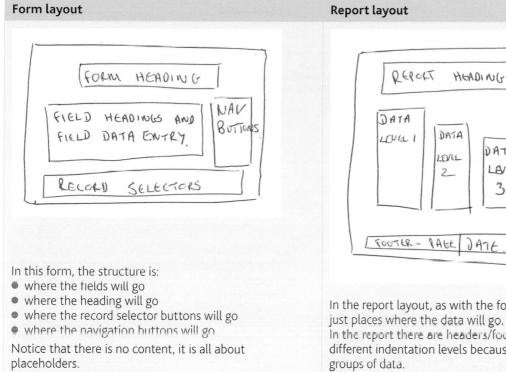

Form layout	Report layout

In this form, the structure is:
- where the fields will go
- where the heading will go
- where the record selector buttons will go
- where the navigation buttons will go

Notice that there is no content, it is all about placeholders.

In the report layout, as with the form, there is no content, just places where the data will go.
In the report there are headers/footers and there are different indentation levels because the report can create groups of data.

You may be asked to design a data capture form. This is just a database form that is paper based (so there will not be any navigation or record selector buttons). It is not possible to have drop-down lists on paper, so you will have either an open-text field or a list of the choices.

The other main type of design is for a spreadsheet. This will follow the same guidelines as for other layout designs, that is no content, just placeholders where the content will go.

Notice how rough the design can be. As long as it is readable and usable, it is fine. It does not have to be ruled or precise.

Content design

Content design is usually created as an example to show what the finished item will look like. It takes the layout design and adds in the content.

Form layout	Content layout
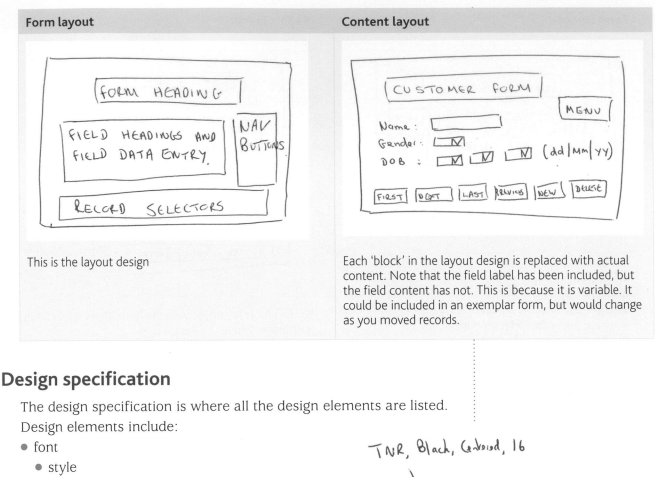	
This is the layout design	Each 'block' in the layout design is replaced with actual content. Note that the field label has been included, but the field content has not. This is because it is variable. It could be included in an exemplar form, but would change as you moved records.

Design specification

The design specification is where all the design elements are listed.
Design elements include:

- font
  - style
  - size
  - type
  - colour
- paragraph
  - alignment
  - spacing
- page
  - size
  - orientation
  - background colour
  - margins.

If there are elements on the page, such as buttons or graphics, the size and location of these elements should be given.

A design specification does not have to be drawn, it can be a style sheet: a word-processed set of instructions.

TNR, Black, Centered, 16

Heading

TNR Black Left 14 → Sub Heading

Body text

TNR, Black, Left, Size 12.

Page: A4, Portrait
Margins. T: 1cm
L: 1cm
B: 1cm
R: 1cm

Colour: White

Figure 10.2 Drawn design specification

Main Title Bold Size 15 Times New Roman Centered

Sub Titles Bold Size 13 Times New Roman Left Aligned,

There are three returns between the main title and the sub title, and one return between the sub title and the main body of text. The main body of the text should be written in Times New Roman size 11, the text should be fully justified – this means that there is a straight left hand edge and a straight right hand edge. The text should be set to one and a half line spacing.

Paragraphs should not be indented but be level all the way done. New paragraphs should have a line left above them. There should be two spaces after a full stop and one space after a

Figures 10.2 and 10.3 are specifications for a document. The same idea can be applied to any piece of software.

Figure 10.3 Document design specification

Navigation design

The navigation design is how the various elements are joined together. A navigation diagram can be used to show links between:

- presentation slides
- worksheets in a spreadsheet
- web pages
- database forms
- games menus and screens
- steps in a macro.

When creating a navigation design:

- do **not** do detailed designs of the elements: they just need a name
- draw lines between the elements that are connected
- put arrows on the lines to show the direction of the link.

The direction of the link is important. For example, if you have a presentation with four slides, a main menu slide and three other slides, each of the three sides returning to the main menu, the navigation diagram would be as shown in Figure 10.4.

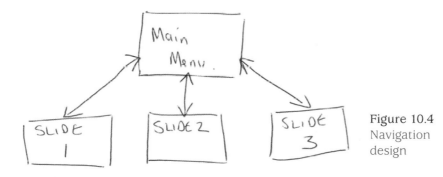

Figure 10.4 Navigation design

Activities

Look at a letter from your school and create a design specification and a layout specification for it. Swap it with another student and see if they can use your designs to reproduce a letter.

An arrow indicates that each slide is accessed by the main menu and returns to the main menu. Notice that the pages have neither content nor layout.

When designing navigation in a system, make sure that there are no dead ends. A dead end is a screen, page or a slide that you can get to but has no links from it.

In most systems (e.g. spreadsheets, presentations and databases), there will be return links from the elements, perhaps to a main menu. With web pages, there will be pages internal to the website and pages external to it. It is unlikely that every external page will have links both ways.

Example

A school requires a website with a home page, a curriculum page, a year group page and an activities page. All the pages need to be accessible from each other. The curriculum page needs also to link to the OCR main web page, and the home page needs to link to an interactive map site showing the location of the school.

There are two elements to this website: internal (the four pages) and external (two pages). All the internal pages need to link together (a straightforward diagram with arrows linking the pages). There is an obvious link from internal to external (the arrow needs to indicate the direction of the link).

However, what about links back from the external pages to the internal site? The only way there will be a link from the OCR page back to the home page is if there is a clickable link on the OCR page. Since it is directing you to link to the main OCR page, this is unlikely. However, with forums on websites, it is possible to add a link and therefore the link could be two way. You need to read the question carefully.

The link back from the interactive mapping page is more complicated. There is a link from the home page to the map page. This is an interactive map, so you can click into the map. When you click into the map, you are interacting with an external website. This website processes your request (maybe to zoom in) and generates a new image, which it then sends back to the internal page. This is what makes it a two-way link (Figure 10.5).

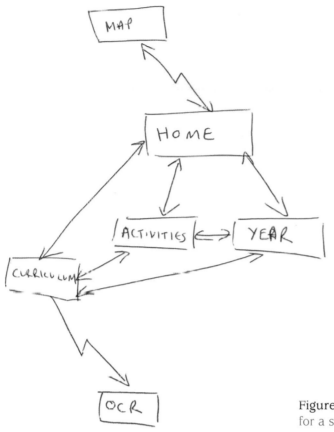

Figure 10.5 Navigation design for a school website

The 'lightning bolt' is used to indicate an external website.

Web pages can also have forms or process data. The results of this processing of data can be a confirmation page. If this is the case, then this also needs to be included in the navigation diagram.

Other designs

There are other areas that you may be asked to design. The most common ones are likely to be:

- storage
- processes
- entity relationship models.

Storage

This is how the data will be stored. It is usually associated with databases – designing the data structure.

A typical layout for a file structure design is:

Field name	Data type	Length	Sample values/range/set	Type of validation expected

When designing data structures, remember the database requirements: primary key, atomic fields etc.

Imagine you have been asked to design a data structure for a garage to hold information on cars for sale. The following might be part of the design that you come up with.

Field name	Data type	Length	Sample values/range/set	Type of validation expected
CarID*	Autonumber	4	0000–9999	Unique, sequential
Manufacturer	Text	15	Ford, Subaru	Presence
Type	Text	15	Ka, Impreza	Presence
Model	Text	15	Studio Edge	
Engine size	Number	4	1600	Range, Type, Presence
Number of doors	Number	1	0–6	Range, Type, Presence
Mileage	Number	6	0–999999	Range, Type, Presence
Colour	Text	15	Red	Drop-down list
Price	Number	6	£5,999	Presence, Type, Range
Registration	Text	9	GU51 0HG	Presence

Processes

This is either the design of the validation (see Chapter 12 on testing) or the design of the data flow through the system.

A flow chart is a specific type of diagram that is used to represent a process. It shows the different steps as boxes, and arrows connecting the boxes together to give an order.

The following table shows some of the boxes that are used.

Activities

Design a data structure for storing information about a student.

Name	Symbol	Description of use
Oval		This is used to indicate the start or end of the process.
Rectangle		This is used to denote a process to be carried out (e.g. addition of data).
Diamond		This is a decision that will determine the route the process takes.
Flow line	⟶	This shows the logical flow of the process.

To create a flowchart:

1 Brainstorm the processes and list them in the order they occur. Ask 'What happens next in the process?', 'Is there a decision to be made?'
2 Draw the oval and label it 'Start'.
3 For the first process/decision, draw rectangle or diamond.
4 Write the process or question inside the shape.
5 Draw a flow line to the next process/decision.
6 Make sure you write the possible outcomes on the lines coming out of decision diamonds.
7 Work through the steps for each process.
8 The end of the process (there may be more than one end) should be an oval marked Finish.
9 Work through the process with different data to see if it works.

Example

A letter needs to be sent to all bank customers. If they have a balance of more than £1000 and have used the account in the last six months, they get letter A. If they have a balance of more than £1000, but have not used the account in the last six months they get letter B. If they have less than £1000 they get letter C.

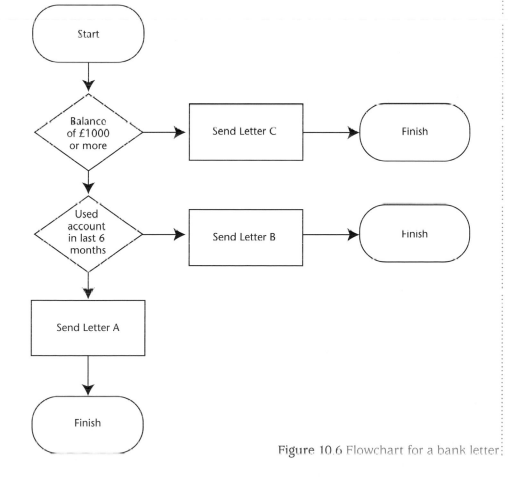

Figure 10.6 Flowchart for a bank letter

Activities

Produce a flowchart for the following system.

An order is received. The stock level is checked to see if the order can be met. If it cannot be met, then an email is sent to the customer telling them the order cannot be fulfilled. If the order can be fulfilled, then the amount required is reduced from the number in stock and an email is sent to the customer telling them that delivery will be the following day.

Entity relationship models

You may be asked to design an entity relationship diagram (ERD). To do this, look at Chapter 5 on databases.

Remember, an entity is something about which we want to store data and a relationship shows how the entities are related to each other.

When designing an ERD:

1 List all the entities.

2 Identify the links that exist between the entities.

3 Identify the degree of the relationship between the entities.

Activities

Design an ERD for the following situation:

A company has many salespeople. When they sell a product, an invoice is written by one salesperson. However, during their time at the company, a salesperson will write many invoices. Each invoice has one or more products on it and each product will be on none, one or more than one invoice. The company buys its products from wholesalers. The wholesaler sells many different products, but each product the company buys is only bought from one wholesaler.

Common errors in design

The following are common errors made in designs:

- Not making it a hand-drawn design – if the task asks for hand drawn, then it must be hand drawn.
- Not including all aspects of the design – particularly in a design specification (e.g. missing out the background colour of the page or the font colour, size or type). A developer should not have to make any decisions about what to do, they should **all** be listed.
- Not doing the correct type of design – producing a content design instead of a layout design, for example.

Tip

If you have a many-to-many relationship between two entities:

- put a new entity in between the entities
- apply the relationships: the outside will be 1, the inside many.

Software development: Interpreting the tasks and **11** producing the evidence

Introduction

This section is about how to understand the requirements of the task and to produce the evidence that is required to obtain the marks. Having the practical skills is one thing, producing the evidence in the format that is required to gain marks is something different. Unless you prove to the examiner that you understand what you have done you will not gain credit.

The tasks

1 When you first receive the tasks, look through them and read them in detail. There may be a sequence to the tasks that you need to follow. For example, task 1 might be to create a logo for the organisation and this logo is to be used in subsequent tasks. If you start task 2 without having completed the logo from task 1 you will not be able to obtain full marks.

2 Look at the software that you need to use to complete the tasks. For some tasks there might be more than one piece of software required. Tasks that require spreadsheets or web pages tend to be more difficult than other tasks.

3 Look at the number of marks available for each task and for each sub-part of the task. This will give you a general idea of how much work is required. Spreadsheet, web and database tasks tend to require more work for the marks.

4 Finally, look at what you are being asked to do. This will involve designing and creating a solution for which you will need to provide evidence and write about what you have done.

The tasks will fall into a number of different skills and a number of different applications. You will be likely to be asked to use the following software:

- Word-processing – This will include creating user guides and help sheets (documentation) and mail merge.
- Spreadsheet – This will involve creating a model using formulae and functions, and is likely to make use of multiple sheets. You might also be asked to use graphs, cell/sheet protection and macros.

Key words

Requirements – These are objectives required by the client that your solution must meet – they are specific and measurable.

Evidence – This is the printed evidence of the solution that you have created – all elements of the solution must be visible.

Annotation – This is text about a screenshot or solution – it is detailed and explains rather than describes what has been done.

Labelling – This is similar to annotation, but does not go into as much depth – it is identifying what has been done or the context and content of a screenshot.

Hand drawn – This means completed by pen or pencil – the drawing can be scanned, but the original must have been completed by hand.

Development – This is the process that you have gone through to create the solution – it is usually combined with annotation.

- Web page authoring – This is to create web pages and forms, and to validate the forms and link them to other applications. You may also have to embed third-party information, such as maps into the website. A part of creating the web pages includes designing the navigation structure that will be used (links between pages/elements) and designing/creating a cascading style sheet (CSS) file.
- Presentation – This will include the use of master pages, animations, transitions and macros.
- Audio – This will include editing and creating sound files. It could be creating from scratch or editing existing files to meet a purpose.
- Video – This will include editing and creating video files. It could be creating from scratch or editing existing files, or integrating titles/subtitles and sound to the video.
- Graphics – This includes creating and editing images, using layers and different types of image (for example, vector and bitmap).
- Animation – This involves creating an animation or using the software to create elements for use in other applications, such as rollover images.

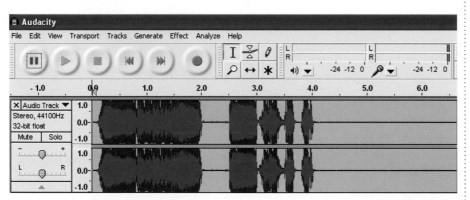

Figure 11.1 Audio editing software

Figure 11.2 Video editing software

Skills required

The skills required to complete the tasks are broken down into four sections:

- Design (see Chapter 10)
- Development
- Testing (see Chapter 12)
- Documentation (see Chapter 13)

The skills required for each section are listed below as a checklist and reminder.

Design

- Design the layout of data capture forms, screen layouts, report layouts and/or other forms of output (e.g. audio output).
- Design how input screens and outputs link together as part of the interface.
- Produce written design specifications.
- Design the data structures/models necessary to solve a given problem.
- Specify any routines using appropriate methods such as flow charts.

Testing

- Select suitable test data that could be used to test a given problem, including normal, invalid and extreme data where appropriate.
- Produce a test plan that could be used to test a solution.
- Test a solution, providing documented evidence that the solution has been tested.

Documentation

- Prepare an instruction guide to show a user how to use/amend/update a system.
- Prepare documentation for a system to include, as appropriate, title page, contents page, page numbers, overview, hardware requirements, software requirements, instruction guide, troubleshooting, glossary of terms and index.
- Prepare documentation in an electronic format using text, images, sound, animation and video.

Example

Read the task introduction and identify the requirements of the client.

Mr Jones requires a database that will store his customers' details. The data entered needs to be protected and checks put in place to stop erroneous data.

Skills required for the development of a solution are specific to the tasks for any year. There are some generic skills that you will need, such as basic spreadsheet, database and word-processing skills, but the higher level skills will come from the client requirements in the task.

Client requirements

The tasks are very specific in the requirements. They are based around a client and the client has requirements that you need to fulfil.

When reading about clients' requirements, make a list of all the things that you are going to need to do. Perhaps you may need to do some research and make some assumptions, or you may have some questions.

Client requirements	Further information/skills
A spreadsheet	
Store details about students by class	A worksheet for each class Details to be stored include forename and surname Possible unique identifier? Do I need to store gender, date of birth?
Store attendance at lessons	Need column for each lesson
Store test scores	Need column for each different test
Work out averages	Function – average
Features to minimise the entry of errors	Use drop-down lists Automatic copying of data where possible (e.g. names from one worksheet automatically populate other worksheets)

Take the task apart and, for each requirement, look at what this requirement means. The task will not list everything in detail; there will be some elements you will need to think about.

Production of evidence

Producing the solution is only one element of the task. You also need to produce evidence of your solution. Each part of the task will have a key set of words that help you decide what is required.

Keywords	Requirements
Produce and print/produce printed evidence of…	A simple printout of what has been created – no need for annotation
Produce a hand-drawn…	Must be hand drawn – can be scanned after being drawn, no annotation required
Print annotated evidence to show…	A printout that has been annotated
Print annotated evidence to explain how…	A printout that explains something so that someone can understand what has been done – it requires a greater degree of annotation than the previous statement; not just a printout of the final version, but of all elements that were done to produce the final version
Produce annotated evidence showing how the requirements were met…	Going through the list of requirements and producing screenshots/printout, with annotation showing how the screenshot meets the requirement
This may be a single screenshot per requirement or a single screenshot may meet more than one requirement

Example

Create a spreadsheet that, for three students, will store their names, the marks for three tests and calculate the total and the average for the tests, and then give a grade based on A = 80, B = 60, C = 40 and lower than 40 is a fail.

Produce and print the spreadsheet that has been created on one side of A4 while remaining readable. Include row and column headings in your printout.

	A	B	C	D	E	F	G	H
1	Name	Test 1	Test 2	Test 3	Total	Average	Grade	
2	Eleanor	78	76	97	251	83.67	A	
3	Jane	54	76	56	186	62.00	B	
4	Oliver	32	54	72	158	52.67	C	
5								
6								
7								
8								
9		Grade Table						
10		0	Fail					
11		40	C					
12		60	B					
13		80	A					
14								
15								

Figure 11.3 Evidence that meets the requirements

This meets the requirements:

- Presentation
  - Row and column headings included
  - On one side of A4
  - Readable.
- Content
  - Names of three students
  - Marks for three tests
  - Total of the tests
  - Average of the tests
  - Grade based on requirements given.

Example

Produce annotated evidence to show how the grade was automatically calculated.
Include row and column headings.

Name	Test 1	Test 2	Test 3	Total	Average	Grade
Eleanor	78	76	97	=SUM(B2:D2)	=AVERAGE(B2:D2)	=VLOOKUP(F2,Gr
Jane	54	76	56	=SUM(B3:D3)	=AVERAGE(B3:D3)	=VLOOKUP(F3,Gr
Oliver	32	54	72	=SUM(B4:D4)	=AVERAGE(B4:D4)	=VLOOKUP(F4,Gr

Grade Table	
0	Fail
40	C
60	B
80	A

This calculated the grade from the table on the right.

Figure 11.4 Annotated evidence that does not meet the requirements

The evidence in Figure 11.4 would not gain the marks for four reasons:
- The function is not completely visible (truncated).
- There is no reference to the named cell.
- There are no row and column headings.
- The annotation is labelling – it is not showing how.

Truncation

It is important to make sure that any functions/formulae that you show are completely visible.

Grade
=VLOOKUP(F2,Gr
=VLOOKUP(F3,Gr
=VLOOKUP(F4,Gr

This is truncated – the whole function cannot be seen.

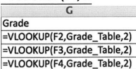

G
Grade
=VLOOKUP(F2,Grade_Table,2)
=VLOOKUP(F3,Grade_Table,2)
=VLOOKUP(F4,Grade_Table,2)

This is not truncated, all parts of
The function can be seen

Figure 11.5 Truncated and complete cell content

Named cell ranges

Where named cell ranges have been used, they should be identified.

	A	B	C	D	E	F	G
1	Name	Test 1	Test 2	Test 3	Total	Average	Grade
2	Eleanor	78	76	97	=SUM(B2:D2)	=AVERAGE(B2:D2)	=VLOOKUP(F2,Grade_Table,2)
3	Jane	54	76	56	=SUM(B3:D3)	=AVERAGE(B3:D3)	=VLOOKUP(F3,Grade_Table,2)
4	Oliver	32	54	72	=SUM(B4:D4)	=AVERAGE(B4:D4)	=VLOOKUP(F4,Grade_Table,2)
5							
6							
7					The reference Grade_Table refers		
8					to the cells:		
9	Grade Table						
10	0	Fail			A9:B13		
11	40	C					
12	60	B					
13	80	A					

Figure 11.6 Named range of cells

This is so that the marker and moderator can look at the functions and formulae you have used and identify whether they are correct.

Labelling and annotating

There is a difference between added text that does not add anything to the function/formula (a label) and text that shows you understand what you have done (annotation).

The text in Figure 11.7 does not add anything to the function – it gives a general description of the function VLookup. This would not get marks.

	A	B	C	D	E	F	G
1	Name	Test 1	Test 2	Test 3	Total	Average	Grade
2	Eleanor	78	76	97	=SUM(B2:D2)	=AVERAGE(B2:D2)	=VLOOKUP(F2,Grade_Table,2)
3	Jane	54	76	56	=SUM(B3:D3)	=AVERAGE(B3:D3)	=VLOOKUP(F3,Grade_Table,2)
4	Oliver	32	54	72	=SUM(B4:D4)	=AVERAGE(B4:D4)	=VLOOKUP(F4,Grade_Table,2)
5							
6							
7					The function in cell G2,3 and 4 is a lookup		
8					function. It looks up the data in the table in cells		
9	**Grade Table**				A9 to B13 and returns the value that matches what		
10	0	Fail			it is looking up.		
11	40	C					
12	60	B					
13	80	A					

Figure 11.7 Annotation that does not meet the requirements – labelling

The text in Figure 11.8 goes through the function step by step, but is repeating what is on the printout, it is not adding anything to the understanding.

	A	B	C	D	E	F	G
1	Name	Test 1	Test 2	Test 3	Total	Average	Grade
2	Eleanor	78	76	97	=SUM(B2:D2)	=AVERAGE(B2:D2)	=VLOOKUP(F2,Grade_Table,2)
3	Jane	54	76	56	=SUM(B3:D3)	=AVERAGE(B3:D3)	=VLOOKUP(F3,Grade_Table,2)
4	Oliver	32	54	72	=SUM(B4:D4)	=AVERAGE(B4:D4)	=VLOOKUP(F4,Grade_Table,2)
5							
6							
7					The Vlookup function takes the value from F2,		
8					looks this up in the Grade_Table (A9:B13) and		
9	**Grade Table**				returns the value in the second column.		
10	0	Fail					
11	40	C					
12	60	B					
13	80	A					

Figure 11.8 Annotation that does not meet the requirements – repetition

The correct annotation is shown in Figure 11.9 – it explains what is happening.

	A	B	C	D	E	F	G
1	Name	Test 1	Test 2	Test 3	Total	Average	Grade
2	Eleanor	78	76	97	=SUM(B2:D2)	=AVERAGE(B2:D2)	=VLOOKUP(F2,Grade_Table,2)
3	Jane	54	76	56	=SUM(B3:D3)	=AVERAGE(B3:D3)	=VLOOKUP(F3,Grade_Table,2)
4	Oliver	32	54	72	=SUM(B4:D4)	=AVERAGE(B4:D4)	=VLOOKUP(F4,Grade_Table,2)
5							
6					The Vlookup function takes the value from F2, the average grade		
7					for all the tests.		
8					It looks this up in the Grade_Table (A9:B13), in the first column		
9	**Grade Table**				matching the row. For example an average of 53.5 would be		
10	0	Fail			matched to row 11 as it meets the criteria for row 11 but has not		
11	40	C			met the criteria for row 12. The Grade Table needs to be sorted.		
12	60	B			The 2 at the end of the function is which column to find the value		
13	80	A			to bring back – Column 1 is A and Column 2 is B. So for a value		

of 53.5, it matches to Row 11, looks in the second column and returns a value of a C.

Figure 11.9 Annotation that does meet the requirements – explanation

How to explain development

There may be occasions where you need to explain how a solution achieves its aim. This may mean showing some of the elements of development.

This does not just want evidence of the final graph, but the processes required to achieve the graph.

Table structure

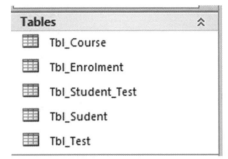

Figure 11.10 Database tables

The first task was to create a query that would allow the teacher to select her class.

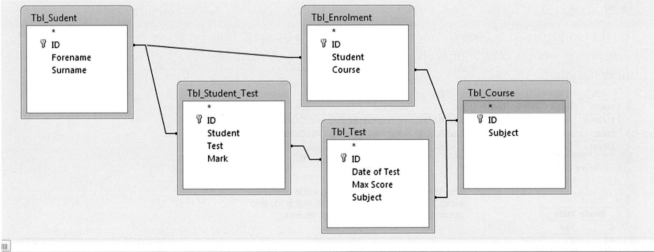

Field:	Forename	Surname	Course	Date of Test	Max Score	Mark	ID
Table:	Tbl_Sudent	Tbl_Sudent	Tbl_Enrolment	Tbl_Test	Tbl_Test	Tbl_Student_Test	Tbl_Test
Sort:							
Show:	☑	☑	☑	☑	☑	☑	☑
Criteria:			[Enter class]				
or:							

This query uses the student details, course and test information. The criterion for Course asks for the Course that is required. The query will return information only for the course selected.

Example

The teacher wants a graph showing the average of the test results of the students in her class.

Produce annotated evidence explaining how the graph was produced. You need to include evidence of any queries, calculations or macros used.

Figure 11.11 Database query

Forename	Surname	Course	Date of Test	Max Score	Mark	ID
Eleanor	Oliver	7W ICT	13/01/2012	20	18	1
Jane	Martin	7W ICT	13/01/2012	20	12	1
Alexandra	Mary	7W ICT	13/01/2012	20	16	1
Eleanor	Oliver	7W ICT	15/01/2012	10	7	2
Jane	Martin	7W ICT	15/01/2012	10	4	2
Alexandra	Mary	7W ICT	15/01/2012	10	8	2
Eleanor	Oliver	7W ICT	18/01/2012	25	21	3
Jane	Martin	7W ICT	18/01/2012	25	22	3
Alexandra	Mary	7W ICT	18/01/2012	25	12	3

This query is used as the basis for the next one, Qry_Average, that takes the information and applies a total to it to calculate the average of the test marks.

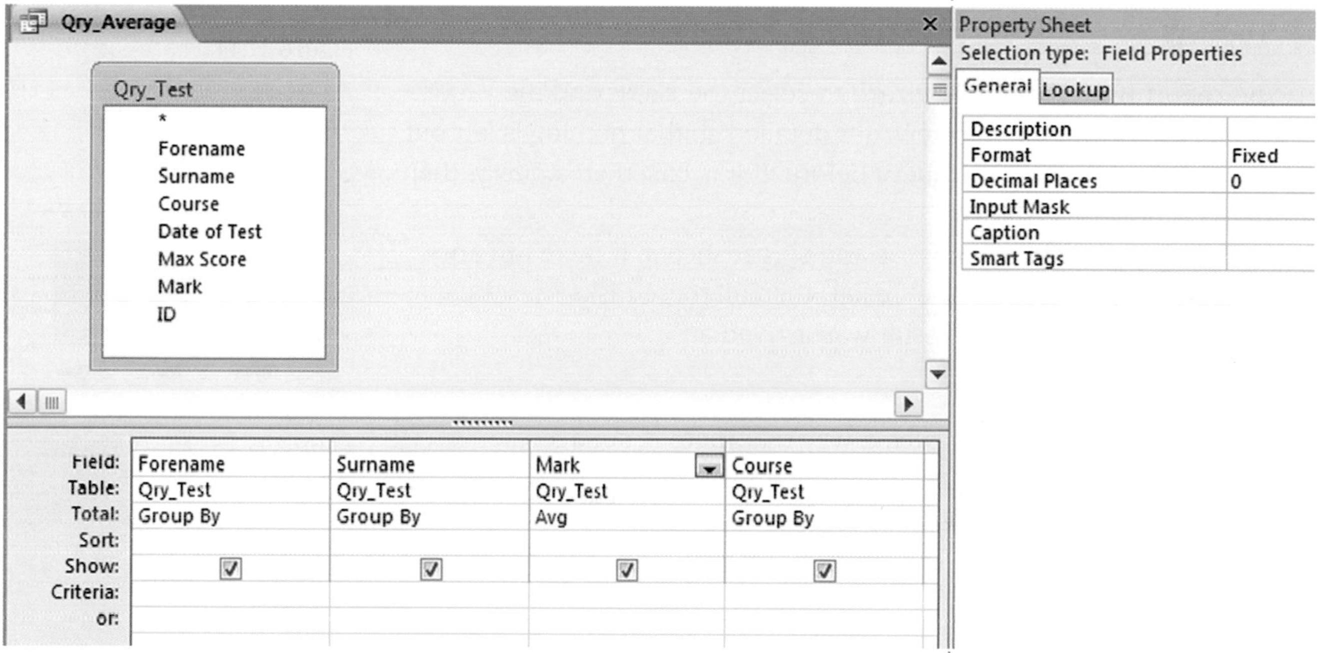

Figure 11.12 Database query result

The format of the Mark column is formatted to be to a fixed number of decimal places – in this case 0.

Figure 11.13 Qry_average database query

This query was used as the basis for the report.

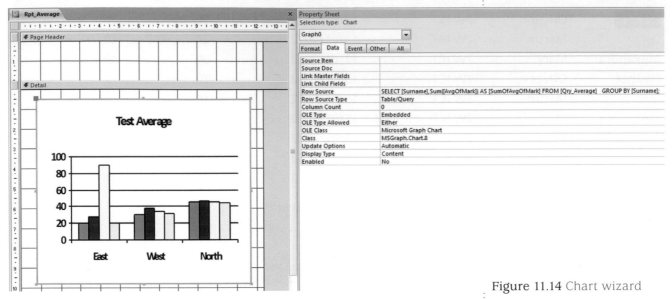

Figure 11.14 Chart wizard

The report used the graph wizard to select the *x*-axis and the *y*-axis.

It is important that all steps are detailed so that nothing is left out. You cannot just show the query before. If it is based on a query, then it also needs to be shown.

The same is true in websites and spreadsheets. If there are any tasks used to create the final result, then all these tasks must be covered to show how the result was arrived at.

Different solutions

The tasks are designed in such a way that there is not a single solution. They can be solved in different ways and each answer, providing it gives the right evidence and is annotated correctly, will gain credit.

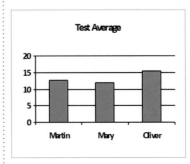

Figure 11.15 Chart of query results

Each example in Figure 11.16 meets the requirements. Each is correct, even though they look different.

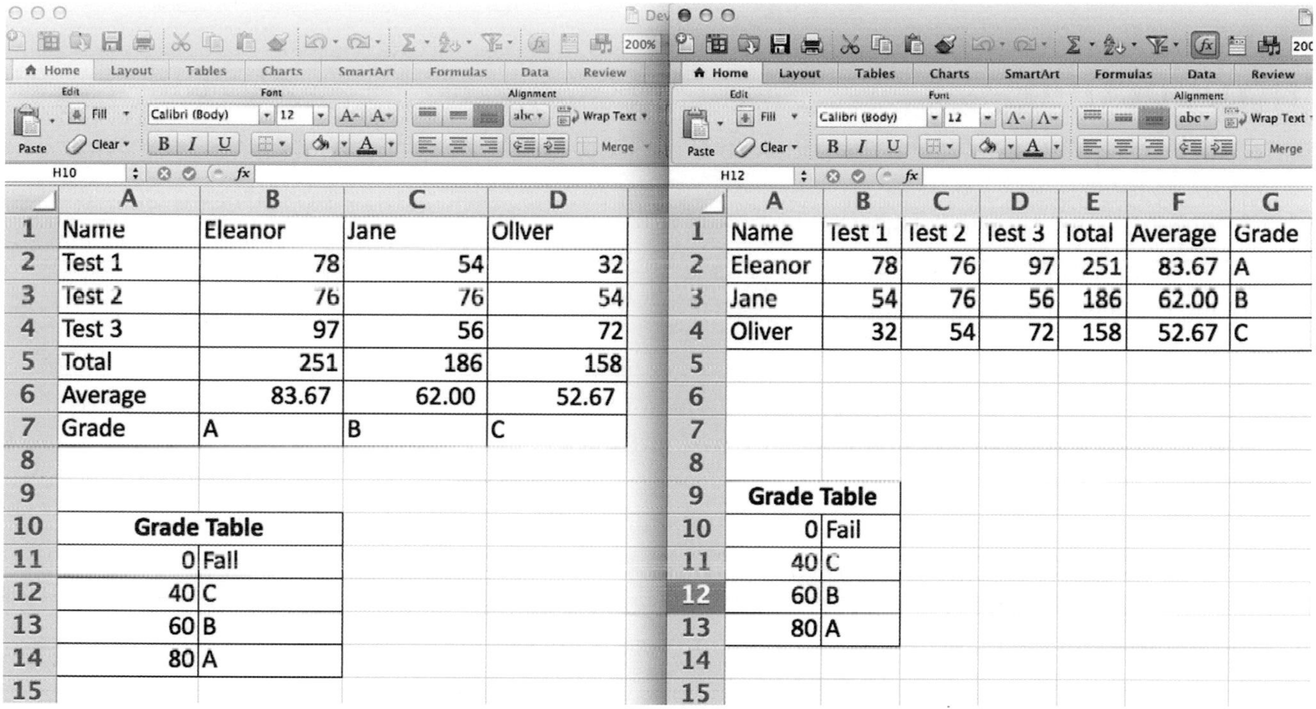

First spreadsheet:

	A	B	C	D
1	Name	Eleanor	Jane	Oliver
2	Test 1	78	54	32
3	Test 2	76	76	54
4	Test 3	97	56	72
5	Total	251	186	158
6	Average	83.67	62.00	52.67
7	Grade	A	B	C
8				
9				
10	Grade Table			
11	0	Fail		
12	40	C		
13	60	B		
14	80	A		
15				

Second spreadsheet:

	A	B	C	D	E	F	G
1	Name	Test 1	Test 2	Test 3	Total	Average	Grade
2	Eleanor	78	76	97	251	83.67	A
3	Jane	54	76	56	186	62.00	B
4	Oliver	32	54	72	158	52.67	C
5							
6							
7							
8							
9	Grade Table						
10	0	Fail					
11	40	C					
12	60	B					
13	80	A					
14							
15							

Figure 11.16 Different ways of achieving the same result

Different software

The tasks do not specify which software package to use. They do, sometimes, specify the type of software (e.g. spreadsheet, database, graphics package) to use.

12 Testing

Introduction

Testing is the process in which the software is put through a series of actions to make sure that:

- it does the job that it is intended to do
- it does not 'crash' if unexpected data is used
- it will cope with all eventualities.

The size and complexity of modern day software mean that it is impossible to be certain that a program will always work and never crash. A lot of work goes into making sure that it does not, but there can never be 100% certainty.

One aspect of testing is to make sure that the end product meets the requirements of the client – does it do the job that it was created for without error? Another aspect is to make sure that if the user does something wrong (e.g. uses the wrong data or presses keys in the wrong order) that the software will continue to function. In addition, there are actions that nobody can predict (e.g. the combination of different things, such as the end user, the hardware, power failures, interaction with other software), all of which can cause problems with a piece of software. The software needs to cope with these unknowns: this is difficult to test.

At the end of testing, there should be confidence that the software will do its job and stand up to whatever is thrown at it.

In this section you will find out about:

- types of tests
- creating test plans
- running test plans.

Test plan

A test plan is a formal document, laid out in a specific way. The test plan you are to use will be given to you. You must **not** deviate from this by changing any of the headings, adding your own columns, or altering anything else.

The following is a standard test plan table:

Test number	Description of test	Type of test	Input data value(s)	Expected output value

Key words

Test data – This is the input that will be used with the tests – it can be input from the user or an action by the user.

Types of test – These are the different categories of test that can be completed by the user using different types of test data.

Normal (valid) – This is a value that is accepted by the system – one that is sensible, reasonable and the system will accept without any problems.

Erroneous (invalid) – This is a value that will generate an error message – one that does not conform to the rules: it could be incomplete, outside of the range or of the wrong data type.

Extreme (boundary) – This is data that is on the edge of what is and is not acceptable.

Test plan – This is a formal structure detailing what needs to be done to test a solution with the different types of test.

- Test number – This is a sequential number starting at 1. It is used, when running tests, to correlate the test in the test plan with the screenshot of the test being run.
- Description of test – This is a text description of what the test is testing.
- Type of test – Whether it is normal, erroneous or extreme.
- Input data value(s) – These are the specific data values that need to be input into the software to run the test. You need to identify what the data value is and where it goes.
- Expected output value – This is the output that will be generated as a result of entering the input data value. If it is a value, you need to identify what the value is and where it can be found. If it is an error message, you need to identify the content of the error message.

Look at the spreadsheet in Figure 12.1. It is a very simple spreadsheet that adds a few numbers together.

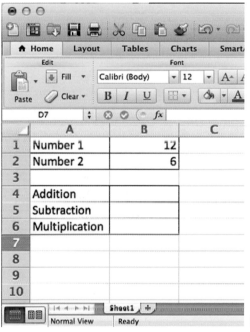

Figure 12.1 Simple spreadsheet

Test number	Description of test	Type of test	Input data value(s)	Expected output value
1	Adding numbers	Normal	12 and 6	18
2	Testing that subtracting number 1 from number 2 gives the correct result	Normal	Sheet 1 6 and 12	Sheet 1 Results of subtraction: 6
3	Testing that multiplying number 1 and number 2 gives the right result	Normal	Sheet 1 B1: 12 B2: 6	Sheet 1 B6: 72

Column	Comment
Test number	• The test number column is sequential and starts from 1 – this column has been filled in correctly for all three tests.
Description of test	• The description of test for test 1 is not in enough detail. It does not say what is being added. • The description of test for test 2 is incorrect. Subtracting number 1 from number 2 is not the same as subtracting number 2 from number 1. • The description for test 3 is a good example – everything is present and it is correct.
Type of test	• In this instance, the type of test used is normal. It will not generate any errors. This column has been filled in correctly for all three tests.
Input data value(s)	• In test 1, although the data values have been given, there is no indication of where they go: in what sheet or what cell. • In test 2, the data values have been given and the sheet has been given, but no cell has been given. • Test 3 shows the sheet and the cell, identifying the specific data value for each cell. This is an example of best practice.
Expected output value	• In test 1, there is no indication of where to look to verify the result. The result is correct, but a test plan is about being able to correlate what is written in the plan with what happens when you physically run the tests. • Test 2 gives the sheet and a text value for where to look. It is possible to work out where to look, but a test plan should not leave any possibility of error. • Test 3 gives the sheet, the cell and the value to look for in that cell.

All tests in the test plan should be repeatable by someone who has never seen the software before. They should be able to complete the tests without having to ask any questions.

Types of test

The type of test determines the type of output that will be received. There are different names for the same type of test, which makes things confusing!

Type of test	Type of output
Normal Valid Correct	The data should be accepted with no problems. No error messages are generated.
Erroneous Invalid Incorrect	The data will not be accepted. The system should stop it being entered and may display an error message.
Extreme (normal)	This is normal data that is on the boundary. It is normal, so it should be accepted without any problems.
Extreme (erroneous)	This is erroneous data on the boundary. It is erroneous, so it should not be accepted and may cause an error message to appear.

If, in a spreadsheet, you had a cell that should only accept numbers between 1 and 20, there are up to five tests that could be performed on the cell:

- 0 – erroneous lower
- 1 – extreme lower normal
- 10 – normal
- 20 – extreme upper normal
- 21 – erroneous upper.

Two of the tests will produce error messages and three will be accepted with no problems.

Activities

Look at the spreadsheet in Figure 12.2 and then copy and complete the following test table. The test number and type of test have been given to you.

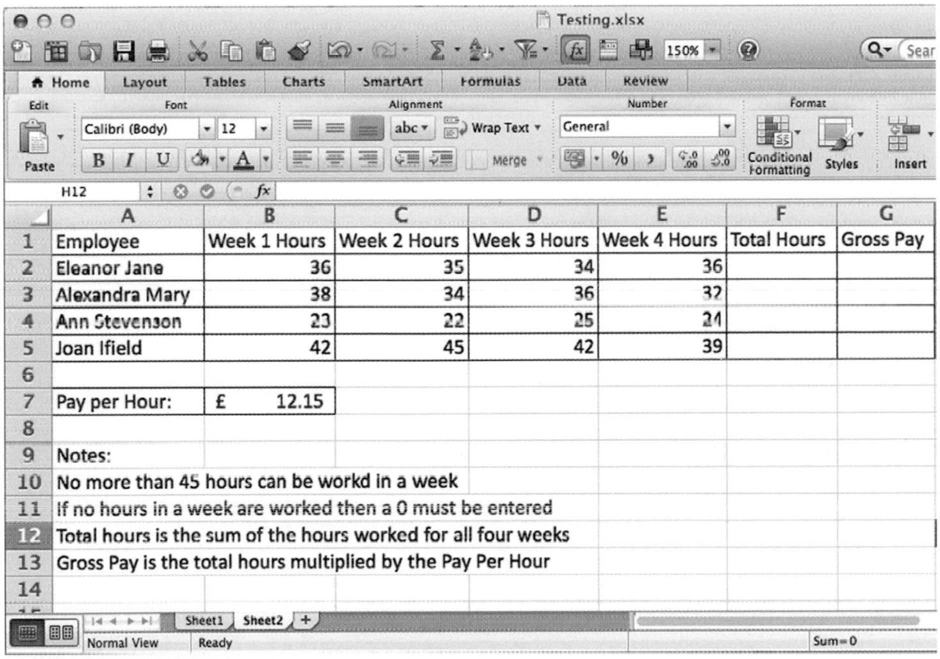

	A	B	C	D	E	F	G
1	Employee	Week 1 Hours	Week 2 Hours	Week 3 Hours	Week 4 Hours	Total Hours	Gross Pay
2	Eleanor Jane	36	35	34	36		
3	Alexandra Mary	38	34	36	32		
4	Ann Stevenson	23	22	25	24		
5	Joan Ifield	42	45	42	39		
6							
7	Pay per Hour:	£ 12.15					
8							
9	Notes:						
10	No more than 45 hours can be workd in a week						
11	If no hours in a week are worked then a 0 must be entered						
12	Total hours is the sum of the hours worked for all four weeks						
13	Gross Pay is the total hours multiplied by the Pay Per Hour						
14							

Figure 12.2 Spreadsheet for testing

Test number	Description of test	Type of test	Input data value(s)	Expected output value
1		Normal		
2		Extreme normal lower		
3		Extreme normal upper		
4		Erroneous lower		
5		Erroneous upper		

Sometimes you will not have created all the elements that are to be tested. In the activity above, you will not have created the error messages, but there should be some listed in the expected output value column. If this happens, you need to use your imagination to give what would be a suitable error message.

Selecting test data

The test data that you select is very important to get the required output. Occasionally, you may be asked to select some test data, giving reasons for your choices. Even if you are not explicitly asked to do this, you should always do this yourself because it will make sure you use the correct data.

Activities

Look at the database form in Figure 12.3.

Figure 12.3 Database form

For each of the input fields in the form, identify normal and extreme normal data that could be used.

There are many elements on this form that can be tested with invalid data. Invalid data for input forms is testing using validation. Validation is when a set of rules are applied to the field that make sure that the data entered is sensible, reasonable and within boundaries.
The most common validation rules are:

- presence
- range
- type
- length
- picture.

Activities

For each of the fields on the following form, identify which validation rule can be applied and select an appropriate piece of data to test it that will generate an error message. An example has been done for you.

Field	Validation rule	Input data value
Postcode	Picture check	ME1234 Q23
Forename		
Surname		
Date of birth		
Number of pets		

When thinking about the data to use, think about the type of test and why that data is being used for that test. For example:

Field	Type of test	Data used	Reason
Telephone number	Normal	01622842167	Correct number of digits. Starts with a 0. All numbers.
Length of back garden	Invalid	Length of a football pitch	Must be a number. Must be between 0 and 1000.

It is possible that a single field will have more than one type of validation associated with it.

Elements that can be tested

There are many different elements that can be tested. The most common are:

- formulae/functions (input and output)
- processes (queries, reports and protection)
- navigation.

Sometimes the testing will be obvious and can be built on something you have already created. Other times you will need to use your imagination to think up the tests and the expected output.

Formulae/functions

These are common within spreadsheets and databases. Each formula/function will have one or more input values and an output. If the input can be validated, then there will be the potential for an erroneous output.

The following table shows some common functions, a description of the function and the inputs that you would need to give.

Function/formula	Description	Input value
=sum(A1:B1)	This will add up a range of numbers	A1 and B1
=if(A2>1,"Y","N")	This will return either a Y or a N based on the value in A2	A2
=left(A2,2)	This will return the first two characters from the text in A2	A2
=vlookup(A3,A3:B5,2)	This will return the value from column B which matches the value in A3	A1 A3, A4, A5 B3, B4, B5

Activities

Use the spreadsheet shown in Figure 12.4 to complete the following test plan for different tests.

	A	B	C	D
1	Name	Number	Username	Password
2	John	123	Joh123	123ohn
3	Fred	124	Fre124	124red
4	Alex	125	Ale125	125lex
5	Mike	126	Mik126	126ike
6				
7				
8			=CONCATENATE(LEFT(A2,3),B2)	=CONCATENATE(B2,RIGHT(A2,3))
9				
10	This column must be at least length 3	This column goes from 100 to 999	This takes the first three letters from the name	This takes the three numbers and adds them to
11			and adds them to the three numbers	the last three letters from the name
12				
13				

Figure 12.4 Spreadsheet for testing

Test number	Description of test	Type of test	Input data value(s)	Expected output value
1		Normal		
2		Normal		
3		Erroneous		
4		Erroneous		

Processes

These are the results of queries. They can be tested using raw results or by using the output formatted in a report.

In the structured tasks, processes can only be tested using normal data – it is testing data that is already in the system, so validation occurs at the point of entry. It is technically possible to validate the search criterion itself and, if you chose to do this and it meets the criterion, you would not lose marks, but there are easier options to choose. Take, for example, the following dataset:

ID	Name	Gender	Date of birth	Town
1	John	Male	1/12/1980	Coventry
2	Ann	Female	24/3/1979	Kenilworth
3	Suzie	Female	13/4/1981	Kenilworth
4	Lorraine	Female	15/2/1978	Birmingham
5	Adam	Male	27/7/1981	Coventry
6	Chloe	Female	11/7/1981	Coventry
7	James	Male	27/8/1983	Birmingham
8	Mike	Male	21/11/1980	Birmingham
9	Andy	Male	11/11/1979	Coventry

Take the query: Find all the men who live in Coventry.

Test number	Description of test	Type of test	Input data value(s)	Expected output value
1	To find all the records where gender = Male and Town = Coventry	Normal	Gender = Male Town = Coventry	Three records: ID = 1 ID = 5 ID = 9

It is unnecessary to specify the whole record; just the ones that have been found.

The results of the query could generate no records. This is not an invalid test because the query itself has worked. For example, in the above dataset, finding all the men who live in Kenilworth will return 0 records. This is a normal test.

To be technically and absolutely correct, you should provide all the data in the dataset as well. However, since this is only an AS-level qualification, this is not required.

Again, using the above dataset, the following queries could be run:

- Find all male/female.
- Find all who live in Coventry/Kenilworth/Birmingham.
- Find all born after a certain date.
- Find all born before a certain date.
- Find all born between two dates.

And any combination:

- Find all men born before 1/1/1982.

You need to read the question and, if appropriate, make sure the tests are testing different aspects of the solution. Wherever possible, the tests should lead to outputs.

Processes also include elements, such as security and cell protection. A security password to gain access can have three tests:

- No password entered (no access).
- Incorrect password entered (no access).
- Correct password entered (access).

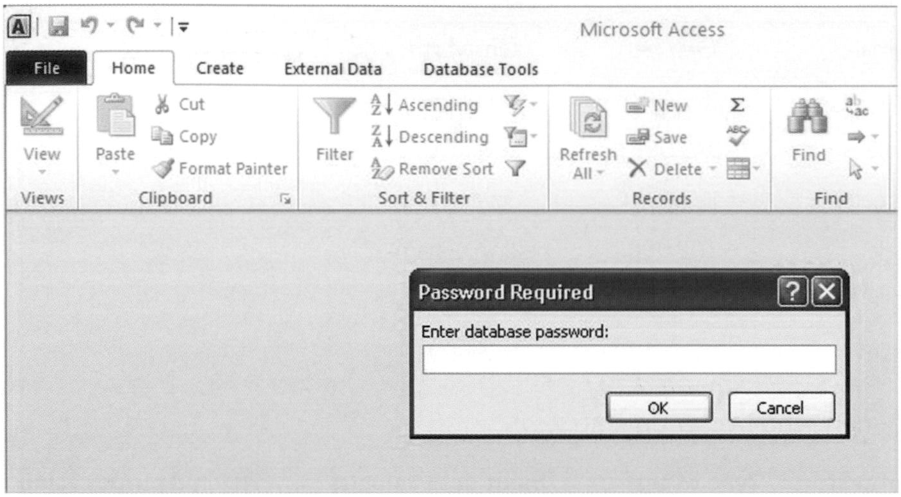

Figure 12.5 Asking for database password

Cell protection, in spreadsheets, can have different outcomes depending on how it has been set up. For example, it is possible to allow users to select, but not change, locked cells. However, it is also possible to stop users from selecting locked cells at all.

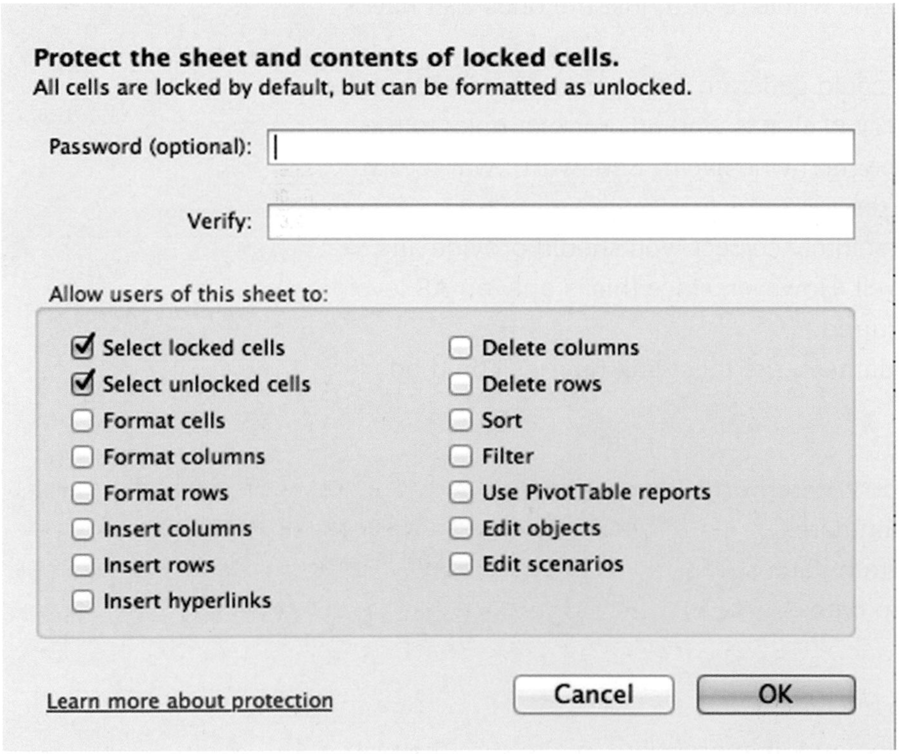

Figure 12.6 Spreadsheet cell protection

Depending on how the cell protection has been set up will change the expected output.

Testing a process can also include an element of validation. For example, a picture check on a postcode is both a process and validation.

The following are the rules for a postcode:

- The first element consists of either one or two letters, followed by either one or two digits.
- The second element consists of one digit followed by two letters. Furthermore, the letters C, I, K, M, O and V never appear in the second element.

Other letter and number combinations that can prove interesting to validate include national insurance and driving licence numbers.

Process testing can also be used when data is being transferred. For example, data entered into a web page being transferred into a database, or from a web page into an email.

Activities

Give **five** tests that could be used to test the input of a postcode.

Navigation

Navigation testing is making sure that hyperlinks and buttons work, for example testing the links between web pages or testing hyperlinks/buttons in spreadsheets/databases/presentations.

Navigation testing is often one test, unless you have implemented the navigation in different ways. Buttons, hyperlinks and hotspots would be three different tests, but testing a button on its own, even if you have many different buttons, is a single test.

Navigation tests are normal tests.

When creating the test plan for navigation testing, make sure that you are very explicit in the input requirements.

Test number	Description of test	Type of test	Input data value(s)	Expected output value
1	Testing navigation link	Normal	Click link	New sheet appears
2	Testing link from menu sheet to data sheet	Normal	Start: menu Click button: Go to data sheet	Data sheet will appear

In the first test, there may be more than one link on the page and the link is not specified: is it a hyperlink, a button etc? It is too vague. The output is also too vague: how do I know that I am on that page?

In the second test, the input data gives the start point and a set of instructions about what to click. The output is very specific.

Other testing

You may be asked to test other elements. These can include such things as web pages and presentations.

The difference between testing these items and the testing of functions/formulae is that the input data values tend to be a little vague. For example, when testing a web page, elements to test can include:

- speed that a page loads
- appearance using different browsers
- consistency of headings/font/font size/colour
- spelling of words on the pages.

When thinking about the input data values and the expected output value, the key is to be specific: the more information you can give the better. It may be that the input data value is a set of instructions rather than a specific data value to be used.

Test number	Description of test	Type of test	Input data value(s)	Expected output value
1	Testing Home page in different browsers	Normal	Open the Home page in Internet Explorer 9 and Google Chrome 16	The pages in the two browsers look the same, the font is Times New Roman and the pictures are in the same place
2	Consistency of font	Normal	Open the Home page and the About page in IE9	The title in the Home page and the About page is centred, Times New Roman, size 16

You need to specify what pages you are looking at and what data, and the format of the data on those pages.

Other aspects of software that can be tested include:

- videos playing
- sound playing
- touch screen presentations
- right clicking (enabled/disabled?)
- animations
- transitions.

Mail-merge results would also be a part of testing. A mail merge can use functions, such as SKIP, IF and so on. These select different records based on criteria and can be used in testing, similar to query testing.

Running tests

Running a test is where the test is carried out. You need to enter the input data, as specified, into the software and compare the output data you get against the output data expected in the test plan. They should be the same. If they are not, there are several explanations:

- The software has a flaw in it: either there is a built-in bug or you have programmed it incorrectly, meaning that it doesn't work as you intended.
- The test is flawed.
- The test data is incorrect.

When running tests:

Activities

A presentation has three slides. It has a background sound track that starts when the presentation is opened and loops with the presentation. The elements on the slides are animated and there are transitions between the slides. There should be no interaction with the slideshow.

Create a test plan for the above slideshow.

- make sure the output is linked to the test number
- the test outputs should be in sequential order
- make sure **all** inputs are identified
- make sure all outputs are identified
- if an error message is generated, make sure that the screenshot shows the input data and the error message.

For example, in the following test plan:

Test number	Description of test	Type of test	Input data value(s)	Expected output value
1	Testing input in cell B1 – must be between 1 and 15	Invalid	Sheet 3 Cell B1 18	Error message – input data must be between 1 and 15

The test output for the preceding test plan is shown in Figure 12.7.

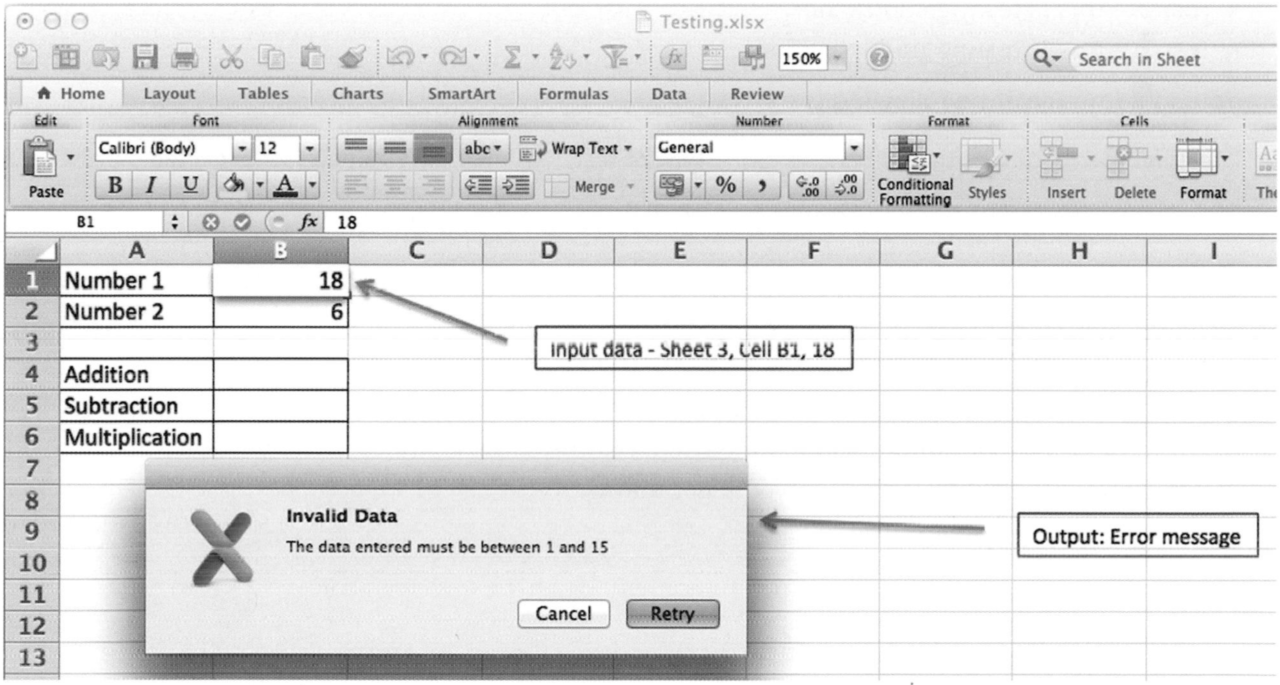

Figure 12.7 Output of test

Points to note:
- Input data has been identified.
- Output has been identified.
- Error message has been moved so that input data can be seen.

Different tests

When designing a test plan, it is important to make sure that you are testing different aspects of the solution. This means that you are testing different function/formulae, processes or navigation. The input data can be the same so long as the actual element being tested is different. For example:

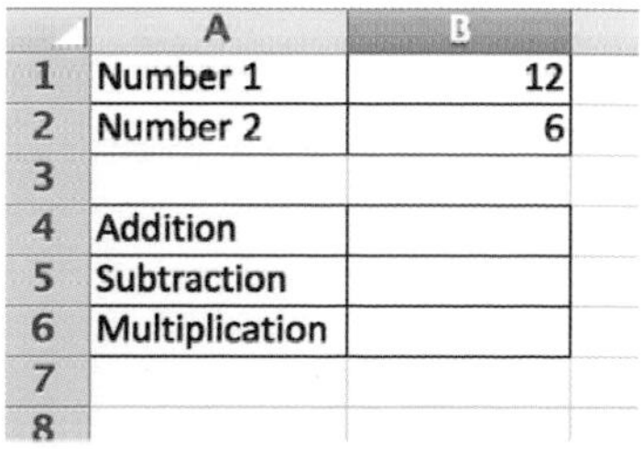

Figure 12.8 Spreadsheet for testing

Test number	Description of test	Type of test	Input data value(s)	Expected output value
1	Testing addition of numbers in B1 and B2	Normal	Sheet 1 Cell B1: 12 Cell B2: 6	Sheet 1 Cell B4: 18
2	Testing subtraction of B2 from B1	Normal	Sheet 1 Cell B1: 12 Cell B2: 6	Sheet 1 Cell B5: 6
3	Testing multiplication of the numbers in B1 and B2	Normal	Sheet 1 Cell B1: 12 Cell B2: 6	Sheet 1 Cell B6: 72

All three tests use the same input values, but the formula/function that is being tested is different:

- Test 1 – this is testing addition
- Test 2 – this is testing subtraction
- Test 3 – this is testing multiplication

You could not give the following tests:

Test number	Description of test	Type of test	Input data value(s)	Expected output value
1	Testing addition of numbers in B1 and B2	Normal	Sheet 1 Cell B1: 12 Cell B2: 6	Sheet 1 Cell B4: 18
2	Testing addition of numbers in B1 and B2	Normal	Sheet 1 Cell B1: 18 Cell B2: 4	Sheet 1 Cell B4: 22

In this case, different numbers are being used, but the same formula is being tested – only the first test would get marks.

13 Documentation

Introduction

Documentation is official evidence, produced by a company, detailing how to make use of its products. There are two main types of documentation: full documentation and help sheets. Both follow the same principles. The audience is important. The documentation may focus on how to use the system or it may be how to support and amend it. The documentation is not about how to build a system, but how to use the finished product.

Help sheets

A help sheet is a stand-alone sheet that details how to complete a specific task. For example, if the task is to create a database with a main menu, a data input form, a report on the number of members and a graph of income, then the help sheets might be:

- how to use the navigation system
- how to use the data input form
- how to use the reports.

Each help sheet would take the user through how to complete that particular element of the finished system.

Marking the help sheet

The mark scheme for the help sheet is given below and is based on the 2010–11 tasks. It is divided into two parts: features and presentation. The features relate to the task that was asked: 'Have you included the instructions within the help sheet?'

Features
- Clear instructions and screenshots that show how to use the following features:
  - Slide master(s) – to achieve a consistent layout
  - Animation – that uses timing so text and images appear automatically
  - Effects on animations and transitions
  - A loop – to restart the presentation.

Presentation
- Must be a stand-alone document with:
  - consistent style throughout
  - use of subtitles
  - appropriate screenshots (clearly visible)
  - text – **not** written as 'I did...'
  - **no** spelling errors.

Key words

User documentation – This is the full guide, the stand-alone book (paper or electronic), that comes with the system – it includes help sheets, index, glossary and troubleshooting.

Help sheet – A sheet on a specific skill or element within the system – it might be stand-alone and target one particular feature.

Index – This is an alphabetical list of names, subjects etc., found at the end of a book, with references to the places where they occur.

Glossary – This is an alphabetical list of terms or words found in the book, with explanations – a brief dictionary.

Troubleshooting – This is a set of instructions to help in solving common faults and problems.

Activities

Plan the contents of the database help sheet for how to use the reports.

Mark	Requirement for the mark
3	All of the features and all of the presentation requirements are covered in the help sheet.
2	All of the features are covered. There are errors or inconsistencies in the presentation of the help sheet.
0–1	At least **three** of the features are covered and there may be errors or inconsistencies in the presentation of the help sheet.

'Presentation' refers to how it looks. There are some very specific elements of the presentation that are being looked for.

Mark scheme	Comment
Must be stand-alone.	It should be possible to remove the help sheet from the work and have no other parts of the coursework tasks on it. It should start at the top of the page, not half way down. You can include your name on it in the header/footer.
Must have consistent style.	The style applies to the heading, the subheading, the body text, header/footer, line style, border style etc. Where used, everything should be consistent: font style, font size, font colour etc.
Must have subtitles.	A help sheet should not be a single continuous set of instructions and images, it should be broken down into parts. Each part should have a heading (the subtitle).
Must have appropriate screenshots.	An appropriate screenshot is one that demonstrates what the help sheet is referring to. It should be of a suitable size so that the content can be seen, cropped and of a similar size to other screenshots in the sheet.
Text not written as 'I did…'.	This is a help sheet to show people how to use the system. It is not a guide to show how you created the system. It should be written as a series of instructions, rather than a step-by-step development of the system.
No spelling errors.	The help sheet should be completed on a computer, so use of the spell checking feature is compulsory. There should be no spelling mistakes. This does not refer just to spelling the word incorrectly, but also the incorrect spelling of the intended work. For example, using 'their' instead of 'there' – both words are spelled correctly, but within the context one is incorrect. This counts as a spelling mistake.

The marks you receive will be based on a combination of presentation and features. The presentation elements do not change. The features are task specific. In order to get over half the marks, you need to make sure that you have covered the features, but that you cannot gain full marks unless all the presentation elements are also included.

Logical order

There should be a logical order to the instructions in a help sheet. They should flow and include everything that needs to be done. If you miss a step out, then someone who does not know what they are doing will not include that step and end up with a different result.

Layout of the help sheet

There are different ways of laying out a help sheet. You need to consider three areas when deciding how the help sheet will look.

- Audience – who will be using it?
- Software – what are you using: a word processor or a desktop publisher?
- Graphics – how does the application handles these? – Some applications have problems with graphics and will move them around the page seemingly at random.

If you are using a word processor, one method of layout is to use a table. This will allow the images to be placed in a cell and for them to remain in a cell (see Figure 13.1).

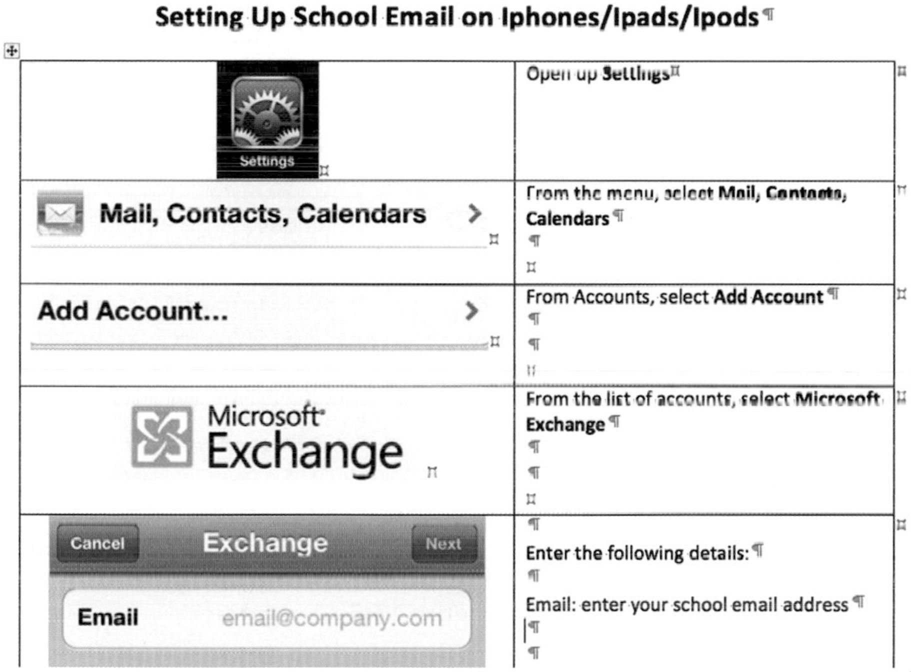

Setting Up School Email on Iphones/Ipads/Ipods

Settings	Open up **Settings**
Mail, Contacts, Calendars	From the menu, select **Mail, Contacts, Calendars**
Add Account...	From Accounts, select **Add Account**
Microsoft Exchange	From the list of accounts, select **Microsoft Exchange**
Cancel Exchange Next Email email@company.com	Enter the following details: Email: enter your school email address

Figure 13.1 Table layout for a help sheet

Alternatively, you could use a sequential method that intersperses text and images as shown in Figure 13.2.

Activities

Think about cleaning your teeth. Write down every step that is involved. When you get home, compare the steps you wrote down with what you actually have to do. Were there any steps missing? What steps were missing, if any, and why do you think you missed them out?

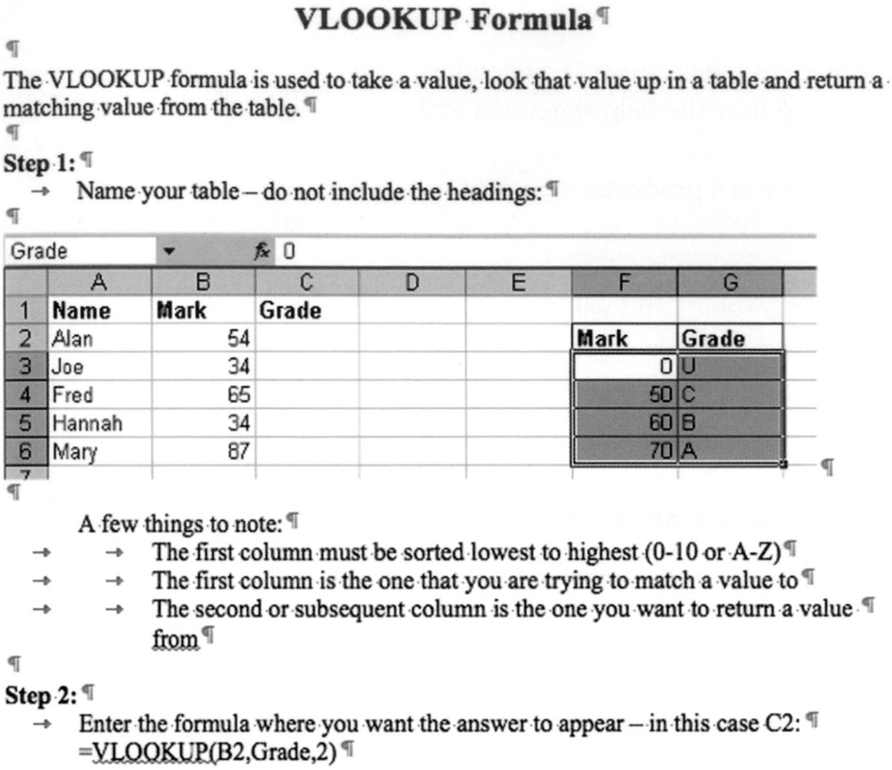

VLOOKUP Formula¶

¶

The VLOOKUP formula is used to take a value, look that value up in a table and return a matching value from the table.¶

¶

Step 1:¶

→ Name your table – do not include the headings:¶

¶

Grade	▼		*fx* 0				
	A	B	C	D	E	F	G
1	**Name**	**Mark**	**Grade**				
2	Alan	54				**Mark**	**Grade**
3	Joe	34				0	U
4	Fred	65				50	C
5	Hannah	34				60	B
6	Mary	87				70	A
7							

¶

A few things to note:¶

→ → The first column must be sorted lowest to highest (0-10 or A-Z)¶

→ → The first column is the one that you are trying to match a value to¶

→ → The second or subsequent column is the one you want to return a value from¶

¶

Step 2:¶

→ Enter the formula where you want the answer to appear – in this case C2:¶
=VLOOKUP(B2,Grade,2)¶

Figure 13.2 Sequential layout of a help sheet

The method you choose does not matter so long as you are consistent.

Screenshots

The screenshots should be appropriate. What does this mean?

- They need to be large enough to see the detail (compare Figures 13.3 and 13.4).
- They need to show enough detail to be able to cross reference the screenshot against what actually appears on the screen. Figure 13.5 shows the detail and is large enough to see, but, because it is just shows the button, it is not clear whereabouts on the screen it is. Figure 13.6 shows what you are looking for and where to find it.
- They must show relevant information only, and not show unnecessary detail (see Figure 13.7). There is no need for the information surrounding the form to be present. The user only needs to see the form. In Figure 13.8, the screenshot has been cropped so that only the window that the end user will see is present. There are no irrelevant details on the screen.
- Similar screenshots should be the same size. In Figure 13.9, the screenshots are different sizes, which gives a negative impact on the presentation. In Figure 13.10, the screenshots are the same size with the same border around them to improve the presentation.

Figure 13.3 Screenshot too small to see detail

Figure 13.4 Screenshot large enough to see detail

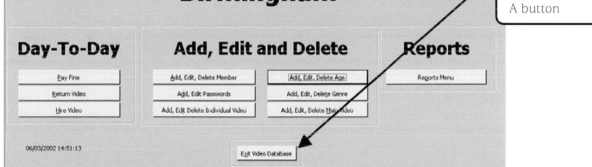

Figure 13.5 A button

Figure 13.6 A button in context

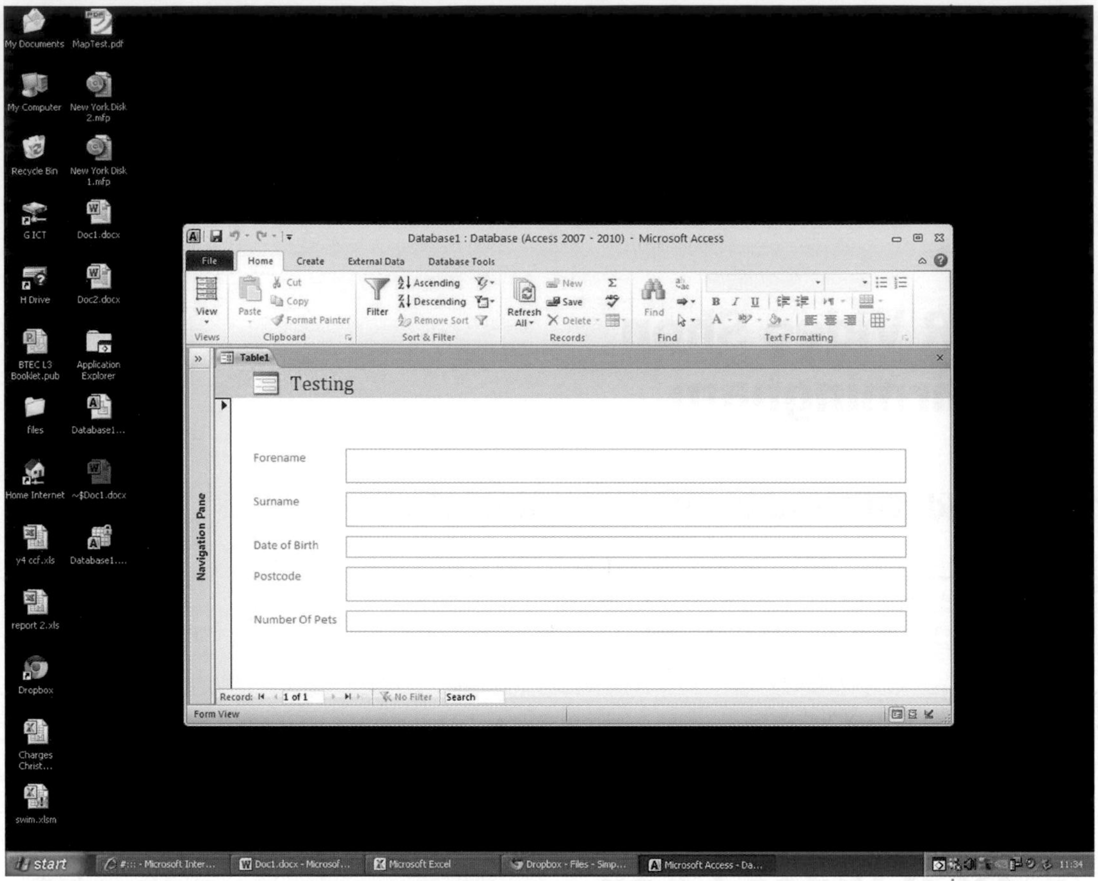
Database1 : Database (Access 2007 - 2010) - Microsoft Access
Testing
Forename
Surname
Date of Birth
Postcode
Number Of Pets

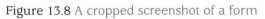

Figure 13.7 A form on a PC desktop

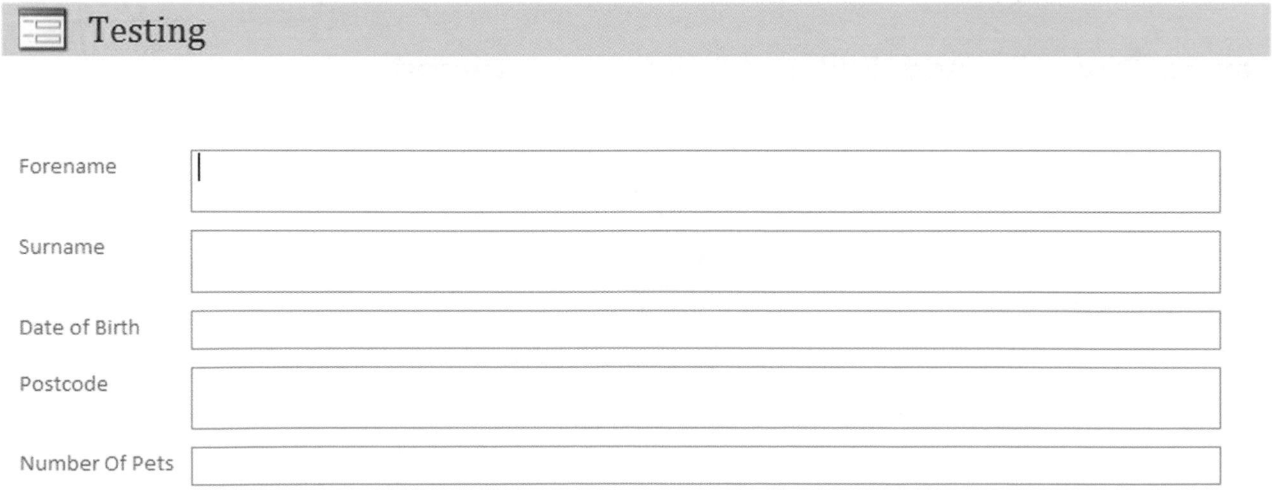
Testing
Forename
Surname
Date of Birth
Postcode
Number Of Pets

Figure 13.8 A cropped screenshot of a form

Error Messages that might Appear

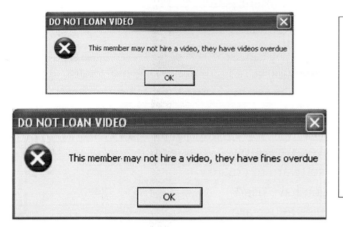

Figure 13.9 Screenshots of different sizes

Error Messages that might Appear

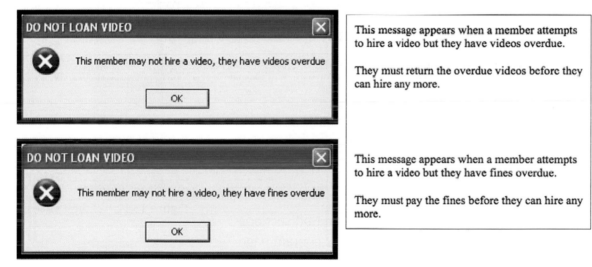

Figure 13.10 Screenshots of the same size

User documentation

User documents are help sheets with additional information presented as a single document. They should be produced entirely on a word processor because they will need to be printed many times. The following pages should be present in user documentation:

- title page
- table of contents
- help sheets
- troubleshooting
- index
- glossary.

Title page

The title page is a single sheet that shows the title of the user guide, the name of the author and an image (optional). It should not have a header or footer. There are options within most word processors to exclude a header or footer from the first page of a document (see Figure 13.11). Alternatively, the first page can be made into a separate section, with the header/footer not applied to that section.

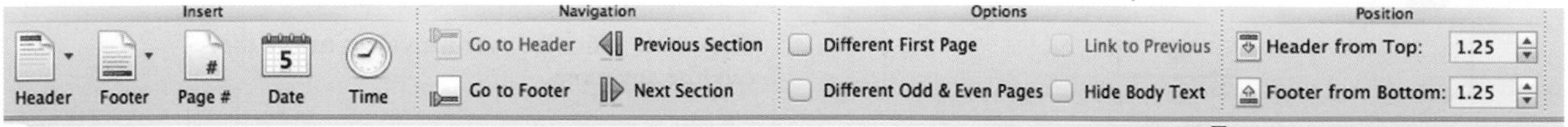

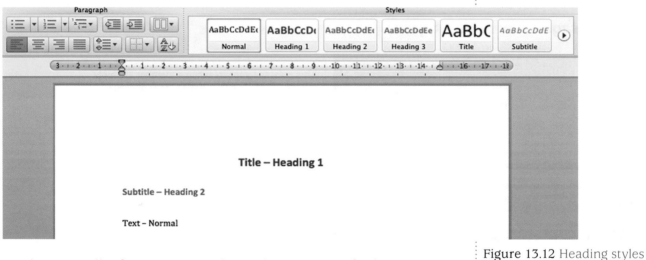

Figure 13.11 Microsoft Word ribbon

Table of contents

A table of contents (TOC) can be manually created or, preferably, automatically created by the software. To use the software to create a TOC automatically, you need to make sure that you have used styles when writing the user guide. The obvious styles to use are Heading 1 and Heading 2 for titles and subtitles, respectively (see Figure 13.12).

Figure 13.12 Heading styles

The TOC will refer to page numbers where you can find sections shown, so you need to include headers/footers that contain page numbers.

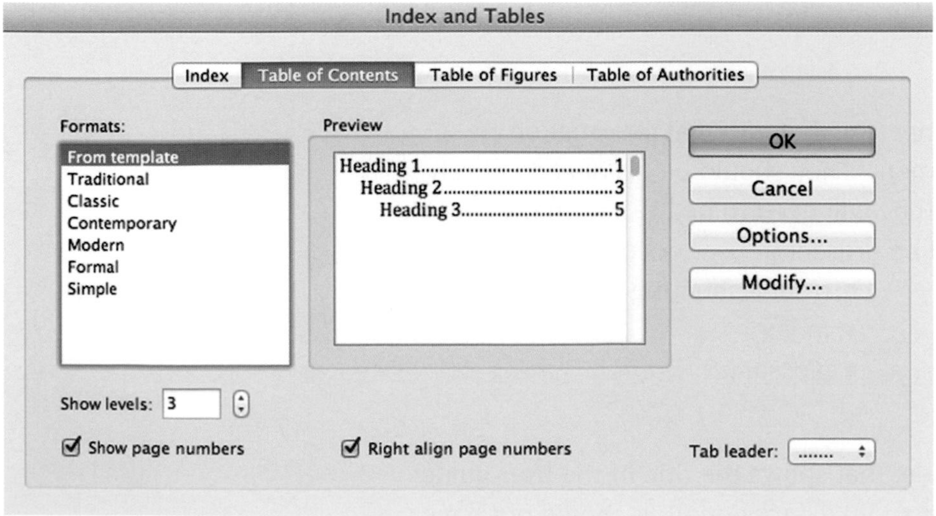

Figure 13.13
Generating a TOC

Help sheets

Help sheets in user documentation are the same as the stand-alone help sheets mentioned before. They should have headings using styles and a header/footer.

Troubleshooting

Troubleshooting is about solving errors. Guidance should focus on the error messages that might occur in a system, and how to deal with them.

Index

An index is where specific terms that occur in the document are listed alphabetically with a page reference to where the term can be found. Turn to pages 248–250 of this book to see an example.

Most word-processing software has a facility to produce an index. You need to 'mark' the entry required to select it for inclusion in the index. In Microsoft Word 2010:

- To use existing text as an index entry, select the text, then click Mark Entry in the Index group on the References ribbon.
- After you have marked all the entries you want, insert the index into your document. Click where you want to add the index and click Insert Index in the Index group on the References ribbon.

Glossary

A glossary is an alphabetic list of terms with a basic description of their meaning. You could create this as a two column table.

Common faults in producing documentation

Not all user guides achieve full marks. There are common mistakes that occur. For example with screenshots:

- Detail not able to be seen.
- Not the same size.
- Show irrelevant information.

Assumptions

Many assumptions are made when using the software. You will know how to use it so including all the steps may seem silly, obvious and a waste of time. However, all the steps must be included. Common assumptions made include:

- How to access software – How do I load and run the software? Is it via a menu, a shortcut?
- File names – What is the name of the file I need to load and where do I find it?

Index